David Simon's American City

Manchester University Press

David Simon's American City

Mikkel Jensen

Manchester University Press

Copyright © Mikkel Jensen 2024

The right of Mikkel Jensen to be identified as the author of this work has been asserted in accordance with the Copyright, Designs and Patents Act 1988.

Published by Manchester University Press
Oxford Road, Manchester, M13 9PL

www.manchesteruniversitypress.co.uk

British Library Cataloguing-in-Publication Data
A catalogue record for this book is available from the British Library

ISBN 978 1 5261 6252 6 hardback
ISBN 978 1 5261 9541 8 paperback

First published 2024
Paperback published 2026

The publisher has no responsibility for the persistence or accuracy of URLs for any external or third-party internet websites referred to in this book, and does not guarantee that any content on such websites is, or will remain, accurate or appropriate.

EU authorised representative for GPSR:
Easy Access System Europe – Mustamäe tee 50,
10621 Tallinn, Estonia
gpsr.requests@easproject.com

Typeset
by New Best-set Typesetters Ltd

Contents

List of Illustrations	*page* vi
Acknowledgments	viii
Introduction	1
1 The Humanized Drug Addict: *The Corner* (2000)	17
2 The Aesthetics of 'Pessimism': *The Wire* (2002–2008)	47
3 The Case for the City: *Treme* (2010–2013)	87
4 The Long Civil Rights Narrative: *Show Me a Hero* (2015)	115
5 Porn and Patriarchy: *The Deuce* (2017–2019)	144
Conclusion	172
References	204
Index	219

Illustrations

1. Sunlit soccer game in the suburbs. *The Wire.* "Old Cases." (S1E4). page 13
2. Mother and children walking on a sidewalk. *The Wire.* "Old Cases." (S1E4). 14
3. Child standing in front of a store. *The Corner.* "Gary's Blues." (E1). 19
4. Gary as a child standing in front of the same store. *The Corner.* "Gary's Blues." (E1). 20
5. McNulty, Bunk, Kima, and Freamon standing in a square. *The Wire.* "The Wire." (S1E6). 55
6. McNulty again faces the train though now lacks the zest he used to have. *The Wire.* "Mission Accomplished." (S3E12). 67
7. Dinner at the McAlary home. *Treme.* "I Thought I Heard Buddy Bolden Say." (S3E5). 99
8. The Lambreaux family celebrating Christmas. *Treme.* "I Thought I Heard Buddy Bolden Say." (S3E5). 100
9. Albert and friends are seeing off a tourist bus. *Treme.* "Right Place, Wrong Time." (S1E3). 106
10. Eileen tries to hide her feelings. *The Deuce.* "Seven-Fifty." (S2E3). 151
11. The model of New York City in the foreground suggests how urban transformation is pivotal to Alston's police work. *The Deuce.* "They Can Never Go Home." (S3E4). 167

| | List of Illustrations | vii |

12 Two boys roughhousing are photographed at the exact moment where it might appear that they are fighting each other in the street and not just playing around. By switching to black and white and using a clicking camera sound, the episode signals what the anti-desegregation advocates choose to document. *Show Me a Hero*. "Part 3." (E3). 175

Acknowledgments

Several sections of this book were published in earlier versions, and I want to express my appreciation to the publishers for letting me use the material in this book in revised form. I want to thank the editors, reviewers, and publishers that worked on these publications: "Social Reproduction and Political Change in *The Wire*" in *Academic Quarter* (vol. 15, 2017), "Intertextual Dialogue and Humanization in David Simon's *The Corner*" in the *European Journal of American Studies* (vol. 13, no. 2, 2018), "The Long Civil Rights Narrative of *Show Me a Hero*" in the *Irish Journal of American Studies* (vol. 8, 2018), "*The Wire* and the Disenchantment of the Outsider" in *American Studies in Scandinavia* (vol. 51, no. 1, 2019), and "'Our future is in the city': Storbyens udfordringer i David Simons tv-serier" in *16:9* (March 7, 2020).

I also want to thank the following people for providing feedback and support during my time writing this book: Steen Ledet Christiansen, Bent Sørensen, Erlend Lavik, Clara Juncker, Kim Toft Hansen, and many other people at Aalborg University, especially our local writing group.

A warm thank you goes to my family: my parents, my brothers, and my extended family for love and support. I will never be able to thank Søren enough. My love and deepest gratitude go to my wife Stephanie and our sons Ebbe and Knud. I gør mig glad hver dag og jeg elsker jer så højt.

Introduction

David Simon's America is an urban one. His television serials are not just set in urban landscapes; the city is their topic. *The Wire* tackles the effects of deindustrialization, *Show Me a Hero* examines the historical roots of residential segregation, and *Treme* emphasizes how lives intersect in the American city. Even when other topics take center stage – sex work and pornography in *The Deuce* and the lives of people struggling with drug addiction in *The Corner* – his serials emphasize how such social issues are framed by their urban contexts. *The Wire* stresses the fact that it is set in Baltimore, but this serial nonetheless engages with issues that many American cities face: the war on drugs, troubled schools, the loss of blue-collar jobs, and so on. Eschewing standard orthography, Simon himself, in an essay outlining his thoughts about *The Wire*, capitalizes "The City" in an effort to stress what he sees as its central issue. To him, this serial was "not about crime. Or punishment. Or the drug war. Or politics. Or race. Or education, labor relations or journalism. It was about The City" (Simon 2009, 3). Indeed, this argument applies more broadly to his career's engagement with American society.

The Wire's first season explores the drug trade in West Baltimore, but each subsequent season expands its storyworld to other parts of Baltimore, making the serial able to address urban issues in a broader sense. In Simon's words, had *The Wire*'s second season just "gone back to the ghetto and continued to plumb the Barksdale story, it would have been a much smaller show, and it would have claimed a much smaller canvas" (Simon in O'Rourke 2006). When its second season shows Nick Sobotka (Pablo Schreiber) to be dismissive about drug culture, drug dealing, and everything associated with it, viewers understand that when he finally does start buying and selling drugs it is because it allows him to provide for his family in a way he was unable to do with his legal work at the Baltimore harbor (*The Wire* [*TW*], S2E6). Nick wasn't getting enough hours to make ends meet. The three subsequent seasons all expand the storyworld in a way that enables *The Wire* to engage with broader themes about the state of the American city.

The Deuce is not focused on the city like *The Wire*, but this serial nonetheless puts a premium on placing its subject matter of sex work, economic exploitation, and pornography in the 1970s and 1980s in a specific urban context. In its first season finale, journalist Sandra Washington (Natalie Paul) discusses with her editor (James McDaniel) her ambitious journalistic piece on the women living and working in the sex industry. Her editor informs her that the newspaper's legal department says that her exposé on the sex work "parlors operating in plain sight" has to be cut from her story because her piece does not name its sources. This editorial decision means that Washington's article will be unable to comment on the structural context in which the sex work industry operates. It will only focus on the human-interest angle, a zoomed-in focus that undercuts Washington's very point in writing the article. Infuriated by this narrowed scope, Washington counters that such a re-framing will reduce her piece to "a sob story about the poor street waifs and their hard-hearted pimps" (*The Deuce* [*TD*], S1E8).

To Washington, this angle marginalizes important societal aspects of sex work and without those elements, and her story is barred from addressing the bigger picture about how City Hall and the NYPD are complicit in the state of the sex work industry in New York City. Her piece will not be able to speak directly to the urban crisis and the maladies of 1970s New York City if its scope does not extend beyond the pimps and sex workers. That is the message she has in mind when she is talking to her primary addressee, her editor. But the viewer is a crucial secondary addressee here; through this self-reflexive piece of dialogue *The Deuce* justifies why it contextualizes sex work within the urban crisis of 1970s New York City. Like Washington's piece, *The Deuce* too wants to situate the sex trade within a larger story of the urban crisis so as not to become a "sob story" with no larger societal agenda. To Simon, *The Deuce* is "an allegory about unencumbered capitalism" (Simon in Rose 2017) and its focus on gender issues and different forms of marginalization and exploitation takes center stage – but not at the expense of the city: when Simon's serials do not have the city as their central topic, they emphasize it as a crucial context.

Show Me a Hero's portrayal of a court case and a vehement popular resistance against a federal judge's ruling to desegregate Yonkers, New York, in the 1980s and 1990s speaks to a central aspect of many American cities: residential segregation (Boustan, 2012; Glaeser and Vigdor 2012). One of this miniseries' accomplishments is the fact that it is able to *dramatize* residential segregation. To identify that one group of people lives in one area and another group lives in another is hardly narrative fodder for an enticing story, but the story of the ambitious Nick Wasicsko (Oscar Isaac) enabled Simon and co-writer William F. Zorzi to bring to life a structural set of circumstances that greatly influence American cities. Indeed, Simon has said that it is Wasicsko's storyline that "drives the piece. [...] This piece doesn't work without it being Nick Wasicsko's story" (Simon in Rose 2015). Wasicsko's journey from ambitious council member to being the mayor and then back again to council member arcs the miniseries in a way that allows Simon and Zorzi to tell a story of how a city tries (not) to deal with its past and present patterns of residential segregation. With this narrative arc as a starting point, *Show Me a Hero* connects the related issues of housing, wealth, and race. These examples demonstrate some main contours in Simon's take on contemporary urbanity.

This urban focus makes Simon an outlier. It sets his serials apart from dominant trends in political and cultural discourse in America. Taking issue with topics such as residential segregation, the war on drugs, failing schools, and a divisive political culture, his serials' exploration of the American city represents a minority voice in American film and television. Urban historian Steven Conn argues that many Americans have embraced an anti-urban sentiment and "have rejected the city" (Conn 2014, 5), and though the city is surely a site of many problems in Simon's work, his serials emphasize that America's future is an urban one. In the late nineteenth century, many Progressives chose not to see the city as the problem itself but instead saw it as a place of problems. As Conn writes, the "Progressives took the problem of the city and turned it into a more manageable set of problems – labor, children and family life, immigrant assimilation, public health, and the like" (Conn 2014, 26).

Simon's take on the city parallels that of the Progressives in this sense. To Simon, the American city surely faces many challenges, but it is not the city itself that is the problem. On the contrary, Simon's serials suggest that the city once again needs to take center stage in terms of addressing core challenges facing American society.

While the city was seen as a central political concern in the first few post-war decades, urban issues have since figured much less prominently in political discussions. Indeed, in 1962, it was possible for intellectual historians Morton and Lucia White to write that it had become "fashionable for many American intellectuals to express tender concern for the city's future" (White and White 1962, 1). Conn, however, argues that the urban issue was all but dropped from the national conversation in the 1980s: "American cities reached a low-water mark during the age of Reagan. If in the Progressive era urban problems were seen as national issues, then by the 1980s that view had been almost entirely negated: urban issues were no longer part of the national agenda" (Conn 2014, 9). "The City" has taken a back seat to other topics and no longer figures prominently in American political discourse the way it once did in America. Simon's oeuvre offers a corrective to this tendency.

Conn notes that contrary to W.E.B. DuBois' famous 1903 prediction about the importance of "the color line" for America in the twentieth century, a much less remembered prediction about that century was uttered five years earlier by Reverend Josiah Strong. Strong had argued that "We must face the inevitable. The new civilization is certain to be urban, and the problem of the twentieth century will be the city" (quoted in Conn 2014, 10). Simon's oeuvre says the same thing about the twenty-first century as Strong did about the twentieth, and while his serials surely tackle racial issues head on, they veer more toward Strong's urban focal point rather than DuBois' racial one. The city – with people of different races and classes living together – represents the central challenge of the twenty-first century for Simon.

Urban historian Jon C. Teaford notes that for much of the twentieth century, urban life "was America's great domestic dilemma" (Teaford 2016, viii). In Simon's case, the same thing could be said about this century but his urban focus is formulated in the context that Conn points to: the city is no longer the central topic it once was in the public conversation. Indeed, Simon has argued that "with more than 80 percent of Americans living in metropolitan areas" the city is "the only future we have." To him, Americans "either live or die based on how we live in cities, and our society is either going to be great or not based on how we perform as creatures of the city" (Simon in Beiser 2011).[1] The city, then, is the central through-line Simon's serials. This book demonstrates how his serials approach this topic from different angles in a way that amounts to a complex and elaborate intervention in public discourse in the U.S.

Two Contextualizations

David Simon holds the unofficial title of being a showrunner, meaning that he is both the head writer and a leading producer on his serials. As head writer he writes teleplays for episodes, is in charge of developing the overall storylines of his serials, as well as doing rewrites on other writers' drafts. But on top of this creative power, his managerial responsibilities that come with being a leading producer also give him a large degree of control over the final product. Yet despite the creative *and* administrative control exerted by the showrunner, the collaborative nature of producing television drama means that we should be careful when discussing Simon's agency in producing his shows. Producers, directors, actors, and writers each weave their separate strands that end up forming the single cord of a television serial. It is crucial to say that the common thread running through Simon's serials is not woven by Simon alone.

The very ambition, however, of tracing the through-line in Simon's serials comes from an ambition to uncover a more complex cultural critique than is possible by examining 'only' one of the serials in isolation from the others. The consistent thematic core and realist aesthetics of Simon's serials is evident despite the fact that important members of the personnel – such as cinematographers, editors, production designers, and many actors – change from serial to serial. This suggests that the core creative and managerial team of, especially, David Simon, Nina Kostroff Noble, Ed Burns, George Pelecanos are able to exert a creative and administrative influence that makes for a consistent and recognizable politics and aesthetics. There are, nonetheless, several aspects about the television that limit the influence of the showrunner.

Since making *The Corner* around the turn of the century Simon has been able to extend his collaboration with HBO, resulting in three multi-season serials and five miniseries. This industrial context is important because a showrunner's influence over 'his serials' is very much shaped by the practical and economic realities of producing multi-season dramas. Television networks do not order a specific number of seasons of a serial before releasing an opening season, meaning that writers and showrunners do not know how long a serial will last. To television scholar Erlend Lavik, this "weakens the creator's control of the work and also weakens our belief in the existence of an authorial intention – a unified plan and will – that ties everything together" (Lavik 2015, 14).

This is important, for instance, when considering the fact that Simon is unable to ascertain which of his ideas HBO will want to produce. When Simon first pitched *The Wire* to HBO they wanted him to do an adaptation of his and Ed Burns's book *The Corner* instead (Simon in Baldwin 2013). Later, Simon and his collaborators believed that they would be making a serial called *Legacy of Ashes* about the CIA after they had concluded *Treme* (Simon 2018). That project did not happen and Simon's next project instead became *Show Me a Hero*. After that HBO called for Simon to produce two pilots. One was filmed, picked up, and became *The Deuce* while a pilot for a political drama, which veteran political journalist Carl Bernstein had been involved in developing, was never shot (Simon in Smith 2017).

In 2015, Simon described his career of making social critiques for the small screen as being "as improbable as it was a decade ago" while also noting that "I get less hours than I used to" (Simon in Woods 2015), which does seem true when one looks at his multiple-season dramas: *The Wire* went on for five seasons and 60 episodes, *Treme* got four seasons and 36 episodes, and then *Legacy of Ashes* did not happen, and Simon was once again producing a six-part miniseries like when he started his career at HBO as a showrunner with *The Corner*. *The Deuce* concluded after three seasons and 25 episodes. From 60 hours on *The Wire*, to 36 on *Treme*, and 25 on *The Deuce*, Simon's societal critiques do still make it to the screen. But they are nevertheless constricted by the hours HBO is giving him. This is but one reason why it is problematic to talk of *Show Me a Hero* and *Treme* as 'Simon's work'; not only are they produced by people other than Simon, they are also HBO's content. What Simon's serials are able to say to and about American culture is fundamentally shaped by and embedded within the context of producing content for HBO.

HBO's decision not to renew *Treme* for a total of five full-length seasons (Andersen 2017, 142) bears witness to the fact that producing television drama is a process with an unknown horizon. Only in the case of his miniseries have Simon and his closest group of collaborators been able structure a narrative knowing how many hours they would get to tell their story. In the case of multi-season serials, it is never set in stone where the writers and producers will want to or be able to take a story. There are, however, also several aspects that speak to the strength of the showrunner, which consequently justifies this book's attempt to explore the through-line in Simon's work. These aspects have to do with the writers' room, the fact that Simon consistently sees his ideas through from conceptualization, to production and release, as well as the relatively 'short' seasons he makes.

Simon can maintain a strong authorial voice in his work due to how the writers' room works where the other writers are supposed to serve the showrunner's overall vision. Playwright and television writer Diana Son explains the difference between writing for television and writing her own plays as a matter of authorial voice: "You're always trying to fulfill the aesthetic of the show and of your showrunner. When you're writing a play, you're writing in your own voice" (Son in Kallas 2014a, 112). The writing of a serial drama is a group effort that serves an overall voice that is shaped at the outset by the creator. The showrunner then manages this vision through his rewrites. George Pelecanos has said that on *The Wire*: "All the scripts [were] minutely mapped out ... [but] In the end, the final word [was] David's" (Pelecanos in Talbot 2007), which is seconded by screenwriter Rafael Alvarez's recollection about how, on *The Wire*, "The final decision was always David's, but he encouraged debate and wanted to be persuaded that there was a better way to go, if you could argue it successfully" (Alvarez in Lynskey 2018). From that starting point, other writers work to support the vision founded by the showrunner. That, however, does not mean that these writers – like Richard Price and George Pelecanos on *The Wire* – do not make a difference in the final outcome of a serial – they most certainly do; but they do so within a paradigm laid down by the creator(s) of the serial, which is an important reason for examining and discussing Simon's works as a whole.

It is also crucial that the showrunner is the person who is able to see the farthest ahead. He is able to set the course for where a serial is going to go (Lavik 2015, 90). That also means that when the showrunner and his closest group of collaborators see what actors and writers, for example, bring to the table as a television serial evolves, they can continually develop their creative vision because they are able to keep an eye on the overall narrative arcs of a serial. This fact of producing television drama shows a part of the showrunner's creative control.

Simon's strong influence on his serials is further enhanced by his participation in all stages from conceptualization to production and release. He has seen all of his serials through to the end of their run. Some serials change showrunners mid-way through their run (e.g. *The West Wing*, 1999–2006, and *The Walking Dead*, 2010–2022), while other productions have what showrunner Chris Downey has termed cradle-to-grave showrunners (Downey in Bennett 2014, 213). It is particularly important that Simon has consistently been a cradle-to-grave showrunner. He has both conceived a vision for his serials and has been involved in developing and administering the execution of his initial ideas. This makes his role more central and adds weight to the rationale of viewing his productions in relation to each other. But the relatively low number of episodes in Simon's multi-season dramas is also important.

Many network television series have 24 episodes per season and the sheer number of teleplays needed for that volume of content requires a group effort (Thompson 2003, 39–40). The seasons in Simon's serials are shorter: *The Wire* averages 12 episodes per season, *Treme*'s first three seasons has 10 or 11 episodes each (with a five-episode final season), and *The Deuce* only has eight or nine episodes per season. In terms of Simon's miniseries, Simon's influence is also very strong as he usually only collaborates with one or two co-writers on these shows: David Mills on *The Corner*, Ed Burns and Evan Wright on *Generation Kill*, William Zorzi on *Show Me a Hero*, Ed Burns and Reena Rexrode on *The Plot Against America*. His latest miniseries, *We Own This City* (2022),[2] however, had three more writers aside from co-creator George Pelecanos: Ed Burns, William

Zorzi, and D. Watkins. In relation to multi-season dramas, television scholar Trisha Dunleavy argues that shorter seasons makes it possible for a showrunner "to sustain a significant level of influence" than in cases where there is a much higher demand for teleplays (Dunleavy 2018, 58). Simon's task of 'only' writing and overseeing this 'small' number of teleplays strengthens his ability to be a strong influence on the production of his serials.

In addition to his importance as a writer on these serials, Simon's role as an on-set collaborator is also important. Screenwriter Christina Kallas writes that one of the characteristic features that has made American television drama so successful is the fact that writers (though not necessarily the showrunner) are often present on the set (Kallas 2014b). This means that though we cannot let all textual components point back to Simon as the sole originator of the textual utterance, his creative and administrative influences on these productions are crucial. This is why it makes sense to explore the through-line in his work as a showrunner. The fact that Simon ended up as a showrunner at age 40, however, has a long backstory.

Simon's first experience in publishing was writing for and editing *The Diamondback*, the college newspaper of the University of Maryland. However, before even graduating Simon had started writing numerous articles for *The Baltimore Sun* on a freelance basis, which subsequently earned him a permanent position in 1983 on his graduation. Here he started out writing very "reactive" pieces about the preceding day's crime, though he later came to cover crime as a social issue. Simon's first brush with the television industry came about when his 1991 journalistic account of a Baltimore homicide unit, *Homicide: A Year on the Killing Streets*, was picked up by Barry Levinson and subsequently served as the inspiration for NBC's *Homicide: Life on the Street* that ended up running for seven seasons (Simon in Baldwin 2013). Set in Baltimore and depicting African Americans with greater nuance compared to other television series of its day (Mascaro 2004; 2005), this series shares common features with the series that Simon would later be the showrunner on. Simon's also earned his first writing credit on *Homicide* by penning with David Mills season two's opening episode "Bop Gun." Half of this episode's script ended up being Simon and Mills's material, because once Robin Williams had been cast, showrunner Tom Fontana had to give him more scenes (Simon 2014a). With 'only' 50 percent of the script having survived, Simon and Mills thought they had not done their part, but the people behind *Homicide* since gave them the chance to write another script.

Then, in 1995, Simon opted to take a buy-out from his position at *The Baltimore Sun*, which he believed to be headed "in a bad direction." Simon wrote two scripts, one for *NYPD Blue* and one for *Homicide*. Crucial to Simon's later career as a showrunner, Fontana promised Simon that he would teach him how to produce television shows while working on *Homicide*. Among other things, this meant that Simon would try his hand at editing and casting, thus enabling him to acquire the skillset required for producing television drama that would be relevant when he transitioned to becoming a showrunner (Simon in Baldwin 2013; Simon in Antholis 2019, Episode 3).

Simon was eventually credited with being a producer on the last two seasons of *Homicide* and was involved with writing a total of 14 *Homicide* teleplays (out of 122 episodes). Simon was never a leading force on that series but played a comparatively minor role in a production spearheaded by Tom Fontana (Lavik 2015, 20). But Simon's time on this NBC production taught him the ropes of the television industry and seems to have been something of a *sine qua non* for Simon's subsequent career with HBO. Given that *Homicide* is more Tom Fontana's production than it is Simon's, I do not explore this show, though Simon's experiences there profoundly inform his subsequent career as a showrunner (Simon in Talbot 2007).

However, trying to understand Simon's serial's engagement with American culture calls for a qualification of how one understands cultural utterances as part of – and as interventions in – a cultural context. To this end, I look to the arguments set forth by intellectual historian Quentin Skinner.

Simon's serials emphasize so strongly their engagement with contemporary American society and culture that we need to look outside the textual boundaries of the serials themselves to see what they are trying to do. This motivates a contextualist approach. Skinner argues that texts are best understood historically by looking at what texts *do* in their historical context(s). During the promotion of *Show Me a Hero*, David Simon and director Paul Haggis were interviewed on *CBS This Morning* where journalist Gayle King commented on this miniseries' depiction of a desegregation case from the 1980s and 1990s in Yonkers, New York. She remarked that when she thought of desegregation, she thought of "the 60s and Alabama and Georgia" (King and Rose 2015). Indeed, an important part of this miniseries' portrayal of desegregation politics lies in its setting. Through Skinner's argument we see how this miniseries *does* something in its historical context. It specifically avoids the 1960s and the South as its setting and thus eschews the mainstream way of talking about and understanding desegregation efforts. Director Paul Haggis says in a piece of promotional material on HBO's YouTube channel that "When you hear forced desegregation you think Birmingham in the '60s, some place in the South, you think civil rights marches. You don't think about New York, 1987 through 1993" (Haggis in HBO 2015). Taking a cue from Skinner's approach attunes our attention to see how this miniseries does not 'just' make a point about public housing and desegregation, but it does so embedded in a historical context, taking an outlier standpoint among other popular culture narratives about race and segregation in America. It expands the depiction of desegregation to another region and era in American history.

In a similar way, media scholar Robin Andersen argues that much of the earliest news coverage of Hurricane Katrina vilified New Orleans and its citizens (Andersen 2018, 3). *Treme*'s sympathetic portrayal of New Orleans thus directly *counters* that media discourse. Indeed, Simon has argued that this serial was "an argument *for* the city. For the idea of American urbanity, for the melting pot, for the idea that our future can't be separated from the fact that we are all going to be increasingly compacted into urban areas, though we're different in race and culture and religion" (Simon in Beiser, 2011; emphasis added). Speaking through the character Creighton Bernette (John Goodman), the serial proclaims its wish for New Orleans to survive Katrina at a point in time where it was still uncertain whether or not – or how – the city would be rebuilt (*Treme*, E1S1). The serial is envisioned as a statement that *aims to do something* in its immediate historical context. By countering some of the negative commentary that New Orleans faced in the aftermath of Katrina, *Treme* engages in debates about the survival of New Orleans and its distinctive culture. It is not merely a story about a place and a group of people; it is a statement directed at both a public debate as well as concrete historical realities.

Such a view of texts as interventions in their immediate contexts is central to understanding Simon's serials' societal critique. This understanding is qualified through Skinner's methodology. To Skinner, texts do not merely *mean* things, they *do* things in and to the context in which they are historically embedded. This idea is premised on the notion that to understand a text in context, it is necessary uncover how it engaged in dialogue with its surroundings and with the key interlocutors. Texts can best be understood as *responses* to the questions that seemed pressing at the time of writing. Skinner argues that one cannot understand what texts "are *doing*, whether they are satirizing, repudiating, ridiculing, ignoring, accepting other points of view" if one reads them without heeding their contexts (Skinner in Pallares-Burke 2002, 219). In Simon's work, this is the dehumanization of people struggling with drug addiction in *The Corner*, Hurricane Katrina in *Treme*, and the segregated city in *Show Me a Hero*. With the above statement as a starting point, the critic's task is then to find out how a text participated in its cultural setting.[3]

This book thus contextualizes Simon's serials in two ways. On the one hand, it places each production in relation to Simon's other serials while it, on the other hand, also situates them in relation to larger social and cultural contexts. However, in order to understand more fully how Simon's television serials participate in the larger cultural debate about the American city, it is insufficient to only examine the serials themselves. One must also outline some of the social issues they speak to. This choice is premised on the idea that the wish to understand any text *in* context is predicated on an understanding of the context in question. Accordingly, to understand Simon's serials *contextually*, one needs to understand at least some of the historical dynamics it addresses. Each chapter therefore outlines some of the socio-historical issues that Simon's serials depict.

David Simon's American City

According to Simon, sociologist William Julius Wilson's 1997 book *When Work Disappears* was an inspiration for the second season of *The Wire*'s exploration of the loss of blue-collar jobs (Simon in Mills 2011). Wilson's study had shown that by the 1990s the scarcity of available jobs made it more common for residents of inner-city

Introduction 13

neighborhoods not to work in a typical week (Wilson 1997, xiii). The industrial jobs that inner-city residents had previously relied on were gone, leaving many people without good chances of solid employment. This development only added to the list of serious problems facing inner-city areas – a situation only exacerbated by the fact that many citizens who could afford it chose to move away from inner cities and out to the suburbs. As more middle-class African Americans from the 1970s were able to move out of ghettos and into, sometimes predominantly white, middle-class suburban neighborhoods, African Americans who still lived in ghettos grew ever more isolated (Wilson 1997, xvii–xviii; Brøndal 2016, 287–288). This massive process of suburbanization resulted in a reduced tax base for many central cities, creating a rising concentration of residents with few choices and resources who needed social and economic support. In the quarter-century following World War II, suburbs grew while inner cities faced decline. Simon's serials dramatize the vestiges of these historical realities.

In an early episode of *The Wire*, police informant *extraordinaire* Bubbles (Andre Royo) rides with police detective Jimmy McNulty (Dominic West) to see the officer's son play a soccer game in the suburbs. When McNulty drops Bubbles off again back in Western Baltimore the bleak *mise en scène* offers a striking contrast to the more colorful suburban scene. Just before McNulty's car rolls into

Figure 1 Sunlit soccer game in the suburbs.

Figure 2 Mother and children walking on a sidewalk.

the frame in the scene in West Baltimore, we see a mother who looks like she is trying to get herself and her children home. This dimly lit scene shows her children playing and running around her feet.

In the light of the preceding suburban scene – which featured a soccer game with many parents looking intently at their kids playing – this change of scenery shows how such a fundamental thing as child's play is profoundly shaped by social environment. Bubbles' remark that "It's a thin line 'tween heaven and here" – the epigraph of the episode – only drives home the point of how quality of life and life opportunities are very much matters of separated social spaces (*TW*, S1E4). In the face of a highly stratified society, Simon asks rhetorically, in his foreword to the 2015 reissue of Lisa Belkin's book *Show Me a Hero*, how much America can be seen as one or as several communities:

> Do all Americans have the same, shared future? Are they all vested in at least a piece – if not an equal share, at least a meaningful portion – in that shared future? Are we all still engaged in the same national experiment? Or not? (Simon 2015, xi)

Martin Luther King's words, uttered in 1963, about the African American living on a "lonely island of poverty in the midst of a vast ocean of material prosperity" (King 1963, 409) came to ring even truer for some groups in the last decades of the twentieth century. Simon broaches the same issue when he raises the question of how to envision American society: as a continuous continent or as a scattered archipelago? For Bubbles, it is, unfortunately, the latter. In *Show Me a Hero*, Norma O'Neal (LaTanya Jackson), one of the residents of the Schlobohm housing project in Yonkers, New York, has a son (McKinley Belcher III) who constructs minivans for a living (*Show Me a Hero* [*SMAH*], E1). Set in 1987, this fact resounds ominously for those viewers who know that the loss of manufacturing jobs has exacerbated social problems in poor neighborhoods. In the post-war era, 40 percent of the workforce in America was employed in the industrial sector. By 2018 that number was down to 13 percent. Because of this shift in the economy, there are today worse job opportunities for low-skilled workers than in the post-war era when there were good-paying jobs in the industrial sector. When those jobs disappear, lower-paying and non-unionized jobs in the service sector are what is left for large groups of the working class (Kollmeyer 2018, 2–3). Even in such subtly presented dialogue, Simon's serials hint at the social-historical context that is relevant for really understanding their thematic core. Such structural issues, however, can be difficult to dramatize and Simon's serials sometimes only hint at such contextual matters without elaborating on them further.

Already before *The Corner* aired, David Simon told a reporter: "TV means finding shorthand ways to reference anything real." In other words, all information about the real world must be presented in a condensed way in order not to let information dumps ruin the flow of televisual storytelling (Simon in Rose 1999). Sometimes such social issues are at the narrative core of Simon's serials and sometimes they serve as the background for other focal points, but they are always present.

This book offers a style of contextualist close reading that examines how the urban interest threads Simon's oeuvre. These analyses examine how Simon's serials engage in discourses about contemporary urban issues in America. The book consequently has two ambitions. First, it reads Simon's serials as a whole and draws connections from serial to serial to present them as a coherent intervention in American culture. A part of this ambition is to devote attention to the parts of Simon's career that so far has received little attention:

The Corner, *Show Me a Hero*, and *The Deuce*. The book's readings of these under-examined shows offers some counterweight to the very strong interest in *The Wire* compared to the rest of Simon's oeuvre. Second, the book contributes to our understanding of Simon's serials commentary on the American city. Chapters 1–5 analyze each of Simon's serials from *The Corner* to *The Deuce*. The conclusion sheds light on the two productions that do not focus on the American city – *Generation Kill* and *The Plot Against America* – and ties together different thematic strands in his work. It lays out Simon's political stance and sums up how his serials engage in public discourse about the state and future of the American city, and how they continually develop Simon's portrait of American urbanity.

Notes

1 According to the 2010 American Census, 80.7 percent of the American population lived in urban areas, corresponding to 249,253,271 people. To qualify that category of urban areas, America Census distinguishes between *urbanized areas* (+50,000 people) and *urban clusters* (2,500–50,000 people). Of those 80.7 percent, 71.2 percent (219,922,123 people) lived in 486 different urbanized areas and 9.5 percent (29,331,148 people) lived in 3,087 different urban clusters. The remaining 19.3 percent (59,492,267 people) lived in rural areas defined as "all population, housing, and territory not included within an urban area" (United States Census 2010). But since the 1970s, urban residents live more in suburbs than in central cities (Teaford 2006, 127).
2 *We Own This City* was released after I had written this book. I therefore do not analyze this miniseries.
3 See Jensen 2017 and Jensen 2021 for an elaboration of my theoretical reflections on how to study David Simon's oeuvre.

1

The Humanized Drug Addict: *The Corner* (2000)

The Corner makes its political intentions clear from the beginning. Its first scene shows its director Charles S. Dutton in Western Baltimore talking about the prevalence of open-air drug markets across major cities in America. This is, he tells us, "the information center of the neighborhood" but also "the place of death, of addiction or the suddenness of gunshots." In Dutton's words, *The Corner* is a story about "the men, women, and children living in the midst of the drug trade," people whose "voices are too rarely heard" (*The Corner* [TC], E1). By presenting itself as a counter-narrative to a media picture that has its focus elsewhere, the miniseries offers its *raison d'être* for its portrayal of a group of marginalized people.

The Wire would later cause quite a stir about how it presented Baltimore to the world and to actor Mike Rowe, this serial, along with NBC's *Homicide*, "convinced millions of Americans that Baltimore is a fantastic place to buy drugs, find a whore, or get murdered. Better yet ... all three at once!" (Rowe 2014). Simon rebutted Rowe's criticisms and did so in a way that also speaks to what *The Corner* aimed to accomplish:

> Mr. Rowe was clearly raising an argument that I find familiar and disturbing: That an undeserving portion of Baltimore has been chronicled at the expense of a Baltimore more deserving of attention, and that the America left behind by deindustrialization, poverty and the depredations of the drug war should just quiet the fuck down while we sell more of the America that has not been so marginalized. (Simon 2014b)

Simon's defense of *The Wire* aligns completely with Dutton's account of *The Corner*'s mission. Their ambition is to tell stories of a forgotten and overlooked part of society that they see the mainstream media not taking any strong interest in. This is why the creators of *The*

Corner and *The Wire* see a need to humanize marginalized inner-city dwellers. *The Corner* does so by embracing both realist and melodramatic ways to depict its marginalized characters. Its realist impulse comes to the fore in its way of stressing that the people shown on screen are real people, while its melodramatic element shows itself in how the series attempts to engender emotions of sympathy in the viewer. *The Corner*'s political ambition is to invite its viewers to recalibrate their conceptualization of the people on screen: from 'merely' being inner-city drug addicts to emerging as torn and ailing human beings. This off-the-beaten-path depiction of this marginalized group is essential to *The Corner*.

The Corner follows Gary McCullough's (T.K. Carter) efforts to make enough money to buy drugs to sustain his addiction. Though Gary studied for a year at Ohio State, he dropped out when he learned that his girlfriend, Fran (Khandi Alexander), was pregnant. He nevertheless built a successful career for himself and was able to provide for his family in a way that allowed them to move out of the city center to a middle-class suburb. But both he and his wife tragically end up addicted to drugs in the years of the crack epidemic (early 1980s–early 1990s). DeAndre McCullough (Sean Nelson), Fran and Gary's son, is shown is helping his mother sustain her drug addiction though he himself is busy selling drugs and trying to either be promoted to the 10th grade or get a job.

While Gary is able to get seasonal employment, DeAndre gets his 15-year-old girlfriend Tyreeka (Toy Connor) pregnant. DeAndre gets a job at a fast food restaurant, but it is the mother of the family, Fran, who offers the positive counterpoint to this story as she, in the end, manages to become clean. Each episode is bookended by fictionalized interview sequences focusing on the person that the episode revolves around – episode two, for example, is titled "DeAndre's Blues" and begins with an interview with DeAndre and ends with an interview with the social worker Miss Ella (Tyra Ferrell) who talks about her work with teenagers in the community. The six-episode miniseries ends with Gary dying from an overdose in his parents' basement and DeAndre becoming addicted to drugs. The final moments of the last episode feature an interview with the real people behind the characters in the miniseries, among others Fran and DeAndre.

Befitting its eye-level portrayal of drug-afflicted Baltimoreans, the miniseries opens with a handheld camera backtracking to follow Gary heading to a corner store. This opening shows how the miniseries

The Humanized Drug Addict: The Corner

is comfortable with a restricted scope that aims to understand and, crucially, to humanize its ailing and struggling characters. This ambition is also forwarded in the title, which indicates a place-specific focus on a concrete, local setting (a corner), while also calling attention to a group of people who are driven into a metaphorical corner with few obvious ways out.

The Corner's liberal use of flashbacks – one of the miniseries' more noticeable stylistic choices – emphasizes the contingency of the present. By showing the neighborhood's decline, the miniseries tries to avoid letting the viewer think that what is seen on screen is to be taken as a given, and by offering a glimpse into Gary's life before he became addicted to drugs, *The Corner* shows viewers the man he was before he became addicted. This historicizes *The Corner*'s portrayal of this Baltimore neighborhood. The first flashback occurs just eleven minutes into its first episode where Gary McCullough is walking down a street and looks over to a store where he worked as a child. The color scheme clearly demonstrates a contrast between a bleak present and a, literally and metaphorically, more colorful past:

Figure 3 Child standing in front of a store.

Figure 4 Gary as a child standing in front of the same store.

The contrast in the color scheme can be interpreted as a way of portraying how things have deteriorated in this area since Gary was a child, but it can also be understood as Gary's romanticized view of the past (Sweeney 2013, 131). The viewer can understand it in either way or as both at the same time. Regardless, this establishes what television scholar Jason Mittell terms an *intrinsic norm:* it teaches viewers how to watch the miniseries and informs them what to expect of subsequent episodes (Mittell 2015, 168). Employed both to explain Gary's backstory and to portray the bigger picture of this West Baltimore community, these flashbacks historicize *The Corner*'s depiction of drug use in inner-city neighborhoods in the early 1990s.

Dutton had initially been reluctant about using flashbacks, believing that only 3 percent of them work; "The other 97 percent don't," he told a journalist in 2000 (Scott 2000). Dutton's point is focused on the aesthetics of the flashbacks; do they "work" or not? Regardless of whether one agrees with Dutton's assessment, *The Corner*'s political argument would be reduced if it had not included the flashbacks.

The Humanized Drug Addict: The Corner

The miniseries would be barred from showing the historical change in the neighborhood if it did not include the flashbacks and it would only be able to show the characters in their present state. That would mean not learning about how Gary had once been on a better path and that this current state is the result of a catastrophic fall from grace. The contingency of Gary's present state would fall away without the flashbacks.

This technique shows how far these characters have fallen from their previously well-sorted lives but it also sets up one of the pivotal scenes of the miniseries, which hinges on the use of flashbacks. Because the viewer has come to expect flashbacks as an intrinsic norm, this instance does not stand out as an unexpected break with the miniseries' overall aesthetics. The scene in question comes at the very end when Gary is overdosing in his parents' basement to the sounds of The Impressions' song "People Get Ready" (E6).

In the last scene of *The Corner*'s first episode, Gary helps DeAndre and his friend R.C. (Corey Parker Robinson) to put up a basketball hoop. DeAndre and Gary do not spend much time with each other due to the father's addiction, but this situation appears to be a rare moment of bonding, or just interaction, between father and son. But the hope that father and son might really spend some time with each other is immediately crushed when Ronnie (Tasha Smith), Gary's girlfriend, shows up and offers Gary drugs. Gary had taken a shot and talked a bit with DeAndre and R.C. DeAndre and Gary had even agreed to play a game against each other, but Gary leaves the second Ronnie appears (*TC*, E1).

In the flashback sequence, when Gary is overdosing in the basement of his parents' house, however, he is shown taking his one shot. The use of extended close-ups, and a shot-reverse-shot that makes it look like Gary and DeAndre are looking at each other rather intensely, shows how Gary's relationship with his son is one of the most important things in his life. The flashback creates a sense of missed opportunity and regret that Gary chose to do drugs instead of spending time with his son and, consequently, this scene shows how Gary failed at this point. His decision to go with Ronnie is surely prompted by his addiction but Gary does not even postpone doing drugs. He abandons DeAndre without even playing basketball with him just for a short while. Through its allusion to Gary's love for his son and his regret about his decisions, *The Corner* emphasizes the importance of the parent–child relationship and consequently criticizes Gary for abandoning his son.

The use of evocative editing, music, and flashbacks in the scene where Gary dies arguably produces *The Corner*'s strongest use of pathos, but The Impressions' song adds an extra layer. Historian Brian Ward points out how this song is associated with 1960s civil rights activism and argues that singer Curtis Mayfield in this track "urged his listeners to 'get on board' the righteous struggle for racial justice" (Ward 2006). This allusion to civil rights activism gives a political dimension to the scene, but Gary's life is over and there is, tragically, nothing for him to 'get ready for.'

Simon and Mills were able to plot *The Corner* to end with Gary's death because they always knew they had only six episodes (Abrams 2018, 7). Unlike multi-season dramas like *The Wire* and *Treme*, the length of a miniseries is usually set in stone from the start and it is therefore possible able to arc such productions in a very strict way. This is a central difference between the serial and the miniseries.

The American television industry does not always adhere to the Aristotelian principle that all narratives are structured around a beginning, middle, and end. Mittell argues that success in this industry means starting a series and then having an infinite middle part that keeps going as long as it is profitable for the network to keep it going. This is why some series end rather abruptly like in the case of, say, *GLOW* (2017–2019) (Mittell 2015, 319–321). This is the direct opposite of the miniseries, which is 'born' with an ending. Just before the release of *Show Me a Hero*, Simon told *Rolling Stone* that creating a miniseries is "still hard work but you know that once you're in, you're in until the end, and you even get to say exactly what you intend" (Simon in Woods 2015), which speaks to the difference in commercial dynamics that shape the outcome of multiple season dramas and miniseries, respectively.

This difference influences how miniseries depict characters. As information accrues across many hours of screen time, the key characters of a multi-season serial usually become more and more complex. While some characters in serials ultimately do evolve over time – such as Eileen in *The Deuce* or McNulty in *The Wire* – television scholar Roberta Pearson argues that in television it is often "more accurate to talk about character accumulation and

The Humanized Drug Addict: The Corner   23

depth than it is to talk about character development" (Pearson 2007, 56). Mittell calls this *character elaboration*, arguing that characters "rarely shift, but our understanding of them often does" (Mittell 2015, 136).

Characters in miniseries work more like characters in films where the writers can carve out a trajectory that will end in a specific way. Simon was able to outline, from the outset, the full storylines for Gary McCullough and Fran Boyd in *The Corner* and Nick Wascisko in *Show Me a Hero*. As the protagonists of both miniseries end up dead, both *The Corner* and *Show Me a Hero* achieve a narrative unity through the narrative arcs of their leading men. This way of being sure to see a narrative arc through by tracing the (rise and) fall of a character is in striking contrast to how HBO cut *Treme* short, long before the creative team wanted to end that serial.

The most central feature of the miniseries, however, is its finite length. Television critics John De Vito and Frank Tropea discuss how the 'Golden Age of the epic miniseries' in the period 1974–1989 saw the release of successful miniseries such as *Rich Man, Poor Man* (ABC, 1976), *Roots* (ABC, 1977), and *Holocaust* (NBC, 1978). In that era, the standard length was eight to twelve episodes (Vito and Tropea 2010, 1). All of Simon's series have either six (*The Corner*, *Show Me a Hero*, *The Plot Against America*, and *We Own This City*) or seven (*Generation Kill*) episodes.

Before *Stranger Things* (2016–) was extended beyond its first season, several critics labeled it a miniseries (Scherstuhl 2016; Weingarten 2016; Carranza 2018) and the same happened in the case of *True Detective* (2014–), which was extended into an anthology series. Indeed, HBO raised something of a stir in the television industry when it decided to submit *True Detective* as a drama series and not a miniseries in that year's Emmy run (Andreeva 2014). People thought of *True Detective* as being a miniseries but people do not discuss *Stranger Things* and *True Detective* as miniseries anymore because they no longer fit that description. If a (mini)series extends beyond the single-season format, it abandons the core feature of the miniseries: being a finite narrative unit from the start. This is important to keep in mind given the fact that Simon so far has created five miniseries and three multi-season serials.

Interlocutors and Intertextual Dialogue

In the first episode, Gary is in his parents' basement reading a chemistry book while a radio call-show in the background discusses racism in America. A caller introduced as "James from Essex" (who sounds very much like David Simon) says:

> Yeah, I wanna comment on what that other caller said earlier. I mean all this crap about slavery and racism and all that be responsible for people who don't wanna work I just think that's a bunch of junk. You know what I mean? You don't hear Italian people or Irish people complain. And they was treated real bad when they got to this country. I mean when are we gonna stop hearing about racism? I mean slavery was more than a hundred years ago. [Indistinct due to diegetic sound effects] ... nobody take no drugs. They just do that to themselves. (*TC*, E1)

This caller's position represents a key interlocutor for *The Corner*. The miniseries rejects the caller's dismissal of the historical record in explaining or dealing with current issues regarding race in America. *The Corner*'s liberal use of flashbacks here come to stand for a belief in the necessity of understanding inner-city issues in a historical perspective. The flashbacks explain the current situation depicted on screen as a result of past developments and thus rebuts the sentiment expressed by the caller on this radio show.

According to sociologist William Julius Wilson, conservatives "tend to stress the importance of values, attitudes, habits, and styles in explaining different experiences, behavior, and outcomes of groups. According to this view, group differences are reflected in the culture" (Wilson 1997, xiv). By attacking the notion that structural racism and historical developments are relevant contexts for understanding current social problems in American ghettos, the caller represents this traditionally conservative sentiment.

The Corner rebuts this understanding of inner-city problems by making the caller's critique clash with what viewers see on screen. The monologue is initially audible in Gary's room, but it then changes to also function as a sound bridge when the image cuts to showing Gary's father, W.M. (J. Valenteen Gregg), coming home from what the viewer soon learns – through dialogue between Gary and W.M. – was a very long shift as a taxi driver. By showing a long shot from outside on the street where Gary's father is parking his taxi outside his home, *The Corner* exploits one of the constitutive elements of audiovisual media: the dual information tracks of sound and visuals. What we *hear* the caller saying does not align with what we are *seeing*. Gary is even shown reading chemistry books while intoxicated, which also counters what the caller is saying on the radio show. Gary struggles with drug addiction, but he is not lazy and W.M. is a hard worker.

The Corner engages with this conservative sentiment by first signaling the discussion it wishes to address and then responds to that discourse head-on. *The Corner* here behaves like a textual expression of what Quentin Skinner calls the "innovating ideologist." Skinner argues that any writer trying to legitimize opinions or actions that could be seen as a form of illegitimate discourse must frame their ideas within certain boundaries. Discursive convention restricts what will be taken seriously at a given point in time and people trying to say 'new' things must do so in a familiar language if they want to legitimize their standpoint. "Every revolutionary is," writes Skinner, "obliged to march backward into battle" in the sense that they must formulate their standpoints in a way that does not come off as illegitimate from the start (Skinner 1974, 294–295).

Intellectual historians Frank Beck Lassen and Mikkel Thorup note that this is a balancing act that the writer has to maintain. By adhering to dominant discursive conventions, the issue that the text activates looks familiar to the viewer but the text then systemically strives to revise the understanding of the issue at hand. In other words, the critical writer needs to play on the existing playing field even if they want to change the rules of the game (Lassen and Thorup 2009, 33). This snippet of dialogue on the radio thus serves as *The Corner*'s way of pointing out the interlocutors that it seeks to engage with and rebut.

Seeing as *The Corner* was one of the first miniseries since *Roots* (1977) and *The Sophisticated Gents* (1981) to feature a mainly Black cast, it has something of a privileged position in terms of engaging in a cultural dialogue about the depiction of African Americans on television and in film. In *The Corner*'s third episode, DeAndre and his girlfriend Tyreeka are watching John Singleton's 1991 hood film *Boyz n the Hood*, and in Dutton's opening interview of episode five with DeAndre, the director asks DeAndre why he and his friends call their basketball team the "Crenshaw Mafia

Brothers" pointing to how "Crenshaw is a boulevard in Los Angeles." DeAndre merely replies "Saw *Boyz n the Hood*. Got it from there." Ed Burns and David Simon write that the boys agreed on the name CMB "after the fourth of fifth viewing of" Singleton's film (Burns and Simon 1998, 21) and this name's acronym, CMB, eventually becomes the name of DeAndre's and his friends' 'gang' when they sell drugs, suggesting how fascinated they are with the South-Central setting depicted in Singleton's film. Film scholar Manthia Diawara sees *Boyz n the Hood* as "a rite of passage film, a film about the Black man's journey in America" (Diawara 1993, 20), and *The Corner*'s storyline about DeAndre parallels this generic affiliation but it makes these two central allusions to *Boyz n the Hood*, to take issue with how some films portray inner-city neighborhoods.

A key difference between *The Corner* and *Boyz n the Hood* is how they depict shootings. In *Boyz n the Hood*, shootings are placed at key dramatic junctures that imbue these acts of violence and murder with a dramatic importance and gravitas. The film's opening intertitles clearly signposts its focus on murder and gun violence: "One out of every twenty-one Black American males will be murdered in their lifetime. Most will die at the hands of another Black male" (*Boyz n the Hood*). This fact surely highlights why shooting scenes are central to the film's narrative structure, but because key dramatic scenes center on violence, violence comes to stand at the center of attention of a film, which otherwise wishes to forward an agenda of non-violence. *The Corner* features only a single shooting and it is interesting to note that the sense of drama that accompanies violence in *Boyz n the Hood* is all but absent from *The Corner*.

The Corner's sole shooting scene is completely disorienting to the viewer in a way that avoids imbuing it with the same degree of dramatic tension and centrality that is characteristic of *Boyz n the Hood* and hood movies in general.[1] Showing the teenagers running around and haphazardly shooting their guns in every which direction, the scene does not even make it clear if anybody is actually shooting at DeAndre and his friends. Shot and edited in a way that confuses the viewer, this scene can hardly be said to romanticize gun violence in any way. But in the ensuing scene DeAndre and his friends are nevertheless standing on a corner boasting about how cool they were and how dramatic that shoot-out was to them.

The Humanized Drug Addict: The Corner

Viewers detect a distinct discrepancy between how they experienced the confusing shooting scene and how the young boys talk about it (*TC*, E5). The young men – the Crenshaw Mafia Brothers as they call themselves – see their experiences through the lens of hood films like *Boyz n the Hood*, and *The Corner* suggests that this form of thinking is not helpful in these children's lives. *The Corner* wants to avoid instilling shooting scenes with the same drama as early 1990s hood films. A somewhat similar shooting scene in *The Wire* with young men hardly taking aim while they shoot at each other ends with a young boy dying from a gunshot wound while he is inside his room in a nearby house (*TW*, S2E9). The mother's grief in this scene in *The Wire* harks back to how *The Corner* lingers on the grief and pain felt by relatives of murder victims.

When the community activist and social worker Miss Ella makes a memorial for a local resident killed during a robbery the previous year, she invites DeAndre and his friends to help out. It turns out that the victim was an uncle to one of DeAndre's friends, Tae (John Epps). Tae and one of the other teenagers therefore decide to help out, but it does not take long before these two friends have spelled out CMB with rocks in the dirt and start rapping "Get your guns out/ Get your guns out!" Their playful way of doing so reveals the childish nature of their fascination with gang culture and guns that they know from popular film and television shows. This scene points out how this fascination plays an unproductive frame of reference for these teenagers; even when they are helping make a memorial garden in honor of Tae's uncle they fall back into their fascination with media representations that depict the sort of violence that caused Tae's uncle to be killed (*TC*, E6).

Miss Ella, whom the teenagers know from a community recreation center where they spend some of their afternoons, stands as an important counterbalance to many other influences in these children's lives that are not as strong and positive as she is. It is later revealed – without Miss Ella's knowledge – that the memorial is also to be dedicated to Miss Ella's daughter who had been killed a few years earlier (*TC*, E6). The inclusion of Miss Ella's storyline is *The Corner*'s way of emphasizing the loss that accompanies violence and killings, but her presence in the miniseries is also important in terms of representational politics; of showing the strong community-oriented people that live in struggling neighborhoods. In this way,

The Corner avoids painting an overly bleak picture of America's inner cities.

This is important to note since *The Wire* later was criticized for *not* portraying the positive work of social workers in the Baltimore communities it centers on. In the words of urban policy analysts Peter Dreier and John Atlas, "*The Wire*'s unrelentingly bleak portrayal missed what's hopeful in Baltimore and, indeed, in other major American cities" (Dreier and Atlas 2009, 330). By including the positive influence of Miss Ella, *The Corner* avoids only displaying the negative elements of life in inner-city neighborhoods. This is important in terms of understanding *The Corner* in a broader context of media depictions of African Americans. American Studies scholar George Lipsitz argues that too many popular films and novels feature "phobic representations of Black people unfit for freedom" (Lipsitz 2011, 13). *The Corner*'s sympathetic and nonphonic depiction of ailing African Americans explicitly steers clear of this tendency. This choice ties in with how ghettos tend to be depicted in American media in general.

In her book on violence and murders in Los Angeles, journalist Jill Leovy writes that the media reported on very few of the many murders that happened in the 1980s and 1990s in poor neighborhoods. When these murders finally did receive mention in the press, however, they were framed improperly:

> Even when cases got some public attention, the tilt often seemed off. Gangs were a big topic, but atrocity, trauma, and lifelong sorrow were not part of the public's vocabulary about black-on-black violence. Somehow, mainstream America had managed to make a fetish of South Central murders yet still ignore them. The principal aspect of the plague – agony – was constantly underrated. (Leovy 2015, 37)

The Corner is also a contrast to the hood film in this way. The murder of Ricky (Morris Chestnut) in *Boyz n the Hood* addresses the terrible consequences of gang violence, but due to its storytelling format, the film is nevertheless unable to speak to the years of grief and trauma that arise from Ricky's death. However, while DeAndre and his friends are shown to be overly fascinated with the setting of the hood film, *The Corner* also shows how schools and recreation centers in Western Baltimore offer the boys with another cultural frame of reference.

The Humanized Drug Addict: The Corner 29

At one point, DeAndre recites Martin Luther King's 1963 "I Have a Dream" speech from the March on Washington for Jobs and Freedom at a public oratory contest. He does so with considerable skill and confidence for his young age and thus proves to himself and his skeptical teacher that his academic abilities are greater than she seems to expect of him (*TC*, E2). Later on, DeAndre and his friends play a basketball game, representing the Martin Luther King Recreation Center where they often spend time after school. But when they huddle up and get ready to play they do not yell "MLK" but "CMB," suggesting that while Martin Luther King represents the cultural frame of reference that their school and recreation center provides, the boys' own cultural frame of reference is culled from Singleton's hood film (*TC*, E5).

The last scene of *Boyz n the Hood* features two of its main characters, Tre Styles (Cuba Gooding Jr.) and Darrin "Doughboy" Baker (Ice Cube), sitting on a porch talking about how the news media that morning did not cover the murder of Doughboy's brother Ricky the day before. Doughboy laments, "Either they don't know, don't show, or don't care about what's going on in the hood. They had all this foreign shit. They didn't have shit on my brother, man" (*Boyz n the Hood*). This scene parallels Charles Dutton's opening monologue where he presents *The Corner* as a story about people whose "voices are too rarely heard." The boys had indeed watched the film in the early 1990s but *The Corner* makes an intertextual reference of this fact in order to express how it opts for a different way of portraying inner-city life. So while both *The Corner* and *Boyz n the Hood* focus on the challenges facing marginalized people living in inner-city neighborhoods, *The Corner* emphasizes that its project of humanizing this group of people is carried out in a different way than was the case with the hood films of the early 1990s.

Given how *The Corner*'s shooting scene is devoid of the drama and suspense characteristic of those featured in *Boyz n the Hood*, the miniseries uses Singleton's debut film as a contrastive frame of reference of how it does and does not portray inner-city neighborhoods. That does not mean that one should overstate the differences between *The Corner* and *Boyz n the Hood*. They share a core ethos but *The Corner* discusses whether the narrative choices *Boyz n the Hood* embodies are fully helpful in dealing with certain social issues in a constructive way.

In the opening interview of the second episode of *The Corner*, DeAndre and Dutton discuss the situation in this West Baltimore neighborhood and DeAndre explains that "Niggers be dying." Dutton replies, "You don't think you're being a little melodramatic?" to which DeAndre shrugs. Dutton's question to DeAndre represents *The Corner*'s way of preempting 'accusations' or reservations about the miniseries overstating its point in order to get its point across.

The Corner's way of ending and opening all its episodes with Dutton interviewing different characters reveals how much it wants to signal a strong commitment to realism. But it is also clear that the miniseries wants us to sympathize with Gary and other struggling addicts on screen. There is a clear emotionality at play. *The Corner* thus embraces both realistic and melodramatic elements. Since the late nineteenth century, however, there has been a tendency to see realism and melodrama as mutually exclusive categories. Seeing realism and melodrama dichotomously is rooted in a condescending view of melodrama, which has often been associated with clichés of rescues that happen only in the nick of time and of villains twirling their mustaches. Film scholar Linda Williams believes that melodrama can work with realism to "generate outrage against realities that could and, according to its creators, should be changed" (Williams 2014, 114). Parallel to this understanding, theater historian Thomas Postlewait argues that we should not see melodrama and realism as a dichotomy where "melodrama distorts, realism reports; melodrama offers escapism, realism offers life; melodrama is conservative, realism is radical; melodrama delivers ideologies (as false consciousness), realism deconstructs ideologies" (Postlewait 1996, 56). In other words, melodrama and realism can overlap in specific texts. They are not mutually exclusive categories.

DeAndre's shrug at Dutton's comment about him maybe being melodramatic makes Dutton explain the concept as "overly dramatic to make a point," revealing that Dutton uses the term in its 'old' usage as if the melodramatic mode undercuts DeAndre's attempts at conveying the realities of living in his neighborhood. Understanding that *The Corner* uses both realism and melodrama shows us how it emphasizes the reality of its subject matter while, at the same time, embracing a pathos-driven style. This instance of self-reflexiveness shows *The Corner* anticipating how it might be received, maybe as "overly dramatic to make a point." DeAndre, however, takes issue with Dutton's remark: "I'm saying niggers be thinking this a game. This shit is for real." Read in this self-reflexive way, DeAndre's anger here is *The Corner*'s anger. *The Corner* objects to the notion that its elements of emotionality and melodrama are textual constructs *imposed* on its real-life subject matter. The self-reflexiveness *The Corner* presents in this dialogue represents an awareness of its communicative situation; it is aware that some viewers may dismiss its portrayal of inner-city problems as manipulative melodrama.

The Corner suggests that its melodramatic elements are part of its realist impulse. In this sense, DeAndre's line that "This shit is for real" is a spelled-out statement of the miniseries' style. It rejects the notion that some viewers might simply see the miniseries as a textual game. *The Corner* wards off potential 'accusations' of sentimentality, which might be acutely important considering how the miniseries has its chief interest in humanizing a marginalized and misrepresented group of people.

Humanization and Dehumanization

Williams defines melodrama as "the fundamental mode of popular American moving pictures" that "is structured upon the 'dual recognition' of how things are and how they should be" (Williams, 1998, 42, 48). *The Corner*'s use of melodrama is embedded in its politics (i.e. its wish that viewers sympathize with Gary and its other characters). In Dutton's interview with Fran, Gary's ex-wife, she describes how she "first started messing with heroin when [her] sister Darlene died. She got burned up in a fire." Fran tells Dutton that a man offered her drugs at her sister's funeral. She accepted them as a way of coping with her loss. The dealer came back the next day, but after that Fran was hooked and had to go find drugs herself (*TC*, E3). The drug dealer's predatory behavior puts Fran's addiction in a new light. To Williams, melodrama works by activating a link between emotionality and morality, which is very much the case here with Fran (Williams 1998, 42). This scene shows how a person targeted Fran in a most fragile state, making the miniseries invite us to sympathize with her, and judge her less harshly. Her addiction is, at least, not only her own fault.

In the fourth episode, Gary goes to see Steven Spielberg's 1993 historical epic *Schindler's List* in a different part of Baltimore. Gary's thoughts on Spielberg's film furthers *The Corner*'s discussion of how its blend of realism and melodrama is connected to its political ambition of humanizing its characters. While doing drugs later that day with Fat Curt (Clarke Peters) and other people, Gary, clearly inspired by *Schindler's List*, talks about the Nazi dehumanization of the Jews in the 1930s and 1940s: "They couldn't see them being anything better than rats or bugs," Gary says, to which Rita (Robin Michelle McClamb) responds, "That sound like a miserable-ass movie." Gary replies, "Yeah, but it was real, all right?" suggesting that the "miserable" content of *Schindler's List* (and, by extension, *The Corner*) is rooted in its truthfulness. The misery is not a form of textual hyperbole. This piece of dialogue thus furthers the miniseries' attempt to ward off accusations of being melodramatic (in the old/pejorative sense of the word) and emphasizes that *The Corner* is rooted in real life.

The few scenes that show Gary in another part of Baltimore are more colorful than the present-day scenes from Western Baltimore and thus suggest how the people at the focus of this miniseries live in a separate reality, divorced from the harbor-adjacent setting that looks more hospitable. While in East Baltimore, Gary is listening to The O'Jays song "Livin' for the Weekend" on a walkman, which contains the lines "You might see me on the east side/ Ha, the west side/ I'm even going cross the bridge/ 'Cause I, 'cause I, 'cause I hear/ They really get down over there." The visual expression and the diegetic music thus create a sense of a divided Baltimore and *The Corner* suggests that this spatial isolation is one prerequisite for the harmful othering of the drug-afflicted citizens living in a marginalized West Baltimore.

It that sense, this scene – along with the scene where Dutton interviews DeAndre in the store – offers the miniseries' poetological manifesto. Referring to the dehumanization of Jews during the 1930s and 1940s, Gary says that "it's happening again" (*TC*, E4). It is completely suiting to Gary – a man shown to have a strong interest in abstract thought – that he says something like this, but it is important that it is Gary that makes this connection. If *The Corner* had made this comparison – without showing it to come from one of its characters who are based on real people – the miniseries might be accused of being hyperbolic by suggesting that there is a similarity between one form of dehumanization (in Nazi Germany) and another (in the U.S.). Spelling out this comparison within the storyworld makes it clear that *The Corner* objects to any discursive dehumanization of people who struggle with drug addiction. This motivates the miniseries' mission to humanize its characters. That is its political core. This also reveals how we are to understand the project of humanization in *The Corner*. It is a discursive phenomenon that has to do with how many people perceive a certain group of people: "They couldn't see them as anything better than rats or bugs," as Gary says.

The Corner's humanization of impoverished drug addicts living in blighted neighborhoods thus has more to do with generating sympathies and changing people's perceptions rather than calling for concrete policy measures. Lavik argues that the politics of *The Wire* are not presented in the form of policy initiatives and concrete plans for societal change: "*The Wire* does not gradually present a chain of argument with well-defined premises and claims. The series creates a complicated network of ideologically and emotionally charged connotations without describing in any detailed fashion the important connections between them" (Lavik 2014, 225). In a similar fashion, *The Corner* tries to engender in its viewers a wish for change by arousing their indignation; it is a counter narrative to those media stories that discursively reduce the humanity of inner-city dwellers and especially drug addicts.

That capacity is directly linked to the amount of screen time devoted to Gary and the other characters. *The Corner*'s project of humanization relies on what film theorist Murray Smith calls structures of sympathy and the fact that it shows people struggling with drug addiction, especially Gary, to be conscientious people. Television scholar Sheamus Sweeney argues that when drug addicts appeared in *Homicide* "they were lacking agency, usually witnesses to a crime and desperate for a fix" (Sweeney 2013, 122), which is a striking contrast to *The Corner*'s focus on Gary and his family. Gary is no bystander in a larger plotline about, say, a murder investigation. He and his family form the crux of the story.

To Murray Smith, viewers can become aligned with certain characters through either spatio-temporal attachment or subjective access (Smith 1995, 142): that is, how much screen time is devoted to a character and how much insight viewers get to a character's emotional life through devices like voice-over. The large amount of screen time devoted to Gary (including interviews with him and the interviews of which he becomes the topic of conversation) aligns the viewer with him in a way not seen in many other depictions of addicts. That feature opens up the possibility that viewers might judge Gary less harshly. We simply see more nuances in Gary because we see him in many different situations like when he is at work and when he muses over the callous attitudes he encounters in his community. In some cases, argues Smith, alignment can even lead to allegiance, which Smith defines as those cases where the viewer extends their sympathy to specific characters. This can, in turn, affect the viewer's moral evaluations of the character's behavior and actions (84–86).

Smith argues that the term "identification" – for the viewer's emotional engagement with characters – is misleading (222). Identification suggests that the viewer mimics what the character is feeling. As film scholar David Bordwell argues, "We might pity a grieving widow, but she isn't feeling pity, she's feeling grief" (Bordwell 2011). Smith's term allegiance, then, shows how we can sympathize with characters like Gary and Fran without suggesting that we feel what they are feeling. Through this terminology we can understand how *The Corner* is able to align its viewers with Gary and, quite possibly, create allegiance with him. Through the time spent with him, the morality he displays, and how he is shown to be less callous than some of the people around him the viewer is invited to sympathize with Gary.

This storytelling choice is directly interrelated to *The Corner*'s politics of humanization. With allegiance having to do with the viewer's "moral evaluation of characters" (Smith 1995, 84), it is important the viewer sees Gary trying to stop his wife's – and, by extension, his and DeAndre's – descent into addiction. These scenes therefore provide the viewer with important information that might well affect their moral evaluation of him. We know how he fought and how he tried to avoid drugs for a long time. This is central to *The Corner*'s overall ambition, which is further underscored by the miniseries' use of flashbacks and interviews.

The Humanized Drug Addict: The Corner

Soon after its release, journalist Janny Scott commented in *The New York Times* that *The Corner* "had shown black inner-city drug addicts as complex and startlingly human" (Scott 2000). Her comment about people struggling with addiction coming across as "startlingly human" surely does not come from her being surprised that people with addictions are human, but is rather motivated by how much *The Corner*'s portrayal of people struggling with drug addiction counters other forms of depicting addiction.

This is particularly poignant in Dutton's opening interview with Gary in episode four. Dutton mentions the books he sees lying around: "You got a library down here I see. James Baldwin, Thoreau, Elie Wiesel. *A History of God*. What's that about?" Gary: "Oh yeah, that's Judaism, Islam, Christianity. It's like it's three paths to the same god" explaining that he, when high, "[tries] to educate [him]self." This surely represents a very untraditional way of depicting drug addicts in popular culture. It adds layers to Gary and stresses the fact that his addiction does not nullify his individuality, which clearly is a representational point in itself. In episode two, Fran has kicked out DeAndre for selling drugs, which has made him move into their former (now abandoned) house. Knowing that his son is holding drugs, Gary sneaks in to steal from him but sees his son having sex with his girlfriend, Tyreeka. The interesting thing here is how, though Gary is stealing from his son, we see him briefly nodding with a slight smile on his face before his face turns back to a sadder expression. In this short glimpse, we see the father – not the drug addict stealing from his son – being glad to learn that DeAndre is growing up and creating his own life experiences (*TC*, E2). The scene embodies the overall aim of *The Corner*: we see the man before seeing his addiction.

"The mentality around here"

Even though we are invited to see the person before the addict, *The Corner* nevertheless emphasizes Gary's moral shortcomings. His choice not to play basketball with his son DeAndre but instead to go shoot drugs with Ronnie can surely be explained by his physical and psychological addiction to drugs. But it is still a rejection of his son who seems to hope that he here had the chance to spend just a little time with his father. But though Gary himself is in no way above reproach he is nonetheless continuously saddened by what he calls "the mentality" in his community (*TC*, E1 and E3). Despite his own poor choices and character flaws, he takes issue with other people's unsympathetic actions.

At one point, Gary is working at a restaurant. Staring down at a barrel full of crustaceans while smoking a cigarette, Gary wonders aloud about what he sees the crustaceans doing. He says to his brother and co-worker, Ricardo McCullough (Antonio D. Charity): "The minute one of them try to break free, the others just snatch him right back down," a metaphorical point about how he sees people in his neighborhood do not always hope for what is best for each other but rather drag each other down. On a very concrete level, this remark speaks to how he and Ronnie's relationship can hinder either of them from getting clean. But on a more general level, this is Gary's indictment of what he considers to be a low level of solidarity in his community. Later on, Ronnie visits Gary while he is at work. She has brought him drugs but Gary wants to keep working. Ronnie snarls, "How long you think this little crab house shit gon' last?!", reflecting how she almost does not want him to succeed in getting clean (*TC*, E4). She takes his wish to do better by himself as a criticism of her and she consequently lashes out at him.

In another scene, Gary has just been acquitted of assault charges falsely filed by Ronnie. After Gary has been released, his mother (Bonita L. Cartwright) tells him that he should stop seeing Ronnie, to which Ronnie's mother takes offense. She says that Gary's mother is "always thinking your family is so high and mighty and churchgoing. Shit, you ain't better than nobody" (*TC*, E4). Gary's musings about the crustaceans is a critique of the sentiment represented by Ronnie's mother who feels talked down to. Her spiteful retort is to criticize Gary's mother's natural hopes about seeing her son get to a place where he will one day be able to get clean. Dutton later told journalist Janny Scott that he had found the scene with the mothers' altercation embarrassing; "There was something about it that was so ghetto, so stereotypical ghetto," and though he did not doubt that it had happened, he feared that some African American viewers would ask why *The Corner* had to include such a scene that depicted inner-city residents in what Dutton saw to be a painfully embarrassing way. He also feared that some white viewers would see the scene as a confirmation of their prejudices about how people in inner-city neighborhoods act (Scott 2000).

The scene with Gary musing about the crustaceans and the scene with the altercation at the courthouse are linked thematically because they articulate concerns about behavior and depict social hierarchies between people in Gary's neighborhood. Ronnie's mother does not see that Ronnie and Gary both suffer from the same addiction, and that it just might be a good idea that they do not stay in a mutually untoward relationship. She focuses on how she feels that Gary's mother talks down to her. In another scene, Fran, while still addicted to drugs, is shown to cuss out her brother Scoogie (Clayton LeBouef), saying "Like you think you better than somebody because you got a car and a job and fucking cable TV" (*TC*, E3). Anybody, it seems, who rises above the mere minimum of just doing drugs is a target for some drug users. That negative attitude to one's fellow people is what Gary has a hard time accepting.

In the restaurant scene with the crustaceans, however, Gary's brother Ricardo questions what Gary is saying. Gary replies: "All I'm saying Card is that when I had it I shared it," which reflects his disappointment with his fellow men and women in his neighborhood. All this builds up to Gary's depressing concluding remark: "I thought when I fell that people would like me more for being like them." Gary's disappointment with the poor degree of solidarity and sense of community that he experiences is a recurring point of dialogue. Later he even learns that his friends use one of his ideas for a caper without including him (*TC*, E5). The characters in the miniseries use the term "caper" without it ever being explained in the way it is in Burns and Simon's book:

> Stick a gun in a man's face and take his wallet; that's a crime and, hey, you're a criminal. But steal the copper plumbing from a rowhouse under construction and sell it for scrap; that's a caper. [...] In Gary's mind, it isn't only the severity of the act that qualifies a crime, but the likelihood that any human being other than yourself might get hurt. In the life of Gary McCullough, this point is essential. (Burns and Simon 1998, 11)

Gary distinguishes between different forms of crime in terms of how severe and dangerous they are. Though he breaks the law, there are some lines that he does not want to cross. He wants to retain his morality in his addiction.

Gary often hauls scrap metal down to a scrapyard to earn $10–20 for the small amounts of metal he is able to deliver, but he realizes that this operation can become much more profitable by towing entire cars down to the junkyard. Gary will only 'steal' a car if he gets the owner's permission to do so, which implies insurance fraud, but this shows how he holds on to a form of morality in his criminal activities. That moral compass, however, is challenged when he learns that the people with whom he had first towed a car down to the scrapyard leave Gary out when they repeat this criminal act. Gary is frustrated to see his friends excluding him and talks about the ethics of doing so with his acquaintance, Scalio (Reg E. Cathey), who merely replies, "Well, Gary. You're the nigger with the ideas, he's the nigger with the truck" (*TC*, E5). Scalio's remark shows how he does not share Gary's point of view; he does not see their actions as a lack of camaraderie or solidarity between friends. To Scalio, that sort of behavior is to be expected and Gary is almost foolish for having hoped for a higher moral standard. Gary, ever hopeful, continues to be disappointed by the people in his community. But it is important that this issue is articulated as the insider's – Gary's – disillusionment with his fellow men and women, and not as the outsider's condemnation of those less fortunate.

When Simon first tried to pitch *The Wire* to HBO, the executives instead wanted him to do an adaption of *The Corner* as a miniseries, and they wanted him to bring aboard more African Americans on the production so it would not look like a case of privileged whites telling a story about under-privileged African Americans (Simon in Baldwin 2013). This was part of the reason why HBO wanted to bring aboard Charles Dutton and co-writer David Mills. According to Janny Scott's 2000 article on *The Corner*, "It was apparent from the line of questioning that a black writer was high on HBO's priority list," which was the reason that Mills was brought on as Simon's co-writer (Scott 2000).

HBO's concerns about *The Corner* come to the fore when Gary is shown being frustrated about "the mentality around here." Even though Burns and Simon's book had been based on a year's worth of observations, this statement could nevertheless be understood as the outsider 'blaming the victim.' This issue is also present when Gary thinks out loud about the crustaceans in the barrel and when Gary listens to the radio caller talking about racial discourses. But seeing as Gary is the one who is frustrated with a culture of non-solidarity we are surely to understand this critique in a different way than that of the privileged outsider passing judgment on those less fortunate. The Corner engages with that discourse and says that it could well be beneficial to address issues like solidarity and personal responsibility, but its take on these issues is different from that of the radio caller, showing an awareness of how these themes can be broached in an unfortunate way.

The Corner: A Year in the Life of an Inner-City Neighborhood features numerous review excerpts on its first few pages, showcasing the praise it received upon publication in 1997. One reviewer from the San Francisco Chronicle is quoted for writing that "Many outsiders who venture into poor urban neighborhoods see only the misbehavior and culpability of the people who live there. In The Corner David Simon and former police detective Edward Burns have broken the mold" (quoted in Burns and Simon 1998, i). The point is that, on the one hand, this reviewer zooms in on how Burns and Simon's book evaded the perspective of blaming the residents of inner-city ghettos for the living standards and the social problems in their area. This is how they 'broke the mold.' But, on the other hand, Gary's repeated frustrations about "the mentality around here" show how The Corner does address the detrimental aspects of some forms of behavior found in impoverished areas. It thus tries to walk a fine line between touching on anti-social behavior in impoverished areas but without engaging in a form of victim blaming.

This arguably sets The Corner apart from much liberal discourse on inner-city problems. Sociologist William Julius Wilson notes that liberal social scientists, journalists, and policymakers in the 1970s shied away from discussing cultural issues in inner-city neighborhoods: "Some scholars, in an effort to avoid the appearance of 'blaming the victim' or to protect their work from charges of racism," Wilson argues, "simply ignore patterns of behavior that might be construed as stigmatizing to particular racial minorities" (Wilson 2012, 149). Through Gary's frustrations with what he calls "the mentality around here," The Corner's evades that traditional liberal position. It actually does tackle "patterns of behavior." Wilson expands on this issue in *When Work Disappears*:

> In emphasizing the powerful role of the environment in shaping the lives of inner-city residents, we should not ignore or deny the existence of unflattering behaviors that emerge from blocked opportunities. [...] The tendency of some liberals to deny the very existence of culturally destructive behavior and attitudes in the inner city is once again to diminish the importance of the environment in determining the outcomes and life chances of individuals. (Wilson 1997, xviii)

Wilson's argument that the untoward living conditions found in impoverished neighborhoods can affect cultural norms is fundamentally a materialist one; it holds that the culture of an area can be shaped by the lack of opportunities experienced by people living. By arguing that poor living conditions help produce unfortunate cultural norms, Wilson makes an even stronger case for why society as a whole should take a strong interest in doing something about the wealth of disadvantages found in some of inner-city neighborhoods. Wilson's point is that if people acknowledge that there are cultural consequences in the impoverishment of certain neighborhoods, the need to do something about poverty in these areas becomes even more pressing. Wilson's perspective is open to also considering other detrimental effects of poverty than what some liberals focus on.

By emphasizing the view that human misery and poverty has consequences for some cultural norms in this West Baltimore neighborhood, *The Corner* aligns itself with Wilson's view. *The Corner* rebuts the radio talk show caller's conservative sentiment on the one hand, but it also evades this 'traditional liberal fear' of not wanting to blame the victim on the other hand. The miniseries is surely not conservative, but it also is not liberal in that tradition that Wilson criticizes.

The Wire would later feature its own variation of this theme. Film scholar Stanley Corkin argues that entrepreneurial characters on *The Wire* like Bodie (J.D. Williams) and Bubbles serve to rebut 'the culture of poverty' discourse put forth by conservative thinkers. Bubbles is incessantly looking for scrap metal to sell and he even starts selling T-shirts to pay for his drug addiction, and Bodie, for his part, embodies a strong work ethic and loyalty in the drug game. Corkin writes that

The Humanized Drug Addict: The Corner

By making enterprise a recurring motif, Simon seems to be directly rebutting notions of the 'culture of poverty' thesis put forth by conservatives, who posit that habits originating from living as a [sic] oppressed minority in the South – such as lack of ambition, criminality, illegitimacy – have affixed themselves to African Americans intergenerationally and have resulted in a persistent inability to participate in the American dream. (Corkin 2017, 13–14)

By portraying these characters as hard working and generally conscientious (though with important exceptions especially for Bodie), *The Wire* contradicts a prevalent discourse in conservative thought. *The Corner*'s engagement with the 'culture of poverty' discourse, however, involves walking tightrope. On the one hand, *The Corner* finds it important to address cultural issues in the ghetto, but on the other hand the miniseries does not want to veer towards a rhetoric of victim blaming or looking like an upper-class or middle-class citizen (Simon) judging those less fortunate. The culture of poverty thesis builds on the notion that poor people are poor due to flawed cultural values, and Gary's frustrations about "the mentality around here" might, to some, look like a similar critique.

As mentioned, this is directly linked to HBO's wish to bring aboard Charles Dutton and David Mills on the project. HBO wanted Dutton to make a statement "describing his reasons for making it" (Scott 2000). Dutton, however, did not want the writers present for the shooting of this opening scene. According to Janny Scott

> HBO asked Mr. Dutton at the last minute to film a personal preamble to the series, describing his reasons for making it. The idea worried Mr. Simon and Mr. Mills; they did not want HBO apologizing for the series in advance. They shipped a draft script to Mr. Dutton. But he sent back a message saying he would write the preamble himself. (Scott 2000)

The result is what ended up being the opening preamble of *The Corner*. However, because *The Corner* is based on Burns and Simon's journalistic account and their year-long observations on the corner, it is harder to suggest that Gary's frustration with his peers is merely Simon and Mills's veiled critique of an inner-city underclass. In Burns and Simon's book, Gary is quoted for lamenting "the mentality" that he encounters and the authors explain that "Gary can't let it go, this idea that some moral thresholds still exist," which emphasizes that while he and his peers may steal, they at least should not steal from their neighbors (Burns and Simon 1998, 188 and 446). While it was the real Gary McCullough who had once made these criticisms of his fellow men and women in West Baltimore, Simon and Mills do not come across – or, at least, come across less strongly – as privileged outsiders criticizing under-privileged African Americans.

Fifteen years later, *Show Me a Hero*'s portrayal of the city of Yonkers' efforts to desegregate housing would subtly touch on a related concern. A federal court has called for the city of Yonkers to construct 200 housing units in Yonkers' predominantly white eastern part of town. *Show Me a Hero*'s version of real-life city architect and city-planner Oscar Newman (Peter Riegert) argues, in a scene set in the judge's office, that the city should make sure not to build too many houses on any single location. The real Oscar Newman made a name for himself arguing for such "scattered-site housing," which stipulates that low-income public housing should be built in many locations. Newman preferred this solution over constructing large public housing projects that, in his view, tended to concentrate social problems in a few isolated areas. Newman's idea was to counter the adverse effects related to social and economic deprivation brought about by concentrated disadvantage in massive public housing high-rises.

Working as a teacher in St. Louis in the 1960s, Newman had, by his own account, witnessed the ambitious Pruitt-Igoe high-rises "go to ruin." In Newman's analysis, the area contained had too many common spaces that the residents did not identify with and which consequently became unsafe. Newman's answer was the principle of *defensible space* which calls for shaping "the physical layout of communities to allow residents to control the areas around their homes," which means reducing the size of common areas that no residents feel personally responsible for. In Newman's eyes, such areas can become sources of insecurity and places for potential crime (Newman 1996, 9–10).

In *Show Me a Hero*, the fictionalized Newman opposes the idea of constructing a total of 48 – and not just 24 – townhouses on a single site. He fears that 48 townhouses will be too many and that the homes consequently will not 'blend in' to the surrounding middle-class neighborhood, a concern that the NAACP lawyer Michael Sussman (Jon Bernthal) takes offense with:

The Humanized Drug Addict: The Corner 43

NEWMAN: ... I can't make the townhouses disappear into the fabric of the middle-class neighborhoods. It's too isolated. And my concern is *that* isolation will allow a criminal element to flourish that the public housing residents alone can't control.

SUSSMAN: Oscar, you're fearmongering and it reflects your ideological baggage. I gotta tell you, this is ... It's basically racist.

NEWMAN: What's so difficult about this!? The smaller the site, the greater the contact, the more the middle-class neighbors are gonna exert their values and control. Simple as that ...

(*SMAH*, E3)

Newman's argument is that the adverse cultural effects of concentrated disadvantage can be alleviated by making sure that public, low-income housing is not clustered together too much. Sussman, it seems, does not buy into the premise of there being cultural or behavioral consequences in concentrating society's most marginalized citizens in isolated spaces. *Show Me a Hero*'s depiction of Sussman thus fits Wilson's description of the liberal who does not want to discuss the cultural and behavioral problems that can arise from concentrated disadvantage.

But even though *The Corner* had evaded the style of liberalism represented by Sussman in this scene, *Show Me a Hero*'s depiction of this lawyer is not critical. It does not portray Sussman as quixotic or naive, which is an important point in itself. The characters Sussman and Newman represent different forms of anti-racist and egalitarian politics. By not vilifying or making a caricature of either man, *Show Me a Hero* grants equal weight to Sussman and Newman's positions. *Show Me a Hero* thus suggests that both perspectives represent relevant and valid positions in discussions about cultural aspects of social problems.

The first episode of *Show Me a Hero* shows drug dealing taking place in the Schlobohm housing area. And one of the miniseries' principle characters living in that area becomes a single mother – the father dies before the child is born – and she cannot cope with her situation and ends up addicted to crack cocaine (*SMAH*, E4). *Show Me a Hero* is thus very direct in portraying the human tragedies and social problems related to drug use, but the miniseries does not depict drug problems in the area in order to vilify Schlobohm.

The miniseries contains several storylines about women who are at a disadvantage because they live in this housing project. *Show Me a Hero* aligns viewers mainly with characters that are frustrated with the crime and drugs in the neighborhood and thus presents a motivation for why it makes sense to attend to the negative consequences of concentrated disadvantage brought about by residential segregation. *Show Me a Hero*'s portrayal of impoverished areas thus aligns closely with the one found in *The Corner*. Neither miniseries shies away from highlighting the cultural problems found in impoverished areas, but both productions try to make the viewer care about social issues in these areas.

This does not mean that Simon's series buy into a conservative rhetoric of blaming the victim, but rather means that the case his productions make for a more inclusive and integrated society is grounded in the idea that residential segregation and concentrated disadvantage do have social and cultural ramifications. This way of discussing these cultural phenomena in the context of broader urban problems suggests that Simon's position aligns with a more leftist position. Showcasing a starting point of sympathy with the inner-city dwellers, Simon's serials are able to veer into discussions of "the mentality around here" and the cultural advantages of scattered site housing without coming across as conservative cases of victim blaming.

Exit

The Corner maintains a strict ethos of neither pitying nor passing harsh judgment on its characters, and though its chief interest is in humanizing Gary, Fran, DeAndre, and its other characters, the miniseries does not shy away from showing how these fictionalized renditions of real people, especially Gary, make some poor life choices. A part of the miniseries' humanization is to meet its characters eye to eye. It does not make excuses for them. As film scholar Jason P. Vest points out, *The Corner*

> refuses the drug-addict-as-unwitting-victim trope that *Hill Street Blues*, *NYPD Blue*, and *Homicide* indulge to illustrate that Gary's problems are at least partly his own fault. The miniseries, however, refutes the

The Humanized Drug Addict: The Corner

drug-addict-as-unsympathetic-criminal trope that cop dramas more frequently portray to demonstrate Gary's inherent goodness even as he commits larceny. (Vest 2011, 129)

The point of *The Corner*'s generally positive depiction of Gary is that he is presented as a person before he is presented as a drug addict. As Vest notes, it is rare to have people struggling with drug addictions as the core protagonists of televisual fictions. This focus allows for a different portrayal of drug addicts and drug addiction compared to, say, many police procedurals where drug addicts might be characters like victims of crimes or as witnesses to them. Indeed, one of the things that attracted Dutton to Simon and Mills' script was that "it was told from the addicts' perspective, not some glamorized dealer's" (Dutton in Scott 2000).

In their 1997 book, Simon and Burns wrote that "In the empty heart of our cities, the culture of drugs has created a wealth-generating structure so elemental and enduring that it can legitimately be called a social compact" (Burns and Simon 1998, 58). Such an ambitious social critique requires a large canvas which extends beyond that of this six-hour adapted miniseries, which instead zeroes in on the human consequences of this 'enduring social compact' without attending to its economic and structural underpinnings. Especially through the characters Bubbles, *The Wire* would revisit the agenda of humanizing Black inner-city drug addicts, but it would do so in a way that *also* considered the structural realities in which this misery exists. Having a core interest in explaining how the war on drugs can perpetuate itself across decades, *The Wire* is able to offer a systemic outlook (Kinder 2008), thus revisiting some of the more structural and societal points found in Burns and Simon's book. *The Wire*'s much broader canvas is used to pick up on the "social compact" that Burns and Simon commented on in their book, but which fell away in the adapted miniseries.

The Corner connects its humanized portrayal of people struggling with drug addiction to the issue of discursive othering. Gary links *Schindler's List*'s depiction of the dehumanization of Jews in Nazi Germany with how he believes he and his peers are seen by society. "No, you ain't human like we human," he says of how Jews were othered in the 1930–1940s in Nazi Germany. But Gary also points the finger at himself: "We're sitting here day after day making ourselves a little bit less human and the world's happy to see it" (*TC*, E4). The miniseries tries to dissuade its viewers from accepting a discourse about inner-city problems that diminishes the humanity of the people living there. *The Corner* zooms in on the dehumanization of people struggling with drug addiction and subtly connects this issue to broader social contexts. Simon's next project, *The Wire*, would focus much more broadly on the city.

Note

1 The early 1990s saw the release of several 'hood films', which had strong links to hip-hop culture through the songs on the soundtrack and the fact that several of them featured rappers such as Tupac, Ice Cube, and Ice-T in leading roles. They tended to focus on impoverished African American communities in Los Angeles and New York and depicted issues like racism, drugs, poverty, crime, and violence. *Boyz n the Hood* and the Hughes Brothers' *Menace II Society* (1993) are the most well-known and successful films in this short-lived cycle (deWaard 2008, 59), but other important films include Mario Van Peebles's *New Jack City* (1991), Ernest R. Dickerson's *Juice* (1992), Steve Anderson's *South Central* (1992), Jeff Pollack's *Above the Rim* (1994), and Spike Lee's *Clockers* (1995). Spike Lee aspired to make *Clockers* "The hood movie to end all hood movies" (quoted in deWaard 2012, 268), and this film cycle did indeed falter in the mid-1990s. By alluding to *Boyz n the Hood*, *The Corner* thus points out one of the central films in this cycle in order to engage with these films more broadly.

2

The Aesthetics of 'Pessimism': *The Wire* (2002–2008)

The opening scene of *The Wire* shows that the serial is not interested in portraying individual criminal cases but instead wants to make a case about systemic violence. Detective Jimmy McNulty is sitting on a stoop talking to a witness, trying to figure out why a young African American nicknamed Snot Boogie has been killed. With a police officer trying to get information from a witness, the sound of sirens, a murder victim lying in the street, and the blueish lights from police cars reflected in trails of blood on the tarmac, this scene invokes many of the classic, generic elements of a police series. Viewers would not be completely off the mark if they expect that the ensuing narrative will follow a police investigation focused on finding and trying Snot Boogie's murderer (*TW*, S1E1). But there is no further mention of Snot Boogie. The dialogue and *mise en scène* of this opening scene suggests that the serial centers on a crime case – but not one about an individual case.

Learning that the murder victim had been known to repeatedly steal the pot at a craps game, McNulty asks his unnamed witness why he and his friends kept including Snot Boogie in the craps game to which the witness replies: "Got to. This America, man," a potently ambiguous line that hints at several of *The Wire*'s themes. To Linda Williams, this scene establishes America both as a place and as an idea. She argues that *The Wire* here challenges 'America' as an *idea* as the serial explores "the failure of American social justice" (Williams 2014, 84–86), yet the wording of the witness' final line also hints of America as a segregated *place*. By omitting the verb *is* in the witness's last line, *The Wire* employs copula deletion – a characteristic feature of African American Vernacular English (Trotta and Blyahher 2011, 21–22) – to thematize the separation of social spaces. It is

"*This* America, man." Not another America, but the one found in ghettos of Western Baltimore. As Simon said in 2016, "You can't see the barbed wire around West Baltimore, but it's there, socioeconomically, it's there and it's been there for generations" (Simon in Rosenberg 2016). Through copula deletion, the ambiguity of this scene invokes the separated reality of urban Baltimore.

As *The Wire*'s mission statement, this scene suggests how the serial examines the roots of "This America," which ties into the ambiguity of the serial's title. Referring both to the idea of a barbed wire separating several Americas as explained by Simon, the title also points out the motif of the wire that the Major Crimes Unit set up in every season. But the title can also be read as pointing to the narrative "wires" that connect so many narrative lines throughout the serial. This highly networked narrative exploits the narrative possibilities of long-form televisual storytelling by offering a social drama that would be difficult to achieve on a smaller canvas. Understanding *The Wire*'s way of portraying the American city, however, requires a closer look at some central developments in American television history.

HBO in the Early 2000s

It is no accident that *The Wire* and David Simon emerged in television history in the earliest years of this millennium. For decades, the three big networks – ABC, CBS, NBC – dominated the American television industry, but with the shift to the multichannel era in the 1980 and 1990s came a window of opportunity for new forms of storytelling for television drama. Home Box Office (HBO) had originally carved out a niche in the American television market by offering films on the small screen. Before the emergence of the VCR and a big video rental industry, HBO thus had a niche business strategy for a segment of the market. But from the mid-1990s, HBO started offering more 'edgy' content (e.g. talk shows fronted by Dennis Miller and Chris Rock) in an effort to carve out a more distinct place in a market that was becoming ever more competitive. HBO's first drama series, *Oz* (1997–2003), showed that the network was willing to push the envelope also in the realm of drama by including transgressive content such as violent homosexual rape. *Oz*, however, was in no way near the commercial hit that HBO's next two series were: *Sex and the City* and *The Sopranos*. But *Oz* showcased HBO as a place where a showrunner like Tom Fontana was able to produce content that could not be made on broadcast networks.

Simon has since said that HBO's decision to do *Oz* was what convinced him that the network "was maybe a possible home for the kind of shit that I was interested in addressing" (Simon in Antholis 2019, episode 3). David Chase's gangster drama *The Sopranos* later cemented HBO as a place for "creator-centered" content, which Simon since has benefitted from and contributed to (Mittell 2012, 19). A different business strategy called for another form of television drama. It is this shift in the television market and at HBO that is the background for Simon's career as a showrunner. Understanding his career in the context of American television is to see how he showed up in the industry at a point in time when major changes were under way.

In 1980, 9 out of 10 American viewers (90%) would tune in to one of the three big networks – ABC, CBS, NBC – during primetime. Twenty-five years later, these channels only had the attention of every third viewer (32%) in that coveted timeslot (Hindman and Wiegand 2008, 119), a share that four years later was down to one in four (25.6%) (Akass 2015, 745). The big networks had been pushed back by cable channels such as HBO, FX, and AMC as well as home viewing technologies like the VCR. The American television market was being segmented into more narrow demographics and this industrial change made way for what Mittell calls "the era of narrative complexity" that started in the 1990s. Before this shift, the industry did not believe that audiences would consistently watch all episodes of a series from week to week, which meant that television series could not afford to embrace seriality as it might lead to alienating especially intermittent viewers. If viewers would not tune in every week the plot could not evolve too much from week to week. And due to the industrial logic of syndication, many series were produced in a way that allowed for episodes to be broadcast out of their original order as was the case with traditional sitcoms and procedural drama (Mittell 2006, 29–30).

This change came from channels needing new ways to attract and maintain viewership. Brett Martin argues that this moment in television history was one of "genuine business and technological upheaval" that came from "people not knowing what the hell to do," which made them "willing to try anything" to succeed on the highly competitive American television market. To Martin, this industrial 'desperation' made possible a situation where the competing interests of art and commerce shifted in favor of art (Martin 2014, 10–11). This structural shift paved the way for a group of creative individuals to exert their artistic agency.

HBO was a frontrunner in the emergent era of ambitious television drama series. In the words of former CEO, Chris Albrecht, HBO "had to go from being an occasional-use medium to something people use on a regular basis in order for people to justify paying us [and] original programming became a tool for doing that" (Albrecht quoted in McCabe and Akass 2008, 84). Consequently, HBO chose to produce content that would set itself apart from the content offered on network television. Beginning in the late 1990s and the early 2000s with *Oz*, *Sex and the City*, *Six Feet Under*, and *The Wire*, this proved a successful strategy for the network. But as is the nature of being a trendsetter, other players since tagged onto HBO's lead and started producing similarly ambitious television series (Miller 2008, ix; McCabe and Akass 2008, 91). In the 2000s, AMC launched *Mad Men* and *Breaking Bad*, Fox launched *24* and *House, M.D.* and in the 2010s, Showtime started broadcasting *Homeland*, *The Affair* and AMC released *The Walking Dead*, also a huge commercial and critical success.

HBO's business decision to start focusing more on original drama series would help the network retain its brand and strategy of trying to set itself apart from 'regular television.' "In its early days," media scholar Dana Polan writes, "HBO worked to achieve brand and product differentiation and spectator fidelity through special offerings primarily in cinema, sports, and sex" (Polan 2009, 188). It focused on sports – especially boxing – and standup shows that pushed the envelope for what you could say on television like George Carlin's monologue "Seven Words You Can Never Say on Television" (Mittell 2012, 17). Its 'edgy' new drama series from the late 1990s and onwards thus played into a long-running strategy at HBO. In an increasingly competitive television market, HBO needed to keep people subscribing and they chose to make original content in order to keep people paying their monthly subscriptions.

HBO, however, nevertheless held on to a branding strategy that labeled the network as the odd one out in American television, epitomized by the slogan it adopted in 1995; "It's not TV. It's HBO"

(Santo 2008, 31). Indeed, television scholars Janet McCabe and Kim Akass argue that HBO has long "made a virtue of its autonomy from the constraints and restrictions that limit network television." It is one thing to produce material under different constraints than the big three broadcasters. Using this industrial fact in one's marketing is something else. David Chase, creator of *The Sopranos*, made a similar point in 1999 when he argued that HBO gave him the opportunity to tell "the story in an unconventional way" (quoted in McCabe and Akass 2008, 87). McCabe and Akass note that it is commonplace for writers, producers, and directors working for HBO to express such attitudes. HBO's discourse is replete with statements where creatives "endlessly speak about and sell themselves, how the media talks about them, and how their customers have come to understand what they are paying for" (McCabe and Akass 2008, 84–89). One such example is Eric Overmyer, co-creator of *Treme*, who argues that HBO offers more creative freedoms compared to broadcast networks where executives tend to interfere more in the creative process (Overmyer in Kallas 2014a, 157).

Simon has also played his part in this branding strategy. In 2015, he acknowledged that he was "part of a brand" but also noted that he was "some weird, little politicized PBS part of it" (Simon in Gura 2015). His work at HBO lends the network an air of being a place for serious drama that tackles important societal issues: a "politicized PBS part of" its brand that appeals to a certain viewership. Lavik, however, notes that the role of a public service broadcaster such as, say, the BBC is to address its audience not as consumers but as citizens (Lavik 2014, 31–32). So while Simon often praises the creative freedom HBO offers him, this comparison to PBS is a way of presenting his productions as content that address viewers as citizens rather than consumers, which arguably also plays into discussions of the distinction of HBO drama. In his first multi-season drama for HBO, Simon used this position and situation to tell a story of social maladies in a somewhat recognizable generic format.

Scope

The Wire tells the story of an urban America in a highly ambitious manner that links formal innovation and aesthetic sophistication with an advanced political argument. Taking on the shape of a police procedural, the first of its five seasons focuses on a police unit's efforts to build a case against a crime ring led by Avon Barksdale (Wood Harris). Set in Baltimore, Maryland, *The Wire* continually expands its portrayal of the contemporary city by adding a new setting with each season. Whereas the first season zooms in on the drug trade and the police's almost futile attempts at stopping – or even containing – it, season two extends and expands narrative arcs from existing storylines. It also establishes Baltimore's harbor as a new setting, depicting a working class facing the risk of losing their unionized jobs. The third season expands the narrative to the political arena by introducing the storyline of a mayoral candidate, Thomas Carcetti (Aidan Gillen), intent on making a positive change in Baltimore while also portraying how a rogue police major, Bunny Colvin (Robert Wisdom), tries to deal with the war on drugs in his own way. Season four looks to the public schools and examines institutional issues that link poverty and social stratification with the reproduction of social ills. The fifth and final season explores the role of the media through a new storyline set at *The Baltimore Sun*. Seen as a whole, the serial demonstrates how these social arenas are interconnected.

Film scholar María del Mar Azcona argues that most films "structure their plots around the trajectory, goals, and desires of a single protagonist" (2). This fact of film history has shaped the way that films portray historical or societal phenomena, and has led historian Robert Rosenstone to argue that the feature film "insists on history as the story of individuals" in the sense that when films tell larger societal stories they do so through the microcosm of the individual (Rosenstone 2001, 55). However, the multi-season, multi-protagonist serialized drama is not narratively restricted in this way. *The Wire* exploits these narrative affordances to trace a plethora of sprawling, ever-meandering, and intersecting lines to tell a story of a complex society. A story that in the long run is not centered on any individual. Different characters' converging storylines makes the multi-protagonist narrative cohere (Bordwell 2006, 99), and *The Wire* uses this fact of storytelling to show how social phenomena are interconnected. We see both the cause and effect of a great many plotlines and this textual feature is intricately connected to the social portrayal that *The Wire* puts forth.

Originally pioneered by *Hill Street Blues* (1981–1987), the use of multiple plotlines has now become a common feature of contemporary television serials (Thompson 2003, 53; Johnson 2006, 66–72). Media scholar Helle Kannik Haastrup argues that the presence of different types of people, views of life, and social and cultural backgrounds is a characteristic feature of multi-protagonist films and that such films emphasize "parallelism rather than causality and narrative drive" (Haastrup 2011, 274). Haastrup's argument about multi-protagonist films is even more true of multi-protagonist television serials. This is why contemporary television serials lend themselves so well to portraying a large social network where many structures and actors are at play in the same environment, a characteristic feature of *The Wire*, *Treme*, and *The Deuce*. The affordances of this narrative structure are central to how Simon's series can envision the city as an interrelated space of converging fates.

The Wire uses this form to create what Mittell calls "centrifugal complexity" in which a "complex web of interconnectivity [is] forged across the social system rather than in the depth of any one individual's role in the narrative or psychological layers." This is in contrast to the so-called "centripetal complexity" of *Breaking Bad* where a focus on a single, central protagonist works to "create a storyworld with unmatched depth of characterization" (Mittell 2015, 222–223). *The Wire* uses this narrative complexity to portray a social complexity, weaving together a multitude of plotlines to create a 'sociological gaze' in which all social phenomena are to be understood in relation to one another.

A perhaps particularly poignant scene in this respect is when Major Bunny Colvin and Bubbles happen upon each other at the site of the former Hamsterdam project, sharing their thoughts about whether Hamsterdam had been a good thing (*TW*, S3E12). A less dramatically charged scene shows ex-convict and ex-gang member Dennis "Cutty" Wise (Chad L. Coleman) trying to get some of the neighborhood children to visit his new boxing gym and Ellis Carver (Seth Gilliam) – who is also trying to be a positive change in the lives of these kids – sees Cutty's efforts as being the positive force for good in that community, just as he himself is trying to be as a police officer (*TW*, S3E10). Making otherwise divergent plotlines intersect in such scenes allows *The*

Wire to make sensible to its viewers how its different social worlds are intertwined.

Bordwell argues that network narratives show the fates of different characters to converge, noting that this feature creates cohesion in such plots. He argues that when network narratives bring "strangers together, the more that the narration emphasizes their separate lives, the more we expect significant encounters among them" (Bordwell 2006, 99). *The Wire* uses this narrative structure to portray an intricately intertwined social reality. But where a show like *The Defenders* (2017) is almost teleological in how it links different narrative lines from earlier series in the Marvel cinematic universe (*Daredevil* (2015–2018), *Jessica Jones* (2015–2019), *Luke Cage* (2016–2018), *Iron Fist* (2017–2018)) in such a way that the viewer will expect the characters' storylines to intersect at some point, *The Wire*'s networked structure is presented more as a side effect to the serial's sociological gaze. *The Wire*'s less strict teleological network narrative underscores its claim to realism. This is not to say that *The Wire* is any less of a constructed aesthetic object than other television series but its narrative structure downplays its own constructedness. Lavik argues that narratives that are told in a looser way than those we know from popular culture tend to appear more realist because "reality itself is marked by coincidence and disorder" (Lavik 2014, 120).

Where several characters' storylines intersect, Simon's serials try to show that they do so because that is how people's lives intertwine in the real world. His series do not try to construct a narrative anticipation so as to make the viewer wait for two specific characters to meet. They try to downplay their own textuality in this way. Simon's storyworlds suggest that they are governed by a sociological logic, not a storytelling one.

"The king stay the king": Social Reproduction

A key scene in *The Wire*'s third episode explores the theme of social reproduction. D'Angelo Barksdale (Lawrence Gilliard Jr.) is explaining the game of chess to two of his subordinates in the drug trade, emphasizing how pawns stay pawns and that "the king stay the king," which, adding to its thematic centrality, is also the epigraph of that episode. D'Angelo's allegory is not lost on his subordinates and one of them, Bodie Broadus, rejects the notion that the stratified 'social structures' of chess should be applicable to his life. Believing in the possibility of social uplift, Bodie accepts that pawns will only stay pawns "unless they some smart-ass pawns" (*TW*, S1E3). It is only much later, in season four, that Bodie realizes that "this game is rigged, man. We like them little bitches on a chessboard" as he puts it to Detective McNulty (*TW*, S4E13).

Bodie's character arc is a long elaboration of how different social phenomena, when seen in relation to each other, compound a network that keeps many individuals in their place. The worldview that D'Angelo outlines at the start of *The Wire* foreshadows how the serial itself will represent a world of social reproduction. But it is only as events unfold across *The Wire*'s seasons that it becomes clear to the viewer and to Bodie that the serial itself aligns with D'Angelo explanations of chess and not Bodie's objections to that outlook. This scene is synecdochic for the serial's systemic portrayal of contemporary urban realities. This is a world of social reproduction rather than one of social uplift and change.

Lavik points out how the *mise en scène* and cinematography in a later scene builds on the parable that D'Angelo makes in the pit in the low rises. Detectives Lester Freamon (Clarke Peters), Bunk Moreland (Wendell Pierce), Kima Greggs (Sonja Sohn), and Jimmy

Figure 5 McNulty, Bunk, Kima, and Freamon standing in a square.

McNulty are standing in a square, venting their frustrations over being forced to push a case prematurely due to pressure concerning clearance rates (*TW*, S1E6). "Just as this institutional dysfunction is most pointedly exposed in the conversation that ensues," Lavik (2012b) argues, "the mise-en-scène alludes to the previous discussion between D'Angelo, Bodie, and Wallace about chess."

In the foreground of the shot, two hands move pieces around a chessboard, making the detectives in the background of the shot look "like pieces in the game." These two chess players in the extreme foreground, Lavik argues, "resemble Olympian Gods pulling the strings from above, making the characters mere puppets, victims of forces beyond their control" (Lavik 2012b).[1] This scene is the visual representation of how *The Wire*'s characters are moved rather than movers. Mittell argues that in *The Wire* "characters' agency is rarely able to make a difference in broader institution systems" (Mittell 2015, 222). The serial's characters are overmatched when facing the force of institutional and socio-economic structures. This is how *The Wire* avoids depicting Baltimore's problems as solvable in any obvious way.

The Wire shows how the police department's focus on clearance rates goes against the detectives' work. They serve an institution that fails to adequately serve the society it is supposed to protect and, consequently, their efforts are counterproductively thwarted by the very institution they operate within. This narrative arc is tied in with the synecdochic chess scene in the low rises and the *mise en scène* of the dialogue in the square, which, seen in relation to one another, makes for a rather eloquent way of criticizing the omnipotence of institutional logic. It is not just the teenage boys selling drugs who are the subjects of larger forces. That also goes for the police detectives.

Just as *The Corner*'s humanization of Gary can be explained through Murray Smith's terminology of *attachment, access, alignment*, and *allegiance*, so too can *The Wire*'s way of critiquing institutional dysfunction be understood through Smith's ideas. Smith defines allegiance as those instances when viewers see a character in a morally positive light. This can invite the viewer to become sympathetic to specific characters (Smith 1995, 84), and viewers may therefore also come to have a parasocial, emotional investment in what happens to them. Drawing on Murray Smith, one could argue that when the police detectives (whom the viewer is aligned with) explicitly criticize the institutional logic, *The Wire* invites its viewers to see things from their perspective rather than from their superiors' standpoint. The viewer's allegiance with, for example, Kima Greggs and Lester Freamon is *The Wire*'s way of inviting the viewer to see the institutional logic as a destructive element in its storyworld.

Systemic Logic

In one of the earliest academic analyses of the serial, media scholar Marsha Kinder argues that *The Wire* serial raises a *systemic* critique but also qualifies that it does not achieve this form of critique by virtue of its urban focus (Kinder 2008, 50). Its systemicness comes from the fact that *The Wire* always contextualizes every social phenomenon it portrays in a broader social world. It shows viewers how, for example, the drug game (the focus of season one) can always recruit new workers to its world of violence because there are not enough jobs left in the legal economy due to deindustrialization (the focus of season two). And the schools are too hard-pressed to really make a positive change in many of the children's lives because there are so many social problems that the schools cannot keep up (focus of season four). It is *The Wire*'s way of linking deindustrialization with the war on drugs and the media's inability to report adequately on these issues that makes the serial's criticism systemic. Important to this critique is the fact that *The Wire* shows that the institutions that are meant to attend to some of society's problems are themselves mired in a situation that keeps them from living up to their overall purpose.

This is especially the case with law enforcement. At one point, Major Bill Rawls (John Doman) lectures McNulty about the importance of clearance rates, which is a quantitative way of measuring the effectiveness of the police force (*TW*, S1E6). Rawls is consistently shown to prioritize a management logic that is detrimental to the police work of the Major Crimes Unit. His focus on clearance rates as the guiding principle for police work dramatizes how a political focus on accountability and measurability negatively affects the priorities of law enforcement. By focalizing its narrative through

McNulty and not Rawls, *The Wire* is clear about who viewers are supposed to side with.

The American social scientist Donald T. Campbell voiced a similar critique of the potentially adverse effects of quantitative measurements in the 1970s. Campbell's point was that measures created to ensure a positive outcome of a public institution's efforts can have the direct opposite effect. In Campbell's words:

> The more any quantitative social indicator is used for social decision-making, the more subject it will be to corruption pressures and the more apt it will be to distort and corrupt the social processes it is intended to monitor. (Campbell 1976, 49)

Campbell's objection, now known as "Campbell's law," is that when faced with certain quantitative social indicators such as clearance rates, an institution's efforts can become mismanaged and misdirected. As philosopher Lawrence Blum notes about *The Wire*: "The rules of the institution are constantly at odds with constructively addressing any of the issues with which the institution is meant to engage" (Blum 2011, NP). Rawls's quantitative way of managing police work adversely affects the overall effectiveness of the police force. That does not mean that there is no valid reason to focus on high clearance rates, especially for homicides. Any society should prosecute murderers to the best of its ability. Journalist Jill Leovy argues that "where the criminal justice system fails to respond vigorously to violent injury and death, homicide becomes endemic" (Leovy 2015, 8). The idea is that there are many important reasons for solving the vast majority of homicide cases. One such reason is that if enough murders go unsolved the police can end up losing the trust of the communities they are supposed to protect. In other words, there is ample reason why the commanding officers in *The Wire* try to ensure that the Baltimore Police Department delivers high clearance rates, especially in murder cases.

The commanders, however, are often struggling to get the clearance rate above the 50 percent mark, but the brass's tunnel vision focus on numbers is nonetheless shown to be detrimental to the overall mission of policing – upholding the law and making a positive change in its community. The Major Crimes Unit's countermeasures against this managerial discourse is shown to attend to society's ills in a way that the police is otherwise unable to do. *The Wire*'s main objection against the brass's focus on clearance rates is that it is shortsighted and is not attuned to building big cases against entire criminal organizations. The outsider unit thus counters the harmful discourse found at the center of power.

The problem that Campbell identifies here thus mirrors the criticism *The Wire* presents, yet it is interesting to note that Campbell published this study as early as 1976. *The Wire*'s critique of institutional dysfunction is not new though it is arguably rarely seen in television series. This logic is what frustrates McNulty in the above-mentioned scene, but it also frustrates Roland Pryzbylewski (Jim True-Frost) in season four when working at Edward Tilghman Middle School. The way that season four introduces the school system as a main setting serves to illustrate how educational institutions, police enforcement, and broader social realities are interrelated, and drawing this connection is very important for *The Wire*'s systemic analysis. Linda Williams points to how season four's opening episode "Boys of Summer" (*TW*, S4E1) cross-cuts between two scenes set at Edward Tilghman Middle School and the police department, respectively. These cross-cuts compare how both teachers and police officers are subjected to similar PowerPoint presentations, showing how these institutions face some of the same problems (Williams 2014, 71). The quantitative logic of measuring effectively redirects efforts away from the highest of goals to more minor aims, which are more easily measurable. As a consequence, the efforts of public institutions are directed not at their overall objective (i.e. teaching children or solving crimes), but are rather aimed at living up to the measurements which have been imposed by an administrative and political logic.

The criticism that Campbell and *The Wire* point to is that certain measures can encumber an institution's functionality, which is reflected when Bill Rawls berates McNulty for having to explain to his boss "why he's getting calls about murders that don't mean a shit to anybody" because one of the murders McNulty has been investigating happened in the previous year and is therefore not interesting in terms of the statistics that Rawls is interested in improving that year (*TW*, S1E1). The callousness of a line about some murders not meaning anything to anybody clearly shows how *The Wire* is critical of this administrative logic.

The first shots of Bill Rawls show him shrouded in black, signaling that McNulty is facing an antagonist when he steps into his commander's office. Their adversarial relationship helps viewers understand how, despite all of *The Wire*'s moral ambiguity, there are still some characters that we are invited to root for such as McNulty. Screenwriter and producer on *The Wire* Ed Burns explains that when he worked as a police detective in Baltimore in the 1980s and 1990s, several leading police officials did not acknowledge the existence of gangs. Like McNulty in *The Wire*, Burns experienced that his superiors did not support important police work. Burns consequently turned to the State's Attorney's Office to have them put pressure on the higher-ups in the police department to establish a unit that could build cases against gangs (Burns in Abrams 2018, 17). This experience informs *The Wire*'s first season and its overall thematization of institutional dysfunction.

Burns's experience as a police officer implicitly supports the societal relevance of *The Wire*'s critique, yet the link between Campbell and *The Wire* may be explained more fruitfully through the affective frustration that *The Wire* engenders by its invitations to align one's sympathy with the Major Crimes Unit. As *The Wire* progresses, McNulty proves to be motivated more by intellectual vanity in wanting to prove himself as the cleverest detective in Western Baltimore than by moral ambitions about bringing criminals to justice. Yet while McNulty is not a very moral character at heart, Rawls's way of dismissing the importance of the murders invokes a moral element to this dynamic. Rawls is shown to be amoral which thus makes McNulty look almost righteous by comparison. Mittell argues that a character's traits or actions do not have to appear moral in any absolute sense to invite viewers to feel allegiance with that character. Viewers just need to see that a character – here McNulty – appears better in comparison with another character, here Rawls. Mittell calls this "relative morality" (Mittell 2015, 143–146). *The Wire* shows that the detrimental administrative logic that Campbell criticized is the logic embraced by a morally questionable character. *The Wire* dramatizes the immorality of this discourse and at the same time places McNulty on the moral high ground.

But, as Lavik points out, Rawls later consoles McNulty after Kima has been shot, showing Rawls to be a caring character. McNulty, ridden with guilt, is distraught in a way we have not seen before, but it is Rawls that – while claiming that McNulty is a "gaping asshole" – convinces him that it was not his fault that his partner was shot (*TW*, S1E11). To Lavik, this makes Rawls a good example of E.M. Forster's concept of the "round character" by being able to surprise viewers in a convincing manner (Lavik 2014, 185). Though Rawls embodies a misdirected police force he also has a human side. He transcends merely being a social function within the police department. This is one of the central examples of how *The Wire* portrays a world of moral ambiguity.

Sociologists Anmol Chadda and William Julius Wilson argue that part of *The Wire*'s accomplishment lies in showing how interconnected the causes of urban inequality are. It is through this interconnectedness that the serial is able to claim urbanity as its topic. Broadening its societal canvas with each season, the serial connects different issues that social science scholars may depict precisely. But they do so on much smaller canvases, which the academic community only implicitly takes to be intertwined, as Chadda and Wilson argue (Chadda and Wilson 2011, 166). In contrast to such approaches that aim to understand different social ills in great detail, the scope of *The Wire* represents an ambitious synthesis that examines the intertwined and networked nature of these different phenomena.

Rosenstone argues that films excel at showing historical developments as "a process of changing social relationships in which political, personal, and social questions and categories are interwoven" (i.e. not examined separately) (Rosenstone 2000, 30), and though *The Wire* is neither a historical drama nor a film, this long serialized narrative excels superbly in showing such social connections. In *The Wire*, all social, political, and cultural factors are interwoven into each other. It is through its format as a sociological network narrative (a formal trait), that *The Wire* successfully demonstrates its political point of showing "the interconnectedness of systemic urban inequality" as Chadda and Wilson (2011, 166) put it. In a classroom discussion on drug dealing, middle schooler Zenobia (Taylor King) stresses this relationship when she says: "We got our thing, but it's just part of the big thing," which is also the epigraph of that episode (*TW*, S4E8). To Zenobia "the big thing" is probably the drug game but through the use of dramatic irony the viewer understands "the big thing" as the entire socio-economic structure that shapes the lives of the students of *The Wire*'s fourth season.

In this detrimentally networked social reality, it is almost to be expected that *The Wire* introduces characters that try to change the untoward and gridlocked social situation the serial portrays. All such attempts, however, are ultimately in vain. Explicitly drawing on Simon's statements from *The Wire* DVD bonus material, critic J.D. Taylor argues that the third season of *The Wire* centers on failed reformers who try to change the institutions they operate within. Stringer Bell (Idris Elba) tries to reform the Barksdale crime organization by making it go legitimate and Major Bunny Colvin tries to create a situation where the police can turn a blind eye to minor drug offenses so the police force once again will be able to fill out a societal function which it has strayed from due to the war on drugs (Taylor 2015, 97). The link between Major Colvin and Stringer Bell is signaled by how they utter the same line when they realize that their projects will fail: "Get on with it, motherfucker." Stringer says this line when Omar Little (Michael K. Williams) and Brother Mouzone (Michael Potts) are about to kill him and, one episode later, Colvin utters these words to his superiors when they are about to suspend and subsequently fire him from the police force. Colvin does not say another word in the rest of this scene (*TW*, S3E11 and S3E12). These characters' failure to reform their institutions cements *The Wire*'s portrayal of institutional dysfunction. Neither Colvin nor Stringer are successful in their endeavors and they are thus both failed reformers. However, while these managerial characters are not effective in making a difference, American television series and films rooted in the crime genre have often positioned the rogue cop as the force that can bring about the change that 'the system' is too corrupt to deliver on, but *The Wire* does not buy into that idea either.

Killing the Cowboy

As a highly skilled, dysfunctional, vigilante police officer, McNulty echoes a wide range of leading men from American police procedurals. Television scholar Trisha Dunleavy argues that "Flawed lead characters have been prevalent in conventional crime dramas, frequently constructed as 'mavericks' who regularly break the rules in their pursuit of justice" (Dunleavy 2018, 109). An important ideological component to this usually male character is that he is often portrayed as being the solution to big societal problems. In the final scene of

The Aesthetics of 'Pessimism': The Wire

Don Siegel's *Dirty Harry* (1971), Harry Callahan (Clint Eastwood) throws his police badge into a lake as a symbolic act of rejecting the institution he works within as being ineffectual in fighting crime; if Dirty Harry will get the job done he will do so in spite of and not because of the police force.

The Wire shuns the ideological premise that this figure embodies. When McNulty and Lester Freamon in season five forge evidence to make it seem that a serial killer is on the loose in Baltimore in order to secure more funding for real police work, the viewer is called to see the problematic things that the outsider rogue cop can lead to. It is important for *The Wire* to not let McNulty go out on a moral high ground. Media scholar Sherryl Vint argues that *The Wire* shows crime "to be the result of systemic problems and thus to require systemic solutions" (Vint 2013, 28), which is why McNulty cannot be shown to be effective in the end. *The Wire* would be not be credible in portraying any problem as being systemic if it only took a maverick policeman to solve the problem. The outsider McNulty cannot therefore be the answer to the systemic reality that *The Wire* portrays. The trope of the rogue police officer elevates the individual to a level that *The Wire* does not believe in and the outsider must therefore be rejected as a solution to societal problems.

This is important to note because it shows an important way that *The Wire* takes issue with certain ideas in American culture. According to historian Grace Hale, there is a strong trend in American culture to imbue people seen as outsiders with a particular power and charisma. This view comes from "the belief that people somehow marginal to society possess cultural resources and values missing among other Americans" (Hale 2011, 1). The idea is that the outsider is able to affect positive change in society because he remains at a distance from society. This idea is, for instance, seen in many westerns.

Lavik argues that *The Wire*'s most central intertextual frame of reference is the western, which it uses to "call forth the mythic, macho ethos of the frontier." *The Wire* mainly alludes to so-called revisionist westerns, which sentimentalize "the ethos of the Old West while exposing it as cynical, hypocritical and/or even dangerous" at the same time (Lavik 2012a, 64–65). Simon explains that that *The Wire*'s shoot-outs were written with the American western in mind, mentioning Sam Peckinpah's *The Wild Bunch* (1969) and

John Ford's *The Searchers* (1956) as sources of inspiration. The cultural importance of these allusions connects to how Simon believes that "in some respects the inner-city crime story or the crime story in general has taken the place in American consciousness of the western" (*TW*, S3E3. DVD bonus features). According to Simon, while working on season two the writers even competed about how many lines they could import from *The Wild Bunch* (Simon in Inskeep 2008).[2] But they did not stop in season two.

Season three's opening episode, "Time After Time", contains several lines that sound like they were lifted straight out of westerns. Cedric Daniels (Lance Reddick) tells the Major Crimes Unit to "Mount up [and] Find your way home." Rawls similarly suggests that the Baltimore Police Department leadership "let no man come back alive" and Lieutenant Dennis Mello (Jay Landsman) says to his officers: "Alright, get outta here, don't get captured." To top things off, Lester Freamon asks McNulty "It's you against the world, is it?" as if McNulty were a vigilante cowboy (*TW*, S3E1). The characters of West Baltimore's Western Police District sometimes even call their place of work "The Western" (*TW*, S1E1, S1E12, S2E12, S3E1). In *The Wire*'s first episode, McNulty tells Jay Landsman (Delaney Williams) that "I came from Western" and is thus only a definite article away from metafictionally saying that he has been drawn in from another genre.

Haastrup notes that intertextual references sometimes create a form of self-reflexive distance between the viewer and the text, but she emphasizes that that is not always the case (Haastrup 2006, 9). Lavik notes that *The Wire*'s intertextual references could be seen as a possible "counterweight to its realist aesthetic" but he argues that the serial's overall 'restricted' use of intertextuality lends the show "a certain *ethos*" (Lavik 2012a, 58). *The Wire*'s references are most often not to other television productions and its allusions do not generally stand as invitations to viewers to play clever a game of 'spot-the-reference.' They are included to "add depth and nuance to key thematic concerns" in *The Wire* (Lavik 2012a, 58, 68). *The Wire*'s references to westerns are not included to suggest that the serial relates more to other texts than to the real-world Baltimore, but seem to be included in order to engage polemically with other texts in American cultural history in order to rebut certain ideas about, for instance, the relationship between the individual and a social order. The restricted use of such intertextual referencing makes it blend into The Wire's realist aesthetic.

The Wire's use of self-reflexivity is similarly restricted and does not call attention to itself in overt ways. Self-reflexivity occurs when a text foregrounds an awareness of itself as text or of its communicative situation as discussed earlier with regards to The Corner's invocation of the melodrama. The use of self-reflexivity in The Wire points to how the serial wants to be watched. The Wire uses the technique of making a discussion on radio show inform the serial's communicative ambitions. In something that resembles a call back to how a radio talk show is used in The Corner while Gary is doing drugs in his parents' basement, The Wire shows Bubbles sitting in a garage while a radio talk show in the background features a journalist's reflections about how he has covered socially important topics:

> crime, violence, drugs, drug addiction, failing schools, all of these social problems in Baltimore city. Over and over again. ... And, you know, the idea of sitting down again and writing another column on this subject. I don't know if it is important. But here I am a citizen of Baltimore, and I take my citizenship as seriously as I take my credentials as a columnist. I said, "what am I gonna say? What can I say about this?" (TW, S4E7)

This monologue self-reflexively brings up the relevance and purpose of telling stories of the harsh conditions in Western Baltimore, which are at the heart of The Wire. What is the social relevance of telling stories in the face of the grim social realities the journalist here is talking about? Here, The Wire points out its own reservations about its way of tackling the social realities it portrays. But this is a self-reflexivity that exists within the storyworld of The Wire, which means that it does not collide fundamentally with its realist mode. It only discreetly calls attention to the fact that The Wire is a television series.

The Wire's use of intertextuality does not tend to collide with the serial's realism. It uses these allusions rhetorically to dismantle the charismatic position of McNulty the outsider. It was not clear that The Wire would be continued after its third season. According to Simon, it was actually cancelled (Simon in Franich 2012) and because of this storytelling reality, the writing team "wrote for closure in case [they] weren't renewed" (Simon in Alvarez 2009, 281). Had *The Wire* ended at the conclusion of season three, they already would have domesticized McNulty by taking him out of the Homicide Unit, making him a beat cop. However, when *The Wire* ultimately was picked up for another two seasons the writers let McNulty exist in his happier family-oriented lifestyle for a while, only to let him go back to being the more unruly McNulty we knew from the start of the serial. However, at the end of season five McNulty is again – like at the end of season three – shown departing from his former lifestyle. *The Wire* thus 'kills off' McNulty-the-vigilante twice, which suggests just how important it was for the writers to have him end up in another place than where he started. Indeed, in season three's final episode Daniels asks McNulty where he will go if he is no longer a part of the Major Crimes Unit. McNulty replies: "The Western, I think. Yeah, Western feels like home" (*TW*, S3E12). He chooses to ride off into the sunset. But the Major Crimes Unit is inside the contemporary city and is even employed by the city.

The cowboy figure embodies the dynamics of the outsider who has the potential to do things that benefit a community, but who also, in the end, cannot live within the confines of established society. The positive valorization of the figure is directly connected to his marginal position. *The Wire*'s revision of the ethos of the western is something that Simon has also forwarded paratextually. Frequently drawing on Greek mythology and other canonical texts from literary history, Simon has often argued that *The Wire* either parallels or avoids ideas found in other narratives. One such example is how Simon frames *The Wire*'s depiction of the power of the individual in relation to the genre conventions of the western:

> "The Wire" has not only gone the opposite way, it's resisted the idea that, in this post-modern America, individuals triumph over institutions. The institution is always bigger. It doesn't tolerate that degree of individuality on any level for any length of time. These moments of epic characterization are inherently false. They're all rooted in, like, old Westerns or something. Guy rides into town, cleans up the town, rides out of town.
>
> There's no cleaning it up anymore. There's no riding in, there's no riding out. The town is what it is. (Simon in Mills 2007)

The bleak outlook of *The Wire* is related to how "the town" is all there is; this is the serial's 'sociological gaze' where all human acts are seen as part of the same social grid. There is no space beyond that grid, not even for the cowboy. *The Wire*'s rejection of the outsider is thus connected to the serial's dismissal of the notion that such a liminal space on the edges of society exists. In the systemic logic of this television serial, all the characters are interlocked within institutional constraints, which stop them from really affecting change on their surroundings. Simon's mention of "epic characterization" speaks to how characters on *The Wire* do not transcend their surrounding environment; they do not rise above it. Without putting it directly, Simon implicitly argues that *The Wire* achieves consistency in its systemic analysis. The traditional cowboy is not part of the town. His marginal position is what enables the cowboy to effect positive change, and *The Wire* simply does not buy into that logic. The Major Crimes Unit are proverbial outsiders who try to clean up the mess that established society is unable/unwilling to really attend to. But in the end, The Major Crimes Unit does not affect any change either.

In the first episode of *The Wire*, McNulty and Bunk are getting drunk just next to a railway track at four o'clock in the morning. McNulty relieves himself while standing on the tracks as a train approaches, only to walk off the tracks in the nick of time to avoid getting hit by an oncoming train. With the oncoming train symbolizing

Figure 6 McNulty again faces the train though now lacks the zest he used to have.

the institution that McNulty-the-vigilante stares down, this gesture foreshadows how the individual will not trump larger social structures in *The Wire*. Inserted in the very first episode, this scene indicates how McNulty will be the one to budge, not the institutions that he tries to take on. When McNulty again is standing on the tracks in the final episode of season three, telling Bunk that "I'm tired, Bunk," *The Wire* is emphasizing the symbolic function of the train and shows that the system beat the unruly outsider.

The dysfunctionality of *The Wire*'s institutions shows viewers that it is 'pessimistic' about the outlook for change from within, but the show also makes a point of rejecting the idea that change can come from the outside(r). It rejects the idea that the 'cowboy within the city' is able to bring about change. In that way, the serial remains consistent in its portrayal of the individual being overpowered by society. No individual is able to clean up society's problems. Indeed, in the final episode of *The Wire* McNulty is sitting in silence with his girlfriend Beadie Russell (Amy Ryan) on the front porch of her house and a train horn can be heard somewhere off in the distance (*TW*, S5E10). This small callback to McNulty staring down oncoming trains shows how he ultimately moves on from taking on the entire world. This scene thus ties *The Wire*'s rejection of the outsider on a political level together with a depiction of McNulty having moved on to a better lifestyle on a more existential and emotional level.

The purpose of the Major Crimes Unit of which McNulty is an important member is to build cases against high-level players in the drug game instead of trying to charge any numbers of street-level drug dealers with minor drug-related offenses. *The Wire* depicts the police force through this unit, which means that the viewer is invited to root for this unit as the solution to the problems the serial portrays. Critics Jasper Schelstraete and Gert Buelens argue that this police unit "is virtually the only unit that is depicted as effective," and its "position as outsiders allows them to circumvent, and sometimes to subvert, the mechanisms of the justice system, which are presented as obstacles for police work" (Schelstraete and Buelens 2013, 290). The institution of the police force is an obstacle for productive police work. This depiction is an important part of *The Wire*'s portrayal of the Major Crimes Unit as a positive force for change that the audience can root for, align with and sympathize with. But *The Wire* ultimately invokes this trope in order to deconstruct it.

Grace Hale's study ends on a normative note by suggesting that American culture needs to move on from the romanticization of the outsider (Hale 2011, 302). *The Wire* would agree. The serial rejects this prevalent trope because it extends from the myth of the lone outsider being able to 'clean up.' Though the serial portrays institutions as being detrimental to many efforts, *The Wire* nonetheless tacitly suggests that the solutions it calls for are based on cooperation between people. Freamon and McNulty do, in a sense, ride off into the sunset. At the end of the serial, Freamon continues to make his hobby-sized furniture and is in a relationship with Shardene Innes (Wendy Grantham) and McNulty finally goes home from a bar without drinking himself senseless (*TW*, S5E10). But in doing so without having effected change, *The Wire* dissuades the viewer from rooting for McNulty and the other 'outsider McNultys' on television. He may be a charismatic outsider but he is impotent in the face of the institutional structures he faces. Given *The Wire*'s emphasis on showing how structural forces trump the ability of individuals to effect change in this system, it follows that the serial must reject the lure of the outsider. That is why McNulty crosses too many lines in the last season. That is the serial telling its viewers that McNulty's outsider mentality must be rejected. But where McNulty fails in the face of institutional adversity, Frank Sobotka's (Chris Bauer) foe, conversely, is the much more amorphous social-historical process of deindustrialization.

"Fuck the wall!"

Season two of *The Wire* focuses on the loss of working-class jobs. Local union leader Frank Sobotka tries to pay off city officials to introduce a grain pier to the Baltimore harbor and dredge its canal to allow larger ships to dock in Baltimore, which would help secure the jobs his union members rely on for their living. The season's first scene shows McNulty on a police boat in the harbor talking to his new partner Claude Diggins (Jeffrey Fugitt) about how McNulty's father and one of Diggins' uncles were laid off from the shipyard Beth Steel in the 1970s. This sets the scene for the season's exploration of the effects of the loss of manufacturing jobs in America.

McNulty and Diggins later approach a party boat and tow it out of the way to let the rich people on it continue their fun. The fact that the boat is allowed to stay in the harbor intimates how the harbor – once a site of many working-class jobs – has become the playground for the wealthy, which is only underscored by the fact that the boat is named "Capitol Gains." The dialogue about the loss of manufacturing jobs and the shots of the old shipyard thus clash with the setting of the upper-class boat. The scene foreshadows how this season will explore the way the American city has been shaped by deindustrialization.

Deindustrialization refers to the process of losing manufacturing jobs and facilities in industrial production, which usually happens when an economy transitions from having a large secondary sector to being dominated by a large tertiary sector. In the post-war era, 40 percent of the workforce in America was employed in the industrial sector. By 2017, that number was down to 13 percent. Because of this shift in the economy, there are today worse job opportunities for skilled workers than in the post-war era where there were many well-paying jobs in the industrial sector. When those jobs disappear, there are many non-unionized jobs in the service sector which pay less (Kollmeyer 2018, 3). Simon's oeuvre shows how this development is linked to the emergence of drug running and ghettoization.

But deindustrialization is also linked to globalization, which *The Wire* alludes to in a scene where Frank Sobotka is attending a seminar about automation in the docking industry. A corporate presenter starts his talk by ominously saying that "The future is now" before showing a video demonstration about how the docks of the port of Rotterdam are using more robots, which is reducing the need for man-hours. The film's voice-over tells the audience that "modern robotics do much of the work in the world's largest sea port, Rotterdam." Sobotka asks the presenter: "What kind of man-hours are the stevedores clocking over there?" The union man has a vested interest in making sure that his union members will be able to hold on to their jobs. Automation is a threat to the livelihood of Frank's union members and his entire community and way of life (*TW*, S2E7).

The facial expressions and gesturing of the characters demonstrate how differently the union representatives take in this new information compared to how the corporate representatives talk enthusiastically about what they are learning about the Rotterdam harbor. Frank Sobotka and his colleague Nat Coxson (Luray Cooper) are not Luddites, but the scene makes it clear that the new technology represents a challenging future for them. Historians Jefferson Cowie and Joseph Heathcott note that

> While economists and business leaders often speak in neutral, even hopeful, terms such as "restructuring," "downsizing," or "creative destruction," metaphors of defeat and subjugation are more appropriate for the workers who banked on good-paying industrial jobs for the livelihoods of their families and their communities. (Cowie and Heathcott 2003, 1)

Symptomatic of this optimistic discourse, an IMF report from 1997 concluded that "Deindustrialization is not a negative phenomenon, but a natural consequence of further growth in advanced economies" (Rowthorn and Ramaswamy 1997, 11). Nat and Frank are thinking about the prospects of their livelihood and most certainly *do* experience this form of deindustrialization as "a negative phenomenon."

The presenter's words in the scene in *The Wire* ring ominously for the stevedores, but for other people that very same presentation holds the promise of increasing their profits when they can reduce wages for dockworkers. The discourse does not consider that what may be a positive development for some people actually represents life-changing realities for others. Sociologist Christopher Kollmeyer argues that for people in the working class holding unionized jobs the problem with deindustrialization is not only the loss of jobs. It is also the fact that the bargaining power of unions is weakened, meaning that their advocate is losing ground in a changing economy (Kollmeyer 2018, 2–4).

According to historian Thomas Sugrue, many people believe that industrial jobs started to disappear from America in 1970s. While many such jobs did disappear in that decade, the loss of manufacturing jobs goes back to the 1950s though the booming of the economy of that era drowned out any discussion of the disappearance of industrial jobs (Sugrue 2014, 6).

Like any character in *The Wire* who tries to make a difference in his community, Frank Sobotka's attempts at preserving the livelihood and lifestyle of the dockworkers in Baltimore are ultimately in vain. At one point, Nick Sobotka (Pablo Schreiber) tells his uncle that that "Today we got ships, uncle Frank. Today. The writing's on the fucking wall" referencing how rarely there is enough work for all of the stevedores on the Baltimore harbor. Frank angrily replies, "Fuck the wall," suggesting that the things people around him consider to be irreversible forces of history are to him things that he can actually help change (*TW*, S2E5).

Though this season continues storylines from the first season about the Major Crimes Unit and the Barksdale organization – and carries them into the third season – the setting of the harbor and the Sobotka family almost completely falls away in subsequent seasons. In season five, however, Mayor Carcetti is cutting the ribbon for a planned development to be called New Westport on the Baltimore harbor front where Frank had worked to place a grain pier. For just a short while viewers get to see Nick Sobotka and some of his friends and former colleagues protesting Carcetti's grand proclamations. Nick's reappearance triggers viewers' memories about the Sobotkas and the harbor front, and this creates a tension between these two characters' storylines. By having aligned viewers with the Sobotkas in season two and still aligning viewers with Carcetti in season five, *The Wire* manages to create a confrontation between two worldviews that *The Wire* has devoted vast amounts of screen time to. In this brief scene, the serial is able to depict the competing interests that are at play in the struggles around how a city like Baltimore is to develop.

Without the season two storyline about the Sobotka family this scene would not take on this added dimension of showing how Carcetti's actions – whom we are otherwise invited to sympathize with to some extent – are complicit in hurting the former stevedores which viewers followed for twelve episodes. When Carcetti asks who that protestor is and real estate developer Andy Krawczyk (Michael Willis) tells him that "that's nobody, Mr. Mayor. Nobody at all" Krawczyk represents an outlook that collides with the viewer's experience (*TW*, S5E6). To us, Nick *is* somebody. Journalist Peter Moskowitz argues that gentrification is "about the decimation of decades-old cultures" (Moskowitz 2017, 4) and here we see how the Sobotkas' way of life is threatened by the real estate developments that Carcetti is complicit in constructing.

Frank does not ultimately change anything but it is important that *The Wire* shows the struggle from his perspective, for viewers will surely know that he is fighting an uphill battle. The British social historian E.P. Thompson once wrote that eighteenth and nineteenth century Luddites' "hostility to the new industrialism may have been backward-looking. Their communitarian ideals may have been fantasies. Their insurrectionary conspiracies may have been foolhardy. But they lived through these times of acute social disturbance, and we did not" (Thompson 1966, 12–13). Thompson's words remind us that even though America has faced the consequences of deindustrialization for decades it is important to heed the voices of those people who most acutely suffer the cost of this development.

In 1982 Barry Bluestone and Bennett Harrison wrote that "By the beginning of the 1980s, every newscast seemed to contain a story about a plant shutting down, another thousand jobs disappearing from a community, or the frustrations of workers unable to find fulltime jobs utilizing their skills and providing enough income to support their families" (Bluestone and Harrison 1982, 4). *The Wire* thus picks up a story that has a long social-historical backstory and the mere fact that season two zooms in on Frank and the dockworkers represents *The Wire*'s declaration of solidarity with the working class. A major political point for the second season is quite simply to align viewers with Frank and his group of peers so that we may feel allegiance with him, so when Andy Krawczyk later dismisses Nick as a mere nobody we are invited to feel that that is wrong. As explained earlier, viewers do not generally identify with characters. Viewers do not necessarily think they are – or are like – Frank or Nick but we have spent enough time with them to see some things from their point of view – certainly more compared to Andy Krawczyk. This is why we understand why Frank prefers looking back in time instead of looking forward to the future. His experience is that things are going the wrong way. Historian Steven High notes that many historians have followed E.P. Thompson's efforts "to avoid obscuring the agency of working people even in political defeat, when history itself seemed to be against them" (High 2013, 1000). *The Wire* imbues the dockworkers with agency in a story that ultimately shows them being defeated but its alignment and allegiance with the Sobotka family make all the difference.

When the Major Crimes Unit has been tasked with going after Sobotka due to the vindictive police commissioner Stan Valchek (Al Brown), Freamon and the rest of the unit ponder how Sobotka is able to donate sizable amounts of money to political players in Baltimore when the union membership at that point in time is down to less than one hundred stevedores from a high point of 300 members in the 1970s (*TW*, S2E6). At that point, the viewer has already seen Sobotka and Father Jerome Lewandowski (Tel Monks) talking to people about getting the harbor canal dredged in order to accommodate more ship traffic in the city. Clay Davis (Isiah Whitlock, Jr.) has apparently received $40,000 from Sobotka (*TW*, S2E3) and viewers are shown how Sobotka and his union members express big hopes for a possible grain pier on the Baltimore docks (*TW*, S2E6). Yet though we are invited to sympathize with Frank we still know that he is deeply involved with facilitating the import of drugs to Baltimore and is thus complicit in some of the misery related to addiction shown in season one – for instance in Johnny Weeks' (Leo Fitzpatrick) and Bubbles' sad lives marked by their struggles with drug addiction.

A key scene in Frank's storyline comes when he meets with lobbyist Bruce DiBiago (Keith Flippen) to discuss the prospects of dredging the Baltimore harbor canal. Sobotka reminisces about how no matter what the kids of his neighborhood had aspired to be when they grew up they all became stevedores. The underlying point is that though the neighborhood children may have had different dreams growing up, there was always going to be a job waiting for them on the docks. The white-collar lobbyist DiBiago, however, counters Frank's story, relating how his great-grandfather was a knife-sharpener but still managed to send his son to high school and now DiBiago's son is attending Princeton. Their different outlooks are rooted in how Frank's experience is one of social reproduction where working-class children grew up to become working-class men and women, and DiBiago's family story is one where his ancestor had managed to lift his family up to the professional middle class. To Frank, the docks once represented a social compact where the children growing up in Sobotka's neighborhood, at the very least, had a future to look forward to. Therefore, when DiBiago tells of his family history of social uplift, Frank says, "You're talking history, right. I'm talking now." DiBiago's great-grandfather had a working-class job that allowed him to provide for his family and enabled his descendants move up in the world, but Sobotka's fear is that the stevedores' jobs are disappearing. The chances of mere social reproduction are falling away, not to speak of the chances of upward social mobility (*TW*, S2E7). Frank is afraid of what the loss of more jobs will do to his community.

This speaks to the stalling of social mobility or, rather, how the working class is barred from maintaining their place in the economy due to the loss of well-paying work. While inner cities have long had high poverty rates, the level of joblessness took off in the 1970s to the point that by the 1990s it was common for people in inner-city neighborhoods to not go to work in the average week. The jobs were not there anymore. To Wilson, a neighborhood being poor is one thing. But when poverty is linked to joblessness a neighborhood can face bigger consequences in terms of, for instance, crime and family dissolution. Wilson argues that joblessness in inner cities has severe consequences for "the social and cultural life" in inner-city neighborhoods, which may ultimately "impede the social mobility of inner-city residents" (Wilson 1997, xviii–xix). The cultural effects of joblessness can thus themselves add to the perpetuation of poverty and social ills. In other words, the causes of concentrated disadvantage give way to additional causes (and not just consequences) of social problems. As Wilson notes about his observations in Chicago "children will seldom interact on a sustained basis with people who are employed or with families with a steady breadwinner." In this way joblessness has detrimental effects for children's cognitive and linguistic skills, which later will harm their chances to become employed in the mainstream economy (Wilson 2012, 57).

Frank vents his anger by throwing a dart in the face of a picture of Robert Irsay who in 1984 moved the NFL team then known as the Baltimore Colts to Indianapolis. This symbolic gesture is a poignant frame of reference when discussing the prospects of keeping jobs in Baltimore. But for Frank it is not only the prospects of keeping jobs in Baltimore that is at stake here. Frank's point about the union represents his sense of community identity. Like he says, "it breaks my heart that there's no future for the Sobotkas on the waterfront" (*TW*, S2E7). The issue is not only the economic challenges facing his community but also of his sense of belonging to a place and his community.

Sobotka's main goal as a union leader is to secure the jobs his members rely on, and so, regardless of his disagreement with DiBiago, Sobotka lines the lobbyist's pockets with money and sends him back to secure political support for a grain pier and the dredging of the canal. When the lobbyist finally, four episodes later, tells Frank that the grain pier is dead and urges him to talk to the FBI who is investigating Sobotka, the union local leader drives home the overall agenda of the season asking the lobbyist "You know what the trouble is, Brucey? We used to make shit in this country, build shit. Now we just put our hand in the next guy's pocket" (*TW*, S2E11), a line Simon has since pointed out as one of his favorite lines of *The Wire* (Simon in McGuire 2012, xviii). Frank's sentiment here reflects his class background in the sense that the lifestyle he leads relies on the existence of manufacturing and shipping, but with the deindustrialization of many American cities, especially in the Rust Belt, his life and his community are threatened.

Simon has said that he wanted season two "to go to the death of work. Because where do these drug corners come from? They come from deindustrialization. Our economy no longer needs mass employment. The only factory in town that's still hiring and is always hiring are the corners." Yet he also remarks that the producers were pressed to find a location that would let them come inside to do "a working-class movie" which is why *The Wire* ended up at the port and not on an assembly line like Paul Schrader's film *Blue Collar* (1978), which Simon had in mind as an inspiration for the season (Simon in Abrams 2018, 99). Sobotka's line about how people "used to make shit in this country" seems to reflect that initial ambition about season two being about the loss of production jobs. But the line also brings the discussion up to a more general level about deindustrialization and the loss of working-class jobs in the U.S.

With season one focusing on the war on drugs and the second season focusing on deindustrialization, the writers needed a narrative strategy to connect these two themes. That connection comes through Nick Sobotka's storyline, Frank's nephew. Though he is both an adult and a father, Nick still lives in the basement of his parents' house. He is portrayed as a mature and generally responsible individual, but he cannot get enough hours on the docks due to his low level of seniority compared to his older colleagues, meaning that he cannot afford to buy a house that he can move into with his girlfriend Aimee (Kristin Proctor) and their daughter. Nick's cousin Ziggy (James Ransone), Frank's son, gets himself into trouble with East Baltimore gangsters Proposition Joe (Robert Chew) and Cheese (Method Man), giving Nick the chance/responsibility of helping his cousin by stealing some chemicals from the docks and delivering them to Proposition Joe's organization. But when Nick must decide whether he wants to be paid for his efforts in money or in drugs – and Ziggy wants to take the drugs – Nick decides to get "Half in cash, half in dope" (*TW*, S2E6). This is a key moment for Nick. His storyline shows us that it is because he needs money to provide a home for his family and the fact that he cannot get enough hours on the docks that he decides to get involved in the drug world.

Sociologist Elijah Anderson notes that many "youngsters dream of leading the drug dealer's life, or at least their highly glamorized conceptions of this life" (Anderson 1999, 111), but that is in no way the case with Nick. After having been paid in drugs, he sets up an operation where the minor character Frog (Gary Senkus) will be responsible for selling the drugs. Nick, however, is skeptical of Frog's way of talking and dressing: "You happen to be white" Nick tells Frog who wears large hip-hop style clothes and tries to emulate African American English. Frog seems to fit Anderson's description of a young man infatuated with the drug dealer's lifestyle, which, in Frog's case, seems closely linked to a fascination with cultural trends associated with African Americans living in inner-city areas.

Nick is not infatuated in any way with the drug dealer lifestyle – or with inner-city African American culture for that matter. To him, drugs are a way of providing for his family. Indeed, Frog's hip-hop style attire is quite the contrast with how Nick dresses as well as the fact that his basement room is draped with posters of white rock bands such Static X, Guided by Voices, Disturbed, Filter, and The Used. The scene where Frog and Nick are talking, however, ends with Nick getting a glimpse of an elderly woman looking out her front door with a worried expression on her face. Nick's facial expression changes. He is not proud of what he is doing (*TW*, S2E7). This scene illustrates the link between drug running and the loss of jobs. Getting hold of drugs will allow Nick to make enough money to provide a home for his family. All of this illustrates his somewhat reluctant way into the drug industry.

Sugrue cites an early-1960s survey conducted in one of Detroit's most hard-pressed inner-city areas, which found that that "Under conditions where a gap in legitimate opportunity exists in the world, such deviant occupations [like drug dealing] grow up to fill the void. The motif is one of survival; it is not based on thrill seeking" (quoted in Sugrue 2014, 261). This description fits well with how *The Wire* paints Nick's motivation for getting involved in drug running. David Simon, however, has also said that the shift to the docks in season two was motivated by not wanting to make a story about drugs an all-Black story. The "last thing I want to do," Simon argues, "is suggest that you can track the drug problem through America by following black people" (Simon in Abrams 2018, 111).

In this sense, season two tells of how the corners portrayed in season one came to be. But it is important to show that Nick was not infatuated with the gangster lifestyle, and *The Wire* thus presents an economic explanation – and not a cultural one – for how he ended up in the drug world. When Nick later comes home to his girlfriend Aimee, he tells her that they now will have enough money to "pay down the truck and still have enough left over for some place nice. Out in the county" (*TW*, S2E7). To Aimee, Nick's words do not sound any alarms; he presents a dream not of flashy cars and fancy clothes like his cousin Ziggy, but a dream about not owing money on their truck and moving out of a struggling city. Nick, however, is not just lying to Aimee about how will earn the extra money. At this point, he is already driving an expensive truck, which suggests that his earnings on drug running is already changing his priorities. Yet, while Nick is struggling to support his family, his uncle Frank has bigger ambitions about also caring for what he considers to be his extended family – his union members.

Early on in season two, one of Frank Sobotka's union members, Ringo (Jon Garcia), comes to him to tell him that he is not doing well financially as he is not getting enough days due to his low level of seniority within the union. Sobotka tells Ringo to go to their regular bar and order a shot and a beer on Frank and a slight smile on Sobotka's face tells us just how pleased he is being able to help this checker (*TW*, S2E3). For Frank everything is about protecting his members and their way of life, so when Ringo later shows up at the bar – in a scene that otherwise focuses on a conversation between Nick and Ziggy – and places his order, he also gets a thick wad of cash in return. The bartender (Jill Redding) tells Ziggy that his dad is a good person, demonstrating to viewers that the money from Sobotka's criminal activities does not go to himself but to his community. When Nick in the following episode is called to meet his uncle Frank on the pier and is scolded for stealing a number of cameras from the docks, Nick defends his actions with references to how Frank and his generation have told the younger crowd how they used to steal goods from the docks. Frank furiously replies: "We ain't back in the day, Nicky. ... The cameras come back" and rhetorically asks his nephew "You think it's for me?! Is that what you think, huh? It ain't about me, Nick!" Nick concedes: "I know, I'm sorry" (*TW*, S2E4). Sobotka sees Nick's theft in the context of possible future job loss on the Baltimore harbor. Due to the global nature of the shipping industry the Baltimore harbor is in danger of being left out of the transmission of goods and due to that fact, there is no room for theft on the docks.

Frank consistently sees things in the bigger picture of the survival of docks. When the police question him and inform him that he can help himself and his union if he tells them of his dealings with The Greek's (Bill Raymond) criminal organization, Frank immediately takes offense with the idea that they would help him and his union: "Help my union? For 25 years we've been dying slow down there. Dry dock's rusting, piers standing empty. My friends and their kids like we got the cancer. No life-line got thrown all that time, nothing from nobody, and now you wanna help us? Help me?!" To Frank, this police officer represents a dominant part of society that has disregarded the working class for decades. He concedes that he knew he "was wrong. But in my head I thought I was wrong for the right reasons, you know?" To him, the ends justified the means. He knows what the full effects of deindustrialization will mean for his community. The community's role as a positive social fabric that ties the neighborhood together is in danger of coming apart. So when Sobotka agrees to cooperate with the police, he has one caveat: "Anything but the union. I ain't putting in no union men" (*TW*, S2E11), reflecting his stance of solidarity with his fellow union members. The union itself is pivotal to Frank's sense of community.

The last time Frank talks to Nick he is infuriated with his nephew for selling heroin: "Heroin? How the fuck did that happen, Nick? Look at me! You ain't much more than a kid. Me, I should've known better. I put you up with them, for what? I flushed my fucking family, for what?" Frank's anger when questioning Nick is just as much directed at himself: "I flushed my fucking family, for what?" Looking at the old shipyard Frank laments that he is looking at what soon will be condominiums (*TW*, S2E11). His mind is right back with the political issue at hand even though he was just admitting to himself what he put his family through.

Season two ends – like all seasons of *The Wire* – with a montage. The union is closed down, Frank's collaborator Horseface (Charley Scalies) is on trial, his son Ziggy is in jail, the corrupt politician Clay Davis marks the construction of condominiums, there is still drug dealing on the streets, stevedores have turned to drinking in the street, and new sex workers are coming off a truck. All these shots show that things are staying the same. The only change is the fact that the elderly woman, whom we have seen growing weary of her neighborhood, has put her house up for sale and the harbor landscape now looks abandoned. The montage paints a picture of social reproduction but also discreetly suggests that things are deteriorating on the harbor and in the white working-class neighborhood (*TW*, S2E12). So despite all of Frank's efforts he – like the Major Crimes Unit – is unable to affect change in his community. In the case of the docks, it is not even a case of social reproduction but one of social deterioration. Frank had hoped that the next generation would be able to secure a livelihood for themselves on the docks, but the loss of working-class jobs will most likely prohibit that scenario. This, however, does not change the fact that *The Wire*, generally speaking, emphasizes social reproduction.

A Form of Politics

But how does all this answer the question of how *The Wire* expresses its politics: that is, the issue that arises from being a political serial that calls for change but which presents a situation as all but unalterable? Every character is shown to be replaceable in its storyworld. When Omar Little dies, he is replaced by Michael Lee (Tristan Wilds) and when Bubbles gets clean Dukie Weems (Jermaine Crawford) is just the next addition to the "dope fiends," as Bubbles would say. When the Barksdale organization crumbles the void is filled out by Marlo Stanfield (Jamie Hector). Similarly, the idealistic mayor Carcetti is faced with the harsh reality that the role of the mayor is to "eat shit" and not really change anything as his predecessor tells him (*TW*, S4E7). This is how *The Wire* portrays a world of social reproduction and though these observations could be seen as justifying Atlas and Dreier's criticism that *The Wire* is defeatist, we need to look outside the text itself why to understand why *The Wire* takes this 'pessimistic' shape.

The Wire's urbanity is marked by moral ambiguity where police officers do not hold a moral high ground and a character who has committed murder like D'Angelo Barksdale is shown to be much less callous and more caring compared to many of the other people involved in the drug game or compared to many police officers. This is one way that the serial tries to bring some nuance to discussions of the war on drugs, which is one of *The Wire*'s most central themes – especially in the first and third seasons. The war on drugs has negatively affected impoverished neighborhoods for decades and civil rights advocate Michelle Alexander argues that this 'war' is the leading cause for the soaring incarceration rates in the U.S., pointing to the fact that "there are more people in prisons and jails today [in 2010] just for drug offenses than were incarcerated for *all* reasons in 1980" (Alexander 2010, 60). *The Wire* shows the war on drugs as a case of social reproduction because that is the only way that it is able to show the viewer how the war on drugs has been perpetuated across decades. The first episode hints as much in a dialogue between the experienced officer Kima Greggs and the newly hired police officers Ellis Carver and Thomas Hauk (Domenick Lombardozzi). Greggs laments their macho statements, like when Hauk says "Fuck the paperwork. Collect bodies, split heads." Carver, however, argues that "You can't even call this shit a war [as] Wars end" (*TW*, S1E1). *The Wire*'s vision of social reproduction emphasizes the continuity of the war on drugs across several decades. Thirty-five episodes later, Bunny Colvin is explaining to Carver the intricacies of this idea, which Carver had only rather flippantly thrown into the conversation in *The Wire*'s first episode. Colvin says:

> I mean you call something a war, and pretty soon everyone gonna be running around acting like warriors. They gonna be running around on a damn crusade, storming corners, slapping on cuffs, racking up

body counts. And when you at war, you need a fucking enemy. And pretty soon, damn near everybody on every corner is your fucking enemy. And soon, the neighborhood you're supposed to be policing, that's just occupied territory. Look here, the point I'm making, Carver, is this: Soldiering and policing, they ain't the same thing. (*TW*, S3E10)

Colvin criticizes the fact that police work has been framed through a war metaphor and argues that that logic has consequences for how police work is carried out. Discourse and powerful acts of framing have redirected the focus of the institution. His argument builds on the idea that how people talk about something affects the way they think about it and consequently how they act. The notion of a war presupposes, as Colvin argues, an enemy and that means that the practice of police work goes from enforcing laws and doing preventive work in the community to "collecting bodies and splitting heads," in Hauk's words. Colvin explicitly criticizes this martial discourse that focuses on "storming corners, slapping on cuffs, racking up body counts." David Simon and Ed Burns are both credited for outlining the story of this episode. Burns, however, is credited for penning this episode and his grievances from his time as a police officer seem to shine through here. Indeed, Burns and Simon's 1997 book is explicitly critical of how some police efforts focus too much on drug-related crimes in a way takes resources away from other important police tasks. They write that in the late 1980s "The police department began using more and more of itself to chase addicts and touts […] so there were fewer resources available to work shooting cases, or rapes, or burglaries" (Burns and Simon 1998, 168).

Much of Colvin's monologue here is a critique of Carver. The inexperienced officer's style of police work does not live up to Colvin's ideals and Colvin even suggests that Carver's entire generation of police officers have generally been brought up on a distorted logic about police work. Thanks to the preceding three seasons the viewer is able to see how both Carver and Hauk have bought into the premise of the war on drugs, and it is especially after season three that Carver tries to live up to Colvin's higher ideals of police work and community service.

The war on drugs had made its mark on police work in the decades before Simon started working on *The Wire*, which emphasizes that it is the systemic nature of this situation that is at the heart of the problem. In the way *The Wire* portrays Baltimore it does not seem likely that one could improve the school system if the children do not have many legitimate job prospects when they grow up. As Wilson shows, the loss of jobs is detrimental to inner-city neighborhoods and that development is directly linked to drug running and the war on drugs. And if city hall is unable to attend to the pressing concerns of the city it is difficult to see how this situation can improve. It would go against the politics of *The Wire* to suggest that the source for a positive change is already present in the current situation. Positive forces are indeed there – Bunk (Wendell Pierce), Kima, Bunny Colvin, Carcetti, Walon (Steve Earle) and so on – but with them being so overpowered by their institutions, the serial's politics rejects the notion that it is all going to work out eventually. In *The Wire*'s vision of social reproduction it seems impossible to change any one thing, such as improving struggling schools, without attending to unemployment, loss of jobs, and the war on drugs at the same time. These different phenomena are interlinked in a way that ensures that this state of affairs reproduces itself. The situation is gridlocked.

The Aesthetics of 'Pessimism'

It then follows that there really is a point to *The Wire*'s 'bleakness.' Because *The Wire* focuses so much on several dysfunctional aspects of American society it, at least implicitly, calls for change, but *The Wire* also shows how networked institutional forces keep at bay any initiative for positive change. This creates a tension between, on the one hand, the hope for a different social order and, on the other hand, pointing out the difficult way to get to that better place. Had the serial been more hopeful it would betray the systemic character of its societal criticism.

Presumably due to *The Wire*'s social indignation and its multi-protagonist structure, some critics likened the serial to the novels of Charles Dickens, which, however, to Simon "fell badly on us." In Simon's view, Dickens "would make the case for a much better social compact than existed in Victorian England, but then his verdict would always be, 'But thank God a nice old uncle or this heroic lawyer is going to make things better.' In the end, the guy would punk out" (Simon in Pearson 2009). Simon's point is that Dickens would write endings that did not follow through on his novels' societal criticism. In Simon's view, there is a mismatch between Dickens's politics and his storytelling choices. His aesthetics end up undercutting the political edge of his stories. To Simon, it seems that positive or hopeful endings console readers or viewers into thinking that, say, the social injustices portrayed will ultimately be corrected, and that society therefore is on the right path after all.

This is why *The Wire* paints a bleak picture of the contemporary city. If there were a potentially redeeming element in this defunct system, viewers would be invited to believe that the potential for improvement was already present in the current state of affairs. *The Wire* does not offer its viewers any invitation to think like that. Indeed, urban policy scholars Peter Dreier and John Atlas have argued that *The Wire*'s portrayal of Baltimore politics leaves too little hope for positive change. They criticize *The Wire* for failing to "to offer viewers any understanding that the problems facing cities and the urban poor are solvable" (Dreier and Atlas 2009, 332). The characters of *The Wire* are all but powerless in their attempts to solve crimes, change the dominant political culture, or alleviate the social ills that affect its rendition of Baltimore.

Dreier and Atlas do have a point about how they characterize *The Wire* as being pessimistic, but they miss the purpose of why *The Wire* paints such a bleak picture. Had it been a more uplifting and redeeming story, the systemic nature of its societal portrayal would fall away and then the serial would, in Simon's words about Dickens, "punk out," in other words, not embrace the logical consequence of the politics it espouses.

Because *The Wire*'s portrayal of society is marked almost solely by reproduction at an institutional and structural level, its call for change seemingly becomes almost paradoxical or quixotic. But it is precisely in doing so that it remains argumentatively consistent in its call for change. The serial's 'bleakness,' then, is at the very heart of *The Wire*'s call for political and social change. So while Kinder correctly identifies the systemicness of *The Wire*'s criticism, she does not connect it to the bleakness that Dreier and Atlas point out. Yet it is only by tracing how these two textual elements are connected that one sees that this is the way that *The Wire*'s social criticism becomes coherent and consistent. *The Wire* is not a flawed call for change; on the contrary, it remains consistent in arguing that such change must address the systemicness of the situation in urban America.

This political point is intimately linked to how *The Wire*'s storytelling choices are intertwined with its politics. In most episodic police procedurals, the viewer is only told the information that has to do directly with solving a specific crime, and such TV series consequently eschew showing the social background that leads to crime. It is the other way around in *The Wire* where the contextualization of crime is key. Critic Alasdair McMillan acutely notes that *The Wire* promotes to center stage those social factors that many police procedurals tend to leave out (McMillan 2009, 53). Because *The Wire* presents a form of 'sociological' network narrative, it is possible to present viewers with both cause and effect as in the case of Nick Sobotka. This sets this serial apart from many more traditional forms of police procedurals. *The Wire* shows both the effects of institutional mismanagement at street level, but also how and why this institutional logic is reproduced politically – a key element in season three. It is in this sense that the serial's politics stress the point that, at a basic structural level, the systemic realities are so crippled that what is needed is a systemic change.

We need to look outside *The Wire*, specifically to the war on drugs, to understand this storytelling choice. Lavik argues that some of the criticism *The Wire* received for being too pessimistic ignored the reasons why the serial is structured as it is. To Lavik, blaming *The Wire* for being too pessimistic or bleak is the equivalent of complaining that a fire alarm is too noisy; it is a complaint that does not consider *why The Wire* looks the way it does (Lavik 2014, 142). It is because *The Wire* focuses so much on critiquing the war on drugs that it almost needs to present this bleak outlook.

Revamped by Ronald Reagan in 1982 before the crack cocaine epidemic of the 1980s and 1990s had become "a crisis in poor black neighborhoods" or a big issue in American media (Alexander 2010, 5), the war on drugs has led to sky-rocketing incarceration rates of African Americans. As Michelle Alexander shows in *The New Jim Crow*, the war on drugs and the rise of mass incarceration has had disastrous consequences for America's poor, especially for Black men (Alexander 2010). In other words, the war on drugs had existed for two decades before HBO started airing *The Wire*. But the war on drugs had not prevented drug use and drug abuse from still being widespread in America. *The Wire* portrays a drug war that has carried on for decades without an end in sight and the show suggests that this situation cannot be fixed by, say, an effective form of policing or through the concerted efforts of a group of determined idealists. The point is that had *The Wire* suggested that the situation it depicts will somehow improve in the future, it would become inconsistent in how it portrays a political culture that is unable to address even the most pressing societal concerns. Had it done so, *The Wire* would have misrepresented the issue it portrays.

The Wire is the first of Simon's serials that is able to really claim the city as its topic. *The Corner* had focused on humanizing people struggling with drug addiction but emphasized – through flashbacks and interview sequences at the opening and ending of every episode – that this project was to be understood in the context of a social deterioration in its West Baltimore setting. But while *The Wire* invoked the genre of the police procedural to somewhat 'pessimistically' discuss the state of the city, Simon's next multi-season serial *Treme* would take a more positive spin on the American city. This serial makes a case for understanding the city as a site and source of cultural strength, and as a place where people of different creeds are able to live together in a vibrant and culturally effervescent community.

Notes

1 Simon's repeated remarks about *The Wire* being indebted to Greek mythology (e.g. Simon in Talbot 2007) is one of the claims that has been repeated numerous times in academic criticism. Other than Lavik's video essay and this book, at least nine other peer-reviewed publications refer to this statement and that does not even consider the journalistic comparisons (Etheridge 2008, 155; McMillan 2009, 50; Sheehan and Sweeney 2009; Love 2010; Vest 173; Crosby 2013, 7; Williams 2014, 4; Lister 2015, 69). It thus seems clear that Simon's statements about *The Wire*'s affinity with Greek drama have influenced many discussions about the serial.
2 See Lavik (2012a) for further examples and a discussion of *The Wire*'s intertextual references to westerns.

3

The Case for the City: *Treme* (2010–2013)

Like *The Corner* and *The Deuce*, the very title of *Treme* refers to a specific place. According to geographer Michael Crutcher Jr., the New Orleans neighborhood Treme, or Fauborg Treme, is known for a strong tradition of African American political influence and its long-running African American cultural traditions such as second-lining, Mardi Gras Indians, and the jazz funeral. But the area is also denigrated as being a "dangerous and violent" neighborhood and the "same tourist publications and Internet sites that tout the neighborhood warn tourists to avoid certain parts of the area at certain times of the day." According to Crutcher, then, the neighborhood has "several public identities" (Crutcher 2010, 15–18).

David Simon and Eric Overmyer's serial speaks into these divergent opinions of the neighborhood but it also engages with more general issues concerning the American City in the singular. Simon says that "In some ways [*Treme* is] an argument for what the American city and multiculturalism can create. In our minds *The Wire* was never an argument *against* the city, but I know some people took it that way. After working on *The Wire*, we all felt particularly proud to make an argument *for* the city" (Simon in HBO 2017). I have italicized the prepositions to stress Simon's point about how *Treme*, to him, makes another and more positive kind of intervention in public discourses about the city, a point that an early scene in *Treme*'s first episode stresses. New Orleans culture zealot and Tulane University English Professor Creighton Bernette is being interviewed by a British news reporter (Sean Gormley). Creighton objects strongly to the reporter's suggestion that what happened to New Orleans was a natural disaster:

> What hit the Mississippi gulf coast was a natural disaster. The flooding of New Orleans was a man-made catastrophe, a federal fuck up of epic proportions and decades in the making. (*Treme*, S1E1)

Creighton's distinction between "what hit the Mississippi gulf coast" and the "flooding of New Orleans" emphasizes the idea that the post-Katrina state of the city was not a result of natural causes; it was a consequence of past political wrongs. Similar to Spike Lee's documentary miniseries *When the Levees Broke* (2006–2007), *Treme* suggests that to understand Katrina and its aftermath requires looking at societal structures and the governmental agencies that had failed to make adequate precautions for a Hurricane Katrina, which ended up displacing tens of thousands of people, especially African Americans. The serial thus reiterates Simon's interest in emphasizing the systemic nature of societal ills.

Creighton goes on to completely lose his temper, throwing the reporter's microphone into the levee when the reporter suggests that New Orleans culture is not what it once was. Creighton's anger, however, is just as much directed at the federal government for not protecting New Orleans as it is directed against the media that he believes – in this scene obviously justly – is hostile to New Orleans. Indeed, a group of sociologists found that some early news reports about Hurricane Katrina vilified New Orleans residents by propagating "myths of looting and violence." At the same time, several government officials talked about the aftermath of Katrina "as if the United States were facing an armed urban insurgency rather than a catastrophic disaster." Since then, some journalists have acknowledged that they told stories "that were based almost entirely on rumor and hearsay" (Tiernay et al. 2006, 74). Having two functions, this scene thus both introduces Creighton – this is the first time the viewer sees him – and establishes the discussion about the survival of New Orleans and its culture and how they are portrayed in the media. This second function of introducing the issue of the survival of New Orleans and the problematic media representations of the city is worked rather seamlessly into the narrative, owing to the scene's primary expository function of introducing Creighton as a character. What otherwise could well have come across as an example of ham-fisted exposition with a character talking about how this disaster could have been avoided, this scene's emphasis on characterizing Creighton as a passionate and political advocate for New Orleans allows *Treme* to weave this cultural critique into the narrative. Another fifteen minutes into this episode, Creighton is having dinner with his wife Toni (Melissa Leo), a civil rights attorney. Creighton and Toni discuss how his anger affects the advancement of his politics: "Is it gonna do your argument any good, that's what I'm asking? Vinegar, no flies. Honey gets the job done" (*Treme*, S1E1), Toni tells her husband, suggesting that his "vinegar" way of framing his politics does not help his argument. Creighton's heated interview thus becomes a pivotal point for a discussion about the packaging of politics in Simon's oeuvre. Where *The Wire* may have focused on "vinegar," *Treme* foregrounds the "honey" way of advancing an argument about the city. In this way, *Treme* explores other sides of the American city, effectively making Simon's oeuvre as a whole embrace a more multifaceted depiction of American urbanity.

As discussed earlier, *The Wire*'s portrayal of social reproduction is linked to the fact that it takes on the war on drugs as a key theme. Launched by Nixon in the early 1970s (Siff 2018), the war on drugs had caused severe social ramifications for several decades when *The Wire* started airing (Jensen et al. 2004). Had *The Wire* merely suggested that its Major Crimes Unit would potentially be able to 'win' the war on drugs, the serial would belie the social history that it engages with. The fact that many commentators have commented on *The Wire*'s bleakness is a testament to the fact that it stands out in this respect. American television entertainment rarely misses an opportunity to suggest to its viewers that things will get better. Indeed, sociologist Kenneth Dowler argues that media depictions of police work are "often over-dramatized and romanticized" for instance by suggesting that "the majority of crimes are solved and criminal suspects are successfully apprehended" (Dowler 2002, 228). *The Wire* takes the road less traveled in American television in this respect.

The Wire's rejection of that idea is an intertextual rebuttal of a dominant tradition in American television. For that reason, in order to be consistent in its social critique of the war on drugs, it had to be 'pessimistic.' It could not show a single police unit to 'solve' an issue that had existed for decades. This would counter its vision of a society shaped by social reproduction. Yet when *Treme* was to make a case for the survival of New Orleans and its culture, it took a different route – one of intriguing second lines and charismatic everyday people going about their lives. It embraced an outlook that, at least in part, *had to* come across as celebratory. For if *Treme* were to embrace the bleakness of *The Wire*, it would be much harder for it to make a case for the continued value of New Orleans culture and its survival.

Had *Treme* taken the same bleak approach in its urban portrait as *The Wire*, it just might have appeared to be yet another criticism of New Orleans at a point in time where the city surely had plenty of critics. In that case, the serial could have been seen as playing into some critics' and real estate developers' discourse about Katrina being a chance to 'clean up' parts of New Orleans. And that is the exact opposite of *Treme*'s purpose. Simon and Overmyer's serial celebrates the culture of New Orleans. It is a *rebuttal* of those critics who did not see the importance of protecting the city's particular culture.

The serial starts with an intertitle that just reads: "Three Months After" (*Treme*, S1E1). It does not say after what. It does not need to and this wording invites viewers to activate their cultural knowledge about Katrina. By starting *Treme* three months after Katrina, Simon and Overmyer avoid touching on many of the events during the flood. Such a focus could surely have fueled an angry story that could speak directly to events like when police officers stopped people trying to flee the flood from crossing the Crescent City Connection, a bridge that crosses the Mississippi River. On September 3, three days after the start of the flood, police officers fired over the heads of people trying to cross the bridge, and one policeman reportedly told them they were not "going to have another Superdome down here," a reference to the violence and turmoil in the sports arena that became a refuge for many people in the city (Andersen 2018, 7–8). *Treme* does not depict such events and its focus on people overcoming Katrina allows for a more uplifting story of New Orleans, one that does not reiterate the anger, fire, and fury of *The Wire*.

In *Treme*'s first episode Albert Lambreaux (Clarke Peters) and his daughter, Davina (Edwina Findley) do discuss these events on the Crescent City Connection while Davina is driving her father back to New Orleans to resume his life after the flood. Yet only mentioning these controversial events is surely much less likely to induce anger in the viewer than if *Treme* had chosen to dramatize these events. Considering the fact that New Orleans was vilified in the wake of Katrina, *Treme*'s more 'positive' spin on the wake of Katrina implicitly counters this discourse from five years earlier. Media scholar Robin Andersen argues that "By challenging previous narratives and creating new ones at the center of the city's cultural life, as seen through the eyes of its inhabitants ... *Treme* offered a different historical narrative of the storm." To Andersen, this battle over the legacy of Katrina may even have consequences for future responses to other domestic crises (Andersen 2018, xix), and in this sense *Treme*'s intervention in public discourse addresses more general issues than the state and future of New Orleans.

Seen in relation to *The Wire*'s angry societal criticism, both the politics and the mood of *Treme* stand out. Indeed, whereas *The Wire*'s first scene featured the scene of a murder, *Treme* opens with a festive second line parading through the streets of Treme, setting the mood for a different kind of urban portrait than *The Wire*; one that also engages with the complexities of the contemporary city but which does so in a decidedly different manner. *Treme* thus avoids reiterating *The Wire*'s opening scene with Omar Isaiah "Snot Boogie" Betts lying dead in the street alone with no loved ones around him. It instead centers on a community coming together to celebrate its perseverance. The scene thus establishes the theme of coming together in a time of hardship.

However, in order to understand with greater nuance *Treme*'s positive attitude about the city, it is helpful to be more specific about the urban state of affairs that the serial speaks to. When the serial started airing in 2010, New Orleans' white population had rebounded to pre-Katrina levels, but by 2017 the city still had 100,000 fewer African American residents than before Katrina. Moskowitz explains that the "chaos of Katrina provided an opportunity to enact gentrification-friendly politics on a condensed timeline" and "the idea that we'd need to get a majority-black, majority-poor city back to its former self seemed unnecessary, even irresponsible" to some of the people who wished to transform the city into something else; that is, to gentrify New Orleans on a much quicker time scale than is normally possible (Moskowitz 2017, 17, 23, 66). In other words, *Treme* aired at a point in time when the city had faced gentrification processes that could change the cultural specificity of New Orleans, and the celebratory style of Simon and Overmyer's serial should be understood as a rebuttal of those discourses and urban realities.

This rebuttal motivates and informs the many music scenes where the music stays in focus. The music is not turned down to blend into the background in order to allow for, say, a conversation between two characters at a concert venue. The concert scenes invite the viewer to see some of the appealing aspects of New Orleans culture, and by dwelling on these performances and letting the music be music – and not background music or a plot device – *Treme* tries to charm its viewers into seeing the continued relevance and vitality of this culture. This harks back to Creighton Bernette's angry manifesto at the start of *Treme*, but this is persuasion through honey. Not vinegar.

However, while Simon and Overmyer made a celebration of New Orleans culture, the serial would continue to also criticize political and cultural issues. In particular, Toni Bernette's storylines about defending her clients, such as LaDonna Batiste-Williams's (Khandi Alexander) attempts at finding her brother, Daymo (Daryl Williams), after Katrina, are important to *Treme*'s political ambitions. Though Toni is shunned by many NOPD police officers due to her work as a civil rights attorney, she has a rapport with Lieutenant Terry Colson (David Morse) with whom she discusses the prospects of bringing about positive change in their community. Terry is more pessimistic than Toni about the prospects of changing things for the better. Indeed, one of his lines in the conservation quoted below echoes *The Wire*'s portrayal of social reproduction:

TERRY: When the rest of the world doesn't really give a fuck, what is it that actually helps?
TONI: Lasting. You gotta outlast the bastards.
TERRY: You can't outlast them. The game is rigged.
TONI: No, Terry. There are rules.
[...]
TONI: A young man comes to town, gets hold of some public records, talks to people, makes some calls, and now look. They're gonna have to deal with it. Now it's a case. [...] NOPD is gonna have to investigate.

TERRY: NOPD? [...] I don't know how you've been doing what you've been doing for so long and you are still so naive. (*Treme*, S3E10)

Some viewers will probably recognize Terry's remark that "the game is rigged" as an echo of the scene in *The Wire* where Bodie tells McNulty that "this game is rigged, man," which reflects how, after four seasons he realizes that he will not be able to advance in the drug game on his own accord (*TW*, S4E13). The idea of upward social mobility does not apply to his situation. He is gridlocked in *The Wire*'s systemic reality where things do not change. By making Terry's line allude to Bodie's remark, *Treme* invokes the notion that societal ills are systemic ones, a consistent theme in Simon's career. But it is important that Toni here counters Terry's comment – and thus *The Wire* – by emphasizing that "there are rules." The issue at stake here, however, is whether *Treme* sides with Terry or Toni.

When a judge (Tim Reid) earlier in the serial ruled in Toni's favor in her attempt to find out where the police might be holding LaDonna's lost brother, Daymo, *Treme* sides with Toni's optimist outlook. The judge says that:

> In my 22 years as a judge I have often felt obligated out of love and loyalty to New Orleans to defend my city from those outsiders who like to speak ill about it. Too many are quick to describe this city as a bastion of corruption, of bureaucratic incompetence, of southern laziness, of ineffectual policing and systemic dysfunction within our legal system. "No," I try to argue, "the city is not that bad. Our reputation is grossly overblown." (*Treme*, S1E7)

The judge emphasizes his loyalty to New Orleans while at the same time acknowledging the gross injustice that LaDonna's family experiences. Given how the judge apologizes to Daymo's mother on behalf of Orleans Parish and orders the state to find him within 72 hours, *Treme* makes Toni's assertion that "there are rules" the position of the entire serial. The system works in this isolated case. In *The Wire*, the police do manage to get Wee-Bey (Hassan Johnson) and Avon Barksdale convicted (*TW*, S1E13), but the serial nonetheless emphasizes – especially through its montage sequences at the ends of its seasons – that police work alone cannot bring about positive social change. Toni's belief in the usefulness of "outlasting the bastards" runs counter to *The Wire*, which suggested that on a long enough timeline the system will reproduce its own malfunctions. Seeing that the judge rules in Toni's favor shows that her strategy of playing the long game is a viable option in *Treme*'s New Orleans. His ruling represents one of the ways that *Treme* is a more positive urban portrait than *The Wire*.

The Wire and *Treme* each have their distinct take on the American city. That does not mean that *The Wire* and *Treme* are so different that one could argue that Simon contradicts himself in how he portrays the American city. Their different depictions of urbanity come from the different 'argumentative purposes' each serial has. These serials take different social realities as their starting points. *The Wire*'s focus on the war on drugs and deindustrialization and *Treme*'s focus on the rebuilding of New Orleans after Katrina simply call for different depictions of the city.

However, though *Treme* sides with Toni in the discussion she has with Terry, we need to remember that that is a court case and Toni and Terry's discussion focuses on how journalism can force legal and political systems to act on social problems. Terry points out how few people read the journalistic exposés on the injustices carried out in the wake of Katrina, effectively asking what kind of work can effect change in a city like New Orleans: police work, legal cases, journalism, or something else. Terry's comment about how Toni's extended experience with working civil rights cases in New Orleans should have changed her outlook reflects a jadedness on his part, but Toni does not even take offense by his accusation of her being naive. Her belief that the accumulated weight of legal and journalistic work will force the system to right its wrongs reflects a much more optimistic view on how the city works. In the shape of *The Corner*'s Miss Ella and *The Wire*'s Walon who helps Bubbles get clean and stay clean, Simon's first two series did feature minor characters who represented forces for positive change in Western Baltimore. With Toni being a much more prominent character, *Treme* is able to embrace a more positive outlook by showing how she is actually able to effect change in her community. This is an important contrast to *The Wire* and thus contributes to *Treme*'s more positive and hopeful portrayal of the American city.

"No Closure in Real Life"

In Spike Jonze and Charlie Kaufman's 2002 metafilm *Adaptation*, the struggling screenwriter Charlie Kaufman (Nicolas Cage) is at a loss about how to adapt a screenplay from journalist Susan Orlean's book *The Orchid Thief* (1998). At the end of his creative ropes, the film's protagonist goes to a screenwriting seminar held by Robert McKee (Brian Cox) and asks the screenwriting guru, "What if a writer is attempting to create a story where nothing much happens, where people don't change, they don't have any epiphanies. They struggle and are frustrated and nothing is resolved. More a reflection of the real world." McKee rejects Kaufman's notion of life "where nothing much happens" as being suitable for filmmaking, yet *Treme* is maybe best understood as that sort of 'plot-deficient' look into a New Orleans populated by 'ordinary people' without life-changing epiphanies.

Like *The Corner*'s self-reflexive discussion of its 'melodramatic' elements, so too does *Treme* occasionally take a break from its fundamentally realist impulse to point out its storytelling choices. In *Treme*'s ninth episode, Creighton Bernette is discussing with his freshman literature class Kate Chopin's 1899 novel *The Awakening*. He tells his students to:

> Pay attention to the language itself, the ideas. Don't think in terms of a beginning and an end, because unlike some plot-driven entertainments, there is no closure in real life. Not really. (*Treme*, S1E9)

Though Creighton is discussing a nineteenth-century novel, it is hard not to draw a comparison to *Treme*, which also cannot be said to be very plot-driven. *Treme* eschews the teleology of the crime show elements that always shaped *The Wire*'s narrative structure and Creighton's words to his students represent *Treme*'s self-reflexive manifesto. This scene signals for viewers to understand how the serial's sprawling storylines are not aimed at an end goal. Toni Bernette does fight to serve the needs of her clients, chef Janette Desautel (Kim Dickens) tries to make a living in different ways, and the violinist Annie (Lucia Micarelli) eventually tries to make a career for herself after been discovered by an agent. But these narrative lines are not teleological in the sense that they aim at a specific end goal in the way that, for instance, season one of *The Wire* aimed at seeing through how the Major Crimes Unit built a case against the Barksdale organization and brought Avon to court.

Though *The Wire* tried to show the socially networked reality of the contemporary city – and thus set itself apart from other police procedurals – it did so through a format that always had a narrative drive to set up a wire and use that wiretap in an investigation to build a case against, say, Stringer Bell. However, in season three of *The Wire*, the Major Crimes Unit does not set up a wiretap on Bell until the tenth episode of that season (TW, S3E10), suggesting how much the serial tried to downplay the role of the police investigation as the guiding narrative principle of the serial as it moved into its later seasons. It tried to move away from the narrative tropes of the police procedural.

Treme represents a different kind of urban portrait. Lavik aphoristically argues that while feature films center their attention on establishing a *narrative drive* accompanied by interspersed elements of characterization and setting, contemporary serials focus on exploring setting and characters and deemphasize narrative drive (Lavik 2014, 201). *Treme* takes this key feature of contemporary television serials to new heights. Davis McAlary (Steve Zahn) aspires to throw parties and make records, but not in a way that can be characterized as a career that makes his character arc seem overly plotted. He is, however, an ardent fan of New Orleans music and culture and through him we see a strong advocate for New Orleans culture. In a similar vein, Albert Lambreaux's efforts at rebuilding his life and sewing his Big Chief Mardi Gras Indian suits are not fleshed out in any overtly plot-driven manner.

Film scholar María del Mar Azcona argues that the multi-protagonist film emphasizes parallelism over causality and narrative drive. This type of films centers on the presence of different types of people, views of life, and social and cultural backgrounds (Azcona 2010, 37–38). Early examples of this genre include Edmund Goulding's *Grand Hotel* (1932), John Ford's *Stagecoach* (1939), and John Guillermin's *The Towering Inferno* (1974). The 1990s, however, saw a proliferation of the genre with Robert Altman's *Short Cuts* (1993), Quentin Tarantino's *Pulp Fiction* (1994), and Paul Thomas Anderson's *Magnolia* (1999). Azcona's argument about how multi-protagonist films emphasize parallelism over causality and narrative drive is arguably equally true – if not more so – with regards to multi-protagonist television serials. In Simon's oeuvre, this textual feature is intricately linked to his urban agenda; the parallel storylines let him show how interconnected the lives of urbanites are.

This overarching focus on painting an urban portrait of New Orleans is reflected in the lack of narrative arcs that tie all of the characters' storylines together. In the first season, civil rights lawyer Toni Bernette tries to find out what happened to LaDonna's brother, Daymo, whom nobody has heard from since Katrina. Janette is forced to close down her restaurant, while Delmond Lambreaux (Rob Brown) comes back to New Orleans to help his father, Albert, rebuild his life. Yet apart from the fact that all of these characters are trying to rebuild their lives in the aftermath of the storm, their stories are not tied together in the same way as was the case on *The Wire*.

As mentioned, the serial's opening scenes center on a second line. It then cuts to the main titles after which a scene introduces Davis McAlary and Janette. After that Davis joins the second line. Two subsequent scenes introduce Janette's troubles with her restaurant and show Albert returning to New Orleans, respectively. After that Antoine Batiste's (Wendell Pierce) parade passes by LaDonna's restaurant where it is clear that she clearly knows Antoine – only later do we learn that they used to be married. This way of introducing several characters through a second line without showing them directly interacting is *Treme*'s way of stressing how its multi-protagonist narrative is supposed to portray an interlinked and spatially confined community where people live parallel lives. *Treme* subtlety establishes how these characters live together in the same part of the city, but its multi-protagonist structure only occasionally knits their storylines together more closely. At one point, Davis is hired to teach Creighton and Toni Bernette's daughter, Sofia Bernette (India Ennenga), the piano (*Treme*, S1E3). This plot point ties together their storylines, but *Treme* does not expand this connection any further. By linking these storylines, *Treme* demonstrates its main interest in portraying a city where people lead parallel lives. It was not until *Show Me a Hero* that the issue of residential segregation would really take center stage in Simon's oeuvre, but *Treme* uses its parallel storylines to portray an interlinked city, showing how different social spaces perceive an issue like housing.

The City and Housing

Barring *Generation Kill* and *The Plot Against America*, Simon's productions all take a strong interest in the state and future of the American city. Sometimes the city is front and center and sometimes it takes a backseat to other focal points. Halfway through season two Davis is promoting the upcoming rapper Lil Calliope (Altonio Jackson), and Davis tries to make the rapper embrace a more political outlook than he otherwise seems interested in. Calliope is confounded by Davis's suggestion:

> LIL CALLIOPE: What you mean, politics?
> DAVIS: I mean, we write the world we know. We get out there in the middle of the argument.
> LIL CALLIOPE: Which argument now?
> DAVIS: The one about the city! Where we've been. Where we are now. Where we're going if we don't stop and think. (*Treme*, S2E6)

Though Davis is often portrayed as a rather comic figure, *Treme* here uses him as a mouthpiece in articulating the series' own ambitions to make an elaborate argument about the state of the city. Calliope never really embraces Davis's ideas about discussing the city in his rap songs, but Davis does not abandon the subject. At a much later point in the serial, Delmond and Albert are part of a group protesting outside a city council meeting that is voting on whether or not to demolish some housing units that were not damaged by the flooding during Katrina. These units would be able to house residents wanting to return to New Orleans. The police, however, mace and taser the protestors (*Treme*, S3E5).

A scene later in the same episode shows Davis and Annie – who are a couple at this point in the series – dining with members of both of their families. Davis's mother, Ramona McAlary (Ann McKenzie), says that a reason for optimism about crime in New Orleans comes from the fact that "the city council just voted to tear down the public housing projects," which the viewer saw Albert and Delmond protesting. Davis replies by saying that that decision is "another great example of this city at war with its cultural essence." Ramona replies: "Oh, Davis, I would hardly call the demolition of the projects a war on our cultural essence." Davis rebuts her argument by listing a parade of musicians – Germaine Bazzle, Willie Tee, Earl Turbinton, and the Neville brothers – who are from the housing projects and who have helped shaped New Orleans culture (*Treme*, S3E5).

By juxtaposing the scene where Albert is protesting the housing issue with the upper-class dinner party at the house belonging to Davis's parents', the McAlarys, *Treme* invokes class disparities in New Orleans. *Treme* furthers this contrast when the scene at the McAlarys' place ends to make way for a scene where Albert is enjoying a Christmas dinner with his family. The *mise en scène* of the rich home is a striking contrast to Albert's home where the drywall shows how their gathering is framed by Katrina in a way that is literally impossible to see in the other scene.

The *mise en scène* alludes to the class conflict at play in post-Katrina New Orleans where poor people's homes (e.g. public housing) were in danger of being torn down to make way for a sped-up process of gentrification. Moskowitz explains that plans "to demolish several New Orleans housing projects [...] were under way years before Katrina, but with tens of thousands still evacuated from the city, and the city's politics shaken up by the storm, the demolitions were able to proceed at a much faster pace. The rhetorical attacks on public housing began just days after the storm" (Moskowitz 2017, 52). On a surface level, Davis and Ramona's discussion is about how she focuses on crime and how Davis, true to form, focuses

Figure 7 Dinner at the McAlary home.

Figure 8 The Lambreaux family celebrating Christmas.

on the city's music heritage. The financial realities of this issue, however, are portrayed by the contrast in art direction between the scene in the McAlarys' dining room and the subsequent scene with Albert and his family. Davis disagrees with his mother, but the conflicting interests in New Orleans become only more pronounced in the juxtaposition of how one home is unscathed by the flood and another is in the process of being rebuilt after it.

Though *Show Me a Hero* really zooms in on the issue of housing, Simon's serials have often had that subject looming in the background. In *The Corner*, the flashbacks to Gary McCullough's suburban home before he became addicted to drugs serve as a strong counterpoint to where he ended up. This urban-suburban dichotomy hints at the structural circumstances that affect the people living in West Baltimore as portrayed in this miniseries. Another example is *The Wire*'s season four police investigation where the Major Crimes Unit cannot figure out how Marlo Stanfield has ascended to the top rung of the drug game without dead bodies showing up in Western Baltimore. Marlo's enforcers, Chris Partlow (Gbenga Akinnagbe) and Snoop (Felicia Pearson), have been killing people in vacant houses and leaving them there so as not to alert the police. Vacant homes serving as tombs is an eerie notion, but these vacants subtly allude to the depopulation that many cities in America have experienced since the 1960s (Teaford 2006, 126–127).

The Case for the City: Treme

Though housing never really takes center stage in *Treme* as it would in *Show Me a Hero*, its first season nevertheless devotes much of Albert Lambreaux's storyline to his activist efforts in trying to open up some blocks of public housing that the city government has sealed off, even though they were not flooded and could house several residents who had left New Orleans when the city was evacuated. In the second episode of the serial, Albert goes out to check on the Calliope housing projects, saying that it "Makes no sense" that the city government will not let people move back into these apartments. This storyline does not explicitly speak to racial issues but public housing in America disproportionately houses large groups of African Americans. In the 1940s and 1950s, public housing was home to both poor white and Black families, but this situation changed during the 1960s to the point that by the early 1970s 70 percent of all households in public housing in America were nonwhite. In the course of the 1960s and 1970s, many whites came to associate public housing "with a culture of poverty that was peculiarly African American" and since the 1970s, public housing has continued to house more people of color than whites (Teaford 2006, 140). Albert's struggle to open the units of public housing thus engages with the racial dynamics of post-Katrina politics.

Later on, a public official stops by the bar where Albert spends much of his time and tells Albert that he can get him a FEMA trailer. Albert does not want to hear of it, declaring: "I believe I asked your boss about housing projects" (*Treme*, S1E6). The scene shows Albert to be a man of principle, and the subtext reads that Albert is not only making a protest about public housing for his own personal benefit but also for other people in his community who want to return to New Orleans. He takes offense when the city offers to give him a FEMA trailer to make him quieten down. Their solution would only help Albert and that individualistic focus completely collides with the more collectivist sentiment that Albert embodies. His activism is rooted in his concern for his community.

Consequently, Albert squats in an apartment in the Calliope housing project. His protest is able to attract some media attention before the police violently arrest him (*Treme*, S1E7), and Albert's storyline represents a New Orleans local's struggle for cultural survival, which is a contrast to other characters who have conflicting agendas.

Season two introduces the character Nelson Hidalgo (Jon Seda), a Texan who comes to New Orleans to make money in the wake of Katrina. Such ambitions surely invite viewers to be skeptical about him and his intentions, but I nonetheless believe that writer Rolf Potts overstates this point when he argues that "Seda's winking, swaggering portrayal of [Nelson Hidalgo] pretty much telegraphs what a douchebag might look like if Naomi Klein were playing charades" (Potts 2013). I believe that *Treme* makes a point of *not* making him an overt, clear-cut villain set on exploiting the city's citizens at a critical juncture. Bent on turning a profit in the wake of Katrina one might expect this character to be portrayed as morally irredeemable, yet – true to Simon's form – he is more nuanced than that, much like Bill Rawls in *The Wire*.

Hidalgo meets with bankers and tries to get government contracts for demolishing buildings, but he also takes an honest interest in New Orleans culture. Linda Williams argues that the most clichéd aspects of melodrama are "victims tied to railroad tracks, villains twirling mustaches, rescues that happen too late or in the nick of time" (Williams 2014, 114). Hidalgo does not twirl any metaphorical mustache and he is often painted as a sympathetic character though he is complicit in doing things that may well be detrimental to the parts of New Orleans that *Treme* roots for. He takes a sincere interest in the city while he engages in projects that can exclude some of the city's exiled residents from returning to their homes and their city. *Treme* devotes adequate screen time to Hidalgo for us to get to see that side of him.

The characterological vocabulary of *alignment* achieved through *attachment* and *access* can explain why some viewers may not see Hidalgo as Naomi Klein's version of a "douchebag" in Rolf Potts's words. As mentioned earlier, Murray Smith explains that spatio-temporal *attachment* occurs when viewers get to follow the experiences of a specific character and *subjective access* comes in instances when we learn of a character's emotions, thoughts, and moral code (Smith 1995, 142). Together, these two features can align viewers with a character as is the case of Nelson Hidalgo where there is no apparent reason that we should dismiss him as a mustachioed villain or Kleinian douchebag. Though viewers may be critical of Hidalgo and his intentions, *Treme* makes a point of allowing him to be a rather round character – and not a mere one-sided villain.

This is why I believe that American Studies scholar Anna Hartnell is too dismissive of how *Treme* presents its political critique. Hartnell writes that "Nelson Hidalgo is the principal representative of disaster capitalism in *Treme*, but his characterization veers increasingly toward the lovable rogue as the series progresses, suggesting just how weak *Treme*'s political critique is" (Hartnell 2017, 211). To Hartnell, the mere fact that there are more flattering aspects to Hidalgo's personality shows how 'weak' *Treme*'s politics are. The idea that likeable characters necessarily embody attitudes that the text presents as an agreeable ideological position is an unfortunate way of assessing a serial's politics. Characters representing what Hartnell – and presumably also Simon and Overmyer – find to be an unsympathetic political position apparently need to be unsympathetic and morally repugnant. This idea, however, runs counter to how Simon's serials portray characters in general.

The first episode of *Treme*'s second season introduces Hidalgo. Hidalgo takes his cousin Arnie (Jeffrey Carisalez) out to lunch at a place he has been recommended. After having a local specialty – a Frenchaletta – Hidalgo proclaims his love for New Orleans:

HIDALGO: I love this town. Why didn't anybody tell me about it before?
ARNIE: I've been calling you for the last six months trying to get you down here.
HIDALGO: Yeah, but you never said how great it was. You just said there was dinero lying in the streets. (*Treme*, S2E1)

Hidalgo's reply to his cousin drives home the fact that his interest in New Orleans goes beyond the money he can earn there. He becomes infatuated with the city. Viewers can find Hidalgo's ambitions about making money in the wake of Katrina and saying things like "Never let a disaster go to waste" to his business partner C.J. Liguori (Dan Ziskie) highly unsympathetic (*Treme*, S2E1). But, as mentioned, that does not change the fact that *Treme* devotes adequate screen time to Hidalgo to make him more than a melodramatic caricature of an exploitative entrepreneur. Rolf Potts's critique of how *Treme* depicts Hidalgo does not hold up; Hidalgo is not villainized.

The fact that Katrina was used to speed up gentrification processes in New Orleans is the relevant background for seeing how Hidalgo's actions could be detrimental to New Orleans's poor and marginalized citizens. Hidalgo comes to New Orleans just as the city is facing the prospect of going through huge changes. But he is no mustache-twirling villain and *Treme* thus reiterates *The Wire*'s trend of portraying almost no characters as fully villainous, except for maybe Police Commissioner Stan Valchek and Marlo Stanfield.

In September 2005, a New Orleans real estate broker said that Katrina "destroyed a great deal ... and there's plenty of space to build houses and sell them for a lot of money." "Most importantly," he continued, "the hurricane drove poor people and criminals out of the city ... and we hope they don't come back. ... The party's finally over for these people ... and now they're going to have to find someplace else to live in the U.S." (Shellnut in Gebauer 2005). Law professor Bill Quigley argued that such discourse represented a more general tendency in Katrina's aftermath. He wrote in 2006 that "No sign outside of New Orleans says, 'If you are poor, sick, elderly, disabled, a child or African-American, you cannot return.' But there might as well be" (Quigley 2006, 158). Quigley's point is that it was not just Katrina that caused problems for under-privileged New Orleanians. Their big problems also came from groups of people who did not want them to return to their homes. The real estate developer's overtly classist statement seems to represent an outlier in the post-Katrina discussions about the rebuilding of New Orleans, but he represents a part of the discourse that *Treme* engages with.

This is quite the contrast to Hidalgo's clearly passionate engagement with New Orleans culture. He may be seen as just as economically exploitative as the real estate broker quoted here, but he does not represent that dismissive attitude towards New Orleans culture. At one point, he and C.J. Liguori are trying to persuade Albert Lambreaux to support the construction of a museum that will, among other things, portray the culture of the Mardi Gras Indians and feature some of Albert's costumes. Albert is skeptical of their entire project and dismisses their ideas, talking about how they do not know or appreciate New Orleans culture and mentions LaDonna's bar, Gigi's, which, the viewer knows, Hidalgo has visited several times. When Hidalgo then drops LaDonna's name in that conversation Albert looks completely dumbfounded but nevertheless ends up giving the project his blessings (*Treme*, S3E9).

This scene invokes what Mittell calls *operational aesthetics* (Mittell 2015, 41–54). It invites viewers to marvel at the *Treme*'s intricately intersecting storylines. Viewers are invited to smile at Albert's reaction because we already know that Nelson knows LaDonna and her bar. Simon and Overmyer use the fact the viewer has been aligned with both Albert and Hidalgo to create a moment of dramatic irony in the sense that the viewer knows something Albert does not. The scene illustrates how sympathetic Hidalgo actually is to New Orleans culture though he may not realize – or admit to himself – the fact that for all of the money he makes in New Orleans, he does not contribute anything to the city itself. In another episode Nelson expresses how he as an outsider is slowly coming to understand how New Orleans works as a city:

> I think I'm starting to figure this place out. It's a village. A village on an island. Everyone's connected. They may love each other. They may hate each other. But they're all related. This week I bought an empty building for a million-one and laid out a couple grand in a little bitty bar at the back of town. Both of them on a handshake and 'cause somebody told me to. It's all connected somehow. And I'm this close to seeing how it all hooks up. (*Treme*, S2E6)

Hidalgo's realization that "everyone's connected" spells out a core point of the intersecting storylines that at this point have been going for 16 episodes. His words, however, also reflect Hidalgo's status as an outsider in New Orleans who only bit by bit is able to decipher how this "village" works. Hidalgo's storyline also speaks to a corrupt system at work in the aftermath of Katrina, that, among other things, led to the fall and conviction of Mayor Ray Nagin. Hidalgo is an outsider opportunist trying to profit from a bad situation, but his position does not call back to *The Wire*'s deromantization of the outsider rogue cop. *Treme*'s discussion of outsiderhood has more to do with cultural belonging and New Orleans' relationship to the outside world. The city relies on the outside world, but this world also represents a challenge for New Orleans.

The Tourist Gaze

Early in the first season, Albert and his friends are eulogizing their deceased friend "Wild Man" Jesse whose body Albert found in the ruins of Jesse's home. Jesse had also been a part of the Mardi Gras

Indian culture so Albert and Jesse's other loved ones pay their respects in accordance with that tradition, singing the songs "Tu es pocky way" and "Indian Red." While this heartfelt goodbye is underway, however, a bus full of tourists stops by, and the driver rolls down his window to ask what Albert and his friends are doing, justifying their stopping by saying that "People wanna see what happened." Being aligned with Albert, viewers immediately recognize how problematic it is for the bus to stop by and stare at this private and emotional event. The group, however, soon convinces the driver that he and the tourists are in the wrong and the bus drives away: "I'm sorry. You're right. I'm sorry," the driver says. Judging from the expression on the driver's face, he is being sincere about his apologies. The last shot of that episode shows Albert and his friends walking out into the street and looking at the bus as it drives off towards the horizon. The last shot of the episode is of the group filmed from behind watching the bus drive away (*Treme*, S1E3).

There is no apparent intentional malice on the part of these 'disaster tourists' who are interested in seeing the destruction of New Orleans with their own eyes. Yet the fact that the viewer is aligned with Albert and that this bus stops by at the exact time when they are saying goodbye to a friend and family member makes it easy for the viewer to see that the tourists' behavior is problematic.

Figure 9 Albert and friends are seeing off a tourist bus.

Albert and the others are not putting on a show for these outsiders but are in the midst of mourning and saying goodbye. That situation is gazed upon and the fact that the scene ends with Albert and the others looking at the bus as it drives away is a reversal of this dynamic. From being looked upon they know who are the ones looking, and the serial thus sides with these New Orleanians' point of view. *Treme*'s viewers are invited to be dumbfounded by the insensitivity that lies in looking at a communal display of mourning as if it were a show for them. Creighton's rants on how America should remain committed to rebuilding New Orleans is surely premised on the importance of the nation taking an interest in New Orleans and its culture. But in this scene with the disaster tourists gazing at Jesse's mourners, *Treme* shows that the shape that this interest takes makes all the difference.

The outsider's interest in New Orleans culture, however, is much more elaborately explored through the character Sonny (Michiel Huisman), a Dutch musician deeply infatuated with New Orleans and its music. Sonny seems to have arrived only quite shortly before Katrina but he is nevertheless very scornful when talking to outsiders coming to New Orleans in the wake of Katrina. Potts argues that Sonny embodies what literary historian Paul Fussell calls the "anti-tourist." Sonny seeks a romanticized authenticity in the things that feel "unique and different about a place" and thus "positions himself in solidarity with locals through the studied mimicry of local patterns and prejudices" (Potts 2013). Sonny is insecure with regard to his own status in New Orleans culture and, in an attempt to safeguard his position there, he rejects the interest that other people from outside take in New Orleans. Sonny seeks authentic New Orleans culture but replies with scornful sarcasm when a few tourists ask Sonny and his girlfriend Annie to play "something authentic" (*Treme*, S1E2). By scorning these outsiders, Sonny tries to assert his own claim to insider status. He's not an interloper, they are.

Writer Dan Kois points out that this scene exposes Sonny as a paradoxically exclusionist cultural consumer rather than as an example of *Treme* bemoaning outsiders' interest in New Orleans (Kois 2010). Yet seen in relation to the scene with the bus tourists gazing at Albert and his friends' ritual, *Treme*'s stance on the issue of tourism takes on greater nuance. In the case of the bus, the viewer is invited to side with the New Orleans residents' scorn of the tourist gaze. But when Sonny is abrasive to the tourists from Wisconsin we are invited to be critical of *his* style of rejecting tourism or outsiders taking an interest in New Orleans more generally. Sonny, however, is not alone in being an aspiring musician seeking authentic music culture. That description also applies to the local Davis McAlary. Film scholar Courtney George argues that:

> Davis romanticizes the jazz community, naively considering himself a cultural insider just because he knows and appreciates the music. Davis buys into the transcendent melting-pot narrative that he feels allows him entrance into the jazz community. (George 2012, 230)

George clearly dismisses the notion that Davis can be seen as an insider in the jazz community merely by virtue of knowing about, participating in, and clearly loving the music and the scene. At one point, however, Davis is conducting a walking tour of key sites in New Orleans where he stops by a house and sees that Delmond Lambreaux, by chance, is there on a visit. When Davis tells Delmond that the group is going to stop by Sidney Bechet's house Delmond is eager to go (*Treme*, S3E5). George would surely consider Delmond, an accomplished jazz trumpet player, to be a "cultural insider" but here Davis seems to be on par with Delmond in terms of knowing about different aspects of New Orleans cultural history. In George's analysis, Davis is not really part of the jazz community even though we see that almost everything he does and cares about has something to do with jazz music culture. George does not see Davis's all-consuming behavior and participation as enough for him to be considered an insider.

George is right, however, in noting how Davis's enthusiasm about New Orleans music leads him to overstep standard racial etiquette. In a much earlier scene set in a bar, Davis uses the N-word and gets punched in the face for it (*Treme*, S1E5). Trying to avoid a fight, Davis says to the man in the bar that "It's OK man. I live in this neighborhood," suggesting that standard norms regarding the use of that racial epithet do not apply to white residents of Treme. Davis crosses a line but is none the wiser for it. Indeed, nine episodes later Davis's friend, Henry (Henry Griffin), says to Davis: "Davis, we're white guys. Deal with it," to which Davis comically replies, "Dude, work in progress" as if racial identity were fully up for negotiation (*Treme*, S2E4).

The Case for the City: Treme 109

The discussion about outsiders and their perceptions of New Orleans is nuanced even more in the second season when Janette Desautel is furious about how New York food critic Alan Richman bashes New Orleans cooking in his reviews. In the first season Janette was forced to close down her restaurant (*Treme*, S1E6) and when she learns of Richman's criticism she stresses how the New Orleans economy depends on out-of-city dollars being spent in the city. Janette says: "Fine, fine, he doesn't like the food … For fuck's sake, it's a service economy! They're fucking hurting. He's gotta write this now? Tell people to stay away from New Orleans, don't come down, don't spend your money in restaurants" (*Treme*, S2E2). The real-life food critic Alan Richman actually did write such a critique in *GQ* in 2006 (Richman 2006), and media scholar Robin Andersen argues that Janette's critique of the prominent food critic has to do with both ethics and timing: "The message is, Richman should have held his criticism until a later date. … The prose not read on screen," Andersen adds, "went far beyond food, or timing, and in fact harkened back to the early press coverage that blamed the victims of the storm for their pain" (Andersen 2018, 106). Janette's opposition to Richman is thus a defense of New Orleans in a broader sense.

Treme thus explores the different ways that the outside world takes an interest in New Orleans. In the funeral scene, the tourists are exposed as insensitive, but *Treme* is also critical of Sonny's knee-jerk way of dismissing outsiders. In the case of Janette's critique of Richman, however, *Treme* stresses the city's economic dependence on tourists and through these different examples, the serial shows the multifaceted nature of tourism that plays a part in this service economy.

Media scholar Joy Fuqua argues that the season one episode "Shame, Shame, Shame" further explores this dynamic. In this episode, an ardent Japanese jazz fan, Koichi Toyama (Tatsuo Ichikawa), visits New Orleans and buys Antoine a new trombone after the recent loss of his instrument as the result of a drunken run-in with two police officers (*Treme*, S1E5). In the same episode, Janette is visited by a group of New York chefs interested in having a taste of the local cuisine. Fuqua argues that "these two encounters require the musician and chef to perform their authenticity" to the point of "being placed in the position of the beholden" (Fuqua 2012,

240) in the sense that these outsiders' expectations of Janette and Antoine almost pigeonhole them in their identities as authentic and expert New Orleanians. To these outsiders, they are not just Antoine and Janette. No, they are expected to embody New Orleans culture. These outsiders' view of Antoine and Janette skews their perception of them as people. There is no intentional malice in this gaze, but *Treme* nevertheless shows how this perspective can potentially hinder the encounter between outsider and insider.

This exploration of the dynamics of outsiders taking an interest in a specific city qualifies Simon's interest in discussing the state of the American city more generally. *The Corner* and *The Wire* were about his adopted hometown of Baltimore – he grew up in Silver Spring, Maryland and did not move to Baltimore until the early 1980s (Simon in Dreifus 2018) – and his experiences in that city made him an insider. When he switched setting for New Orleans, however, his exploration of the American city was challenged by the fact that he could not speak with the same insiderhood about New Orleans. Co-creator Eric Overmyer, however, had lived in New Orleans part-time for many years (Mason 2010). Albert, Janette, and Sonny's storylines portray some of the dynamics about city identity, but Simon and Overmyer's portrayal of New Orleans is just as much about American urbanity in general as it is about that specific city. Their serial ultimately addresses the status of the discourses around the American city. In their view, the discourse on the city's challenges must regain some of its former centrality.

Can a City Work?

David Simon and Eric Overmyer first worked together on *Homicide* in the second half of the 1990s, which was when they first started talking about how they might be able to tell a story centered on New Orleans culture. But ideas for how to how to tell the story of what they saw as a highly charismatic city did not make themselves readily apparent (Mason 2010). With this long background in mind, it may seem a bit off to say that *Treme* is the belated positive spin on "The City" after *The Wire*'s more 'pessimistic' view on urbanity. But it is difficult not to think along those lines when you see them in relation to each other. Indeed, Simon himself has asked "'What does the American city promise? What has it given us?' The multiculturalism by which New Orleans has given us our greatest gifts seemed a particularly apt response to what was clearly missing in 'The Wire,' which was the argument for the city" (Simon in Saraiya 2015). I quoted Simon for saying something very similar at the start of this chapter, suggesting that this comparison seems to have been a veritable talking point for him when discussing *Treme*.

So the idea of *Treme* being the positive spin on the American city is indeed a part of Simon's motivations – or, at least, belated reflections – for making the serial. Yet *Treme*'s positive spin on American urbanity perhaps becomes more interesting when situating it not just within Simon's oeuvre, but in the longer sweep of American thought on the city. According to Conn, there is a prevalent anti-urban sentiment in American culture. One part of this tradition is an "unwillingness to acknowledge the urban – and metropolitan – nature of American society, and a refusal to embrace the essentially collective, rather than individual nature of urban life" (Conn 2014, 7). Treme is presented as a location for strong and positive traditions and of a productive and vibrant life. While *Treme* does not gloss over social problems in the Treme neighborhood like when Harley Wyatt (Steve Earle) is killed in a heinous act of random violence (*Treme*, S2E9) or when LaDonna is raped (*Treme*, S2E3), it does present the community as a positive place in general.

It is crucial to *Treme*'s depiction of New Orleans that the biggest threats to the city's survival and culture all come from outside the local communities. Albert Lambreaux's fight for the Calliope housing projects is a testament to that. Davis McAlary's music heritage tour in season three's opening episode offers some comic relief on a sad background. His walking tour of key sites in New Orleans music history stops by a building that once was a recording studio that was important in developing early rock and roll, a park that has been closed off for two years since Katrina, and he talks about how Louis Armstrong's childhood home was demolished in the 1960s (*Treme*, S3E1). None of these places is memorialized today. *Treme* laments this lack of respect for the New Orleans music history and questions the power dynamics that go into such priorities.

While the serial engages directly with the trials faced by New Orleans in the wake of Katrina, it also rebuts an American tradition of anti-urbanism. Its emphasis on urbanity is a defense of the collectivist sentiment, which serves to counter the individualistic tendency that Conn points out. The city has been a subject for leading American intellectuals since the early years of the republic. Thomas Jefferson's agrarian beliefs are especially famous. In a 1787 letter to James Madison, he forwarded the virtues of rural life. To him, America's "governments will remain virtuous … as long as they are chiefly agricultural; and this will be as long as there shall be vacant lands in any part of America." Jefferson believed that urbanity signaled corruption and argued that when people "get piled upon one another in large cities, as in Europe, they will become corrupt as in Europe" (Jefferson 1787). Urbanity was simply the other side of the coin of corruption to Jefferson and this anti-urban sentiment continues to make its mark on twenty-first-century American culture (Conn 2014, 5–10). Simon himself situates his depictions and discussions of urbanity in the tradition going back to Jefferson's skepticism. As he told journalist Sonia Saraiya in 2015:

> Hamilton and Jefferson had that argument [about the city], and guess what? Jefferson lost. We're not going back to some agrarian ideal. Our future is in the city. We need to figure out how to prevail with this increasingly compacted multicultural beast, or we fail as a society (Simon in Saraiya 2015).

Near the end of *Treme*, Albert Lambreaux tells his daughter Davina about his childhood memories of how racial dynamics worked in the Seventh Ward – a neighborhood just north of Treme. "Before things blew up and got pretty ugly in the '60s," he says. Albert reminisces about riding the bus with his father. One day a white friend of theirs came back to sit with them, and this resulted in the bus driver throwing all three of them off the bus. "It was a white man that did us wrong," Albert tells Davina, "and it was a white man that stood by us, too. And that's how it was around here back then" (*Treme*, S4E2). This anecdote forwards New Orleans' history as a testament to how a multiracial community can work. Albert's memories illustrate a functional city. Albert's childhood story does not evade the issue of Jim Crow-style segregation, but it still emphasizes that "it was a white man that stood by us." The Seventh Ward's past here exemplifies the potential promise of the American city in Simon's oeuvre.

Indeed, the agrarian ideal that Simon rejects in the quote has a strong tradition in American intellectual history. Frederick Jackson

Turner's widely influential frontier thesis is premised on the idea that it is the frontier – emphatically *not* the nation's cities – that represents the origins of the American 'national character.' Pivotal to Turner's thesis was the fact that it cast the "Great West" – and thus discarded the urbanity of the east coast – as the "true point of view in the history of this nation" (Turner 1998/1893, 32). To historian Inga Floto, the fact that every subsequent generation of historians after Turner has found it relevant to criticize Turner's thesis illustrates how deeply his ideas are rooted in America's understanding of itself (Floto 2007, 48).

Conn argues that though many Americans in the nineteenth century often considered cities to be problems in and of themselves, Progressive Era reformers (1890s–1920s) saw in the city the place where the fight over future of America was to be fought: "they believed that the future of the nation would be won precisely in the city" (Conn 2014, 8). I am not suggesting that we label Simon a Progressive Era reformer but he does share with them a distinct view on the city, that is, he shares with them a strong interest in attending to the challenges facing troubles in America's cities.

Conn notes that while anti-urbanism has a strong tradition in American intellectual history, skepticism of the city grew in the post-war years due to racial issues as African Americans left the rural South in increasing numbers and became northern urbanites. Today, Conn argues, the American tradition of "anti-urban rejection of cities ... has left [Americans] with an indifference to the problems of the city" (7). *Treme* marks the city as America's core challenge. At a fundamental level, it counters the indifference to urban problems that Conn describes. Because of that fact, Simon and Overmyer's New Orleans serial plays a pivotal role in Simon's oeuvre. Simon and Overmyer stress the urban and metropolitan nature of American society. Sometimes this point is subtly dramatized in serials themselves, but Simon repeatedly emphasizes this agenda in interviews and lectures.

Treme is a positive take on American urbanity in general, but this upbeat angle is particularly acute because the serial is about post-Katrina New Orleans. Simon and Overmyer's show therefore rebuts American anti-urbanism as such while also articulating a defense of a specific city at a critical juncture. One of the ways *Treme* expresses this defense is through its polyphonic depiction of how New Orleans engages with the outsider world, which is poignantly addressed in the storylines of Janette, Antoine, and Albert. *Treme* extends this theme through Nelson Hidalgo's complex way of interacting with New Orleans. These elements are important for *Treme*'s politics but its take on urbanity is also marked by an important aesthetic component. It avoids a teleological narrative structure – like that of the police procedural – that brings with it significant generic markers that would challenge the way that Simon and Overmyer tried to depict New Orleans. *Treme*'s takes on New Orleans is fundamentally shaped by its attempts to avoid filtering its urban portrait through the narrative conventions of generic storytelling templates.

Simon says of his approach to his continuing career that he keeps "slicing up society, taking a different slice each time, thinking, eventually I'll have a cake" (Simon in Dreifus 2018). The part of the cake that is *Treme* thus laid forth a city that offers more promise for the city. It rebuts the tradition of anti-urbanism in American culture. Simon's next project, *Show Me a Hero*, would end on a note that holds promise for a more racially integrated future city while still taking issue with a core fact of many of America's cities: residential segregation.

4

The Long Civil Rights Narrative: *Show Me a Hero* (2015)

The Corner, *The Wire*, and *Treme* all briefly touch on the issue of housing but it is in *Show Me a Hero* that housing and residential segregation take center stage in Simon's work. Based on Lisa Belkin's 1999 500-page journalistic tome about real events in Yonkers, New York in the late 1980s and early 1990s, this miniseries portrays efforts to desegregate a city in the face of staunch opposition. Co-written by William F. Zorzi and Simon, *Show Me a Hero* adds a historical dimension to Simon's depiction of the American city and though Simon's series all feature many African American characters, *Show Me a Hero* breaks new ground in depicting race and the city.

The miniseries portrays how, in 1987, the 28-year-old Democratic politician Nick Wasicsko runs for mayor of Yonkers against the incumbent Republican, Angelo Martinelli (James Belushi). While initially having trouble gaining momentum for his mayoral campaign, Wasicsko finds a cause célèbre in calling for resistance to a federal court order that stipulates that the city must construct 200 units of public housing in its predominantly white, middle-class neighborhoods.

Early on in the twentieth century, Yonkers had been an industrial center in Westchester County (Belkin 2015a, 24), which formed the basis for a strong labor movement, where, for instance, one could see a plant with a unionization rate over 90 percent (Friedman 2003, 24). To Belkin, the city forms a "working-class bridge" between New York City and what she calls "the pampered hills of the rest of Westchester County to the north" (Belkin 2015a, 23). Yonkers' strong industrial economy had enabled immigrant workers to form communities "that felt less like America and more like whichever country used to be home" (24). This historical background would ultimately come to shape a pattern of racial residential segregation that Judge Sand of United States District Court for the Southern District of New York found illegal and consequently "ordered Yonkers to redraw the map … and rework its view of itself" (13).

The court found that Yonkers had for 40 years discriminated against African Americans and Hispanics in schools and housing by effectively excluding these groups from certain neighborhoods. The court's order to construct housing units in the eastern part of Yonkers was to remedy this state of affairs (Pastore 2007). Though Wasicsko wins the election he soon realizes he will not be able to win in court, and he therefore changes his stance from fighting the court-mandated public housing project to instead fighting for Yonkers' compliance with the court's order to desegregate.

In his fight for the housing projects, Wasicsko faces a divided city council that will not cooperate with him due to his new political stance, and, led by councilman Hank Spallone (Alfred Molina), several council members refuse to enact the changes that the court has called for. In an attempt to make the city comply with its decision, the court decides that the city must pay daily fines that will bankrupt the city in a matter of weeks *(SMAH*, E2). But Wasicsko does not just face political pressure from the city council; the housing plans also face massive popular protests. The core struggle of the narrative is the fight over the planning and construction of these new homes. While the city council does finally concede to the plans, several units are vandalized at night during the period of construction (*SMAH*, E4). After he has successfully made the city comply with the court's order, Wasicsko loses the following mayoral election – a massive blow to the young and ambitious politician. Unable to get re-elected to political office, Wasicsko is both distraught and disillusioned, and keeps spiraling down. At the end of the miniseries' sixth and final episode, he commits suicide next to his father's grave (*SMAH*, E6).

Show Me a Hero's opening scene shows a distressed Wasicsko sitting at his father's grave after which the camera cuts to show a beeper saying "911 – 911 – 911," foreshadowing the crisis lying ahead. After this scene, *Show Me a Hero* uses a montage to establish its exploration of residential segregation. Set to Bruce Springsteen's song "Gave It a Name," this sequence cross-cuts between different settings in Yonkers. From clips from suburban streets with white people sitting on porches and young white people sitting on a park bench, the miniseries cuts to scenes from housing projects that are comparably dimmer; fewer characters – Hispanics and African Americans – are in sunlight, and the *mise en scène* is decidedly bleaker. This form of cross-cutting establishes Yonkers as a divided city and invites the viewer to ponder the living conditions of the different parts of the city. This montage also shows Wasicsko looking through the windows of what the viewer later learns is his dream house, thus establishing the dream of a pleasant home as a central desire for the characters in this miniseries.

"Gave It a Name" was not released until 1998 as part of Springsteen's box-set *Tracks*, which makes it an anachronism in this 1987 setting. The song nonetheless sets the tone for *Show Me a Hero*'s use of a total of twelve Springsteen tracks, which became a "musical identity for Nick" (Madden 2020, 173). By alluding to the positive and sympathetic way that Springsteen portrays working-class characters, *Show Me a Hero* creates a similarly sympathetic portrayal of Nick Wasicsko, a lawyer and former police officer turned politician. Film critic Caroline Madden notes that "Springsteen's extratextual canonical concerns with race, community, and American democracy align" with *Show Me a Hero*'s politics (Madden 2020, 173). Yet the central purpose of this montage is not only about setting up this musical connection between Springsteen and Wasicsko. It sets a somewhat melancholy tone for the miniseries' establishment of the two important social environments that the miniseries portrays.

Springsteen's lyrics, however, foreshadow Wasicsko's development as a character: "In the fields of the lord, stood Abel and Cain/ Cain slew Abel 'neath the black rain/ At night he couldn't stand the guilt or the blame … Billy got drunk, angry at his wife/ He hit her once, he hit her twice/ At night he'd lie in bed, he couldn't stand the shame/ Give it a name." Springsteen's own understanding of these words are interesting. Downplaying the religious elements of the lyrics, Springsteen noted that he thought song was "a study of what people do with the parts of themselves they don't like very much" (Springsteen 1998, 108). In other words, to 'give something a name' is to externalize it from yourself. In Wasicsko's case this externalization is the delayed acknowledgment that he played to racist fears to get elected.

The cross-cutting montage of Yonkers stops and the montage instead centers on single a character that will later be introduced as the sociologist Oscar Newman who is, by helicopter, flown over the city, taking photographs of the different sections of the city. This section further illustrates the residential segregation of Yonkers but at this point in the show viewers do not know to whose benefit this person is working. Already knowing that the miniseries will focus on different groups of people and their interests, this montage speaks to power dynamics. The use of the bird's eye view here suggests that the person in the helicopter possesses some degree of agency over the people on the ground. This montage overflight of Yonkers ends by panning to Yonkers's city hall. It thus ends up as an establishing shot on the setting which will become the center of the dramatic action in the ensuing story about ensuring the civil rights of Yonkers's minority citizens.

Civil Rights Narratives

Film scholar Delphine Letort notes that the civil rights film emerged in the 1980s and 1990s with titles such as *Mississippi Burning* (Alan Parker, 1988) and *The Long Walk Home* (Richard Pearce, 1990), which were "dedicated to recounting the fight for desegregation in *the southern states*" (Letort 2012, 31–32; emphasis added). *Show Me a Hero* is also a civil rights narrative but it eschews the traditional understanding of the civil rights struggle as being only located in the South in the 1950s–1960s. In the first episode, NAACP lawyer Michael Sussman argues that the court's decision to make Yonkers desegregate is "a big win for the movement." The leader of the NAACP, Benjamin Hooks (Clayton LeBouef), however, seems almost despondent as he reflects on "watching how this has played out over the last seven years, how much we are going through for a few hundred units of scattered housing." The city's resistance seems nearly to have worn him down:

> MICHAEL SUSSMAN: The executive director of the NAACP is arguing against integration. Who'd have thought it?
> BENJAMIN HOOKS: I'm not arguing against anything, Mike. I'm just tired. (*SMAH*, E1)

Such dialogue suggests how the miniseries depicts just one chapter of a much longer battle in the courts. Yonkers is part of the larger struggle for "the movement." Pointing to how the civil rights movement kept on fighting injustices after the 1960s, the scene echoes how contemporary historians argue that civil rights activism continued well after that decade. In the words of Sugrue, "Conventional histories of the civil rights movement begin with 1954 and the landmark Supreme Court decision *Brown v. Board of Education*, and they culminate in the passage of the Civil Rights Act of 1964 and the Voting Rights Act of 1965, which together unraveled southern-style racial segregation" (Sugrue 2009, xiii). *Show Me a Hero* avoids this narrative, which in itself is a politically charged decision. According to American Studies scholar Carl Pedersen, this – in Sugrue's words – "conventional narrative" is used, often by Republicans, to argue that the civil rights movement achieved its goals in the 1960s, and that racial issues consequently now can be dealt with in a non-structural way (Pedersen 2015, 317). Suggesting that the civil rights movement achieved its goals in the 1960s reduces the civil rights movement to only focusing on formal inequality. But a narrative that also takes socio-economic inequality into consideration cannot be so triumphalist.

The historiographical debate about how to understand the civil rights movement thus contains a political element. Like Sugrue, historian Stephen Tuck argues that the movement is best understood as a struggle that is much longer than the traditionalist focus on its heyday in the 1950s and 1960s. Contrary to that narrative, Tuck proposes to expand it to go "from Emancipation to Obama," as the subtitle of his book reads. Sugrue's and Tuck's narratives are diachronically much more inclusive, and in Tuck's words, "the struggle of black Americans for meaningful freedom was not confined to the world-famous southern Civil Rights Movement of the 1960s" (Tuck 2012, 1). In this perspective, *Show Me a Hero*'s portrayal of a segregation case from the 1980s and 1990s reads like an argument for the long civil rights movement narrative. In the foundational historiographic article on this discussion, historian Jacqueline Dowd Hall argues that the 'classical narrative' also eschews many central aspects of the civil rights struggle. It is not only a matter of periodization:

> Centering on what Bayard Rustin in 1965 called the "classical" phase of the struggle, the dominant narrative chronicles a short civil rights

movement that begins with the 1954 *Brown v. Board of Education* decision, proceeds through public protests, and culminates with the passage of the Civil Rights Act of 1964 and the Voting Rights Act of 1965. Then comes the decline. After a season of moral clarity, the country is beset by the Vietnam War, urban riots, and reaction against the excesses of the late 1960s and the 1970s, understood variously as student rebellion, black militancy, feminism, busing, affirmative action, or an overweening welfare state. (Hall 2005, 1234)

By focusing on the Yonkers case of the late 1980s and early 1990s, *Show Me a Hero* broadens the narrative of the struggle for racial equality insofar as it zeroes in on one of the core issues that the civil rights movement never really succeeded in addressing: housing. To Sherrilyn Ifill, President of the NAACP Legal Defense and Education Fund, "Housing discrimination is the unfinished business of civil rights" (Ifill in Badger 2015).

Show Me a Hero explores some problematic aspects of residential segregation through the storyline of Carmen Febles (Ilfenesh Hadera) who lives in the Schlobohm housing projects. A single Dominican mother who, despite working long hours at a furniture workshop, has trouble making ends meet, Carmen decides to move back to the Dominican Republic (*SMAH*, E1 and E2). She later changes her mind and ultimately decides to live her life in America (*SMAH*, E4), where she and her children later end up as some of the lucky ones who are chosen to move into one of the new townhouses at the end of the miniseries (*SMAH*, E6). In the first episode, while carrying bags of groceries, Carmen tries to take the elevator up to her apartment, but is barred from doing so because the elevator is occupied by drug dealers. This scene shows some of the social problems found in Schlobohm – and thus demonstrates the need for something to be done about that – but also stresses that Carmen is not a part of those problems. On the contrary, she is one of the people whose life is made harder by living in a neighborhood marked by poverty and drug-related crimes. Carmen and her children are worse off because of the residential segregation of Yonkers. Her storyline is important because it devotes screen time to a highly sympathetic and conscientious character. She wants to escape Schlobohm and the new townhouses allows her to do so. Her storyline explores the persistence of residential segregation and thus bears witness to the challenges that civil rights activism had to attend to after the 1960s. Extending from the opinion that the civil rights movement achieved all of its goals, economist Glenn Loury argues that "The civil rights struggle, which succeeded brilliantly in winning for blacks the right to be free of discrimination, failed for the most part to secure a national commitment toward eradicating the effects of discrimination which had already occurred" (Loury 1998, 121). While there is some truth to the narrative Loury presents here, his phrase that Blacks won "the right to be free of discrimination" could be read as suggesting that discriminatory *practices* in, for instance, trying to rent an apartment disappeared. Indeed, a report from the United States Department of Housing and Urban Development in 2009 argued that while housing discrimination is on the wane, African Americans still face discrimination one in five times (20.3%) when trying to rent an apartment and one in six times (16.8%) when trying to buy a home (Trifun 2009). This fact challenges the triumphalist sentiment found in Loury's statement.

Given the fact that the landmark Civil Rights Acts of 1964, the Votings Rights Act of 1965, and the Fair Housing Act of 1968 criminalized formal discrimination, Loury's argument does ring true. But to only focus on the word of the law can be read as arguing that discrimination had ended and 'all' that was left after these victories were the structural and institutional vestiges of past discrimination, which then had to be rectified. *Show Me a Hero* counters this idea by showing that discrimination *did persist* after the 1960s with regards to housing; Yonkers continued to segregate its housing and schools up until the 1980s. The miniseries challenges the triumphalist narratives about a civil rights movement that "succeeded brilliantly" in overcoming discrimination. Where Loury presents a narrative of rupture, *Show Me a Hero* emphasizes an element of continuity in discriminatory practices. Extending from this emphasis, its portrayal of residential segregation speaks to the distinction between *de jure* and *de facto* segregation.

In 1985, historian Kenneth Jackson wrote that "No agency of the United States government has had a more pervasive and powerful impact on the American people over the past half-century than the Federal Housing Administration." The agency was created to improve housing standards, secure reasonable ways of financing, and to stabilize the mortgage market (Jackson 1985, 203). But its work was racially biased. To this day, the FHA's earlier work continues to influence how segregated American cities are (Rothstein 2018, 50, 84–85). Arguing that the American government at different levels has played a part in creating and sustaining residential segregation, historian Richard Rothstein emphasizes how the FHA profoundly impacted residential segregation when it funded entire residential areas, and sometimes even entire suburbs, as exclusively white areas.

Show Me a Hero emulates this residential segregation by choosing to not have the storylines of its characters intersect very much. The miniseries furthers this portrayal of segregated spaces through its use of diegetic music, featuring, for instance, rock songs by Bruce Springsteen ("Racing in the Street") and Jethro Tull ("The Whistler") in scenes with Wasicsko to set up a white setting, while scenes set in the Schlobohm housing projects feature hip-hop songs by African American acts like Public Enemy ("Welcome to the Terrordome") and Digable Planets ("Rebirth of Slick (Cool Like Dat)") (*SMAH*, E5). This use of music helps create a sense of separate social spaces in a story whose storylines are more parallel to each other than they intersect with one another. Simon and Zorzi's use of a multi-protagonist narrative structure to signal the residential segregation of Yonkers works to show that the different characters, though living in a segregated city, are all part of the same urban reality.

The classic example of federal policies that helped create residential segregation was the construction of Levittowns in the post-war era, which were conceived as a part of bigger plan of trying to provide housing for WWII veterans returning from war. The U.S. faced a national shortage of five million homes at that point in time (Nicolaides and Wiese 2017, 2–5). Conceived by real-estate developer William Levitt, the construction of these towns depended on the financial backing from the FHA and the Veterans' Administration. Important to the FHA's influence on residential segregation was the fact that the plans the FHA approved did not only outline information about construction materials and sales prices, but also contained guarantees that the homes would not be sold to African Americans (Rothstein 2018, 70–71).

The Long Civil Rights Narrative: Show Me a Hero 123

To Rothstein, this historical fact problematizes the distinction between so-called *de jure* and *de facto* segregation. Whereas the former refers to forms of segregation that the government has a hand in shaping, the latter term refers to forms of segregation that allegedly arise due to actions of citizens, not the government (Rothstein 2018, vii–viii). Rothstein argues that residential segregation in American cities today "is not the unintended consequence of individual choices and of otherwise well-meaning law or regulation but of unhidden public policy that explicitly segregated every metropolitan area in the United States" (Rothstein 2018, viii, xiv). *Show Me a Hero* parallels Rothstein's argument by also giving lie to the distinction between *de facto* and *de jure* segregation. Challenging the belief that *de facto* segregated cities are the result of private practices and not of government policy or legislation, Rothstein argues that, though private agency plays a part in creating a perpetuating residential segregation, the American government at different levels has also played its part. *Show Me a Hero* shows the City Council of Yonkers to be complicit in perpetuating segregationist practices and thus illustrates how the government after the 1960s continued to play a part in creating forms of residential and educational segregation. The miniseries' emphasis on dramatizing the massive public protests against the housing plans further shows what civil rights activists had to fight against after the classical era of the civil rights movement.

Historians often use the dichotomy of *change* and *continuity* to discuss whether a specific development, event, or decision represents a significant historical change or whether the topic in question more likely represents a history of things staying the same with only the details having changed. Read from this perspective, *Show Me a Hero* shows that the triumphalist narrative of the civil rights movement overemphasizes how much the civil rights victories of 1960s represent a decisive shift in American history. To accentuate the changes that certainly did result as consequences of the struggles of the 1950s–1960s can have the unfortunate effect of downplaying the continuities of racial inequality that continued to exist. This is a key point of the Yonkers story in *Show Me a Hero*; discrimination did persist. The battle over the Yonkers housing units in the late 1980s showed how minorities had still not secured their rights. *Show Me a Hero* both extends the narrative of the civil rights struggle and thematizes the roots of residential segregation.

After having lost his campaign for being re-elected as mayor of Yonkers, *Show Me a Hero* briefly shows Wasicsko packing down a copy of J. Anthony Lukas's book *Common Ground* (1985) into a box in his office (*SMAH*, E4). Chronicling the lives of three families in Boston, Massachusetts during the decade from 1968–1978, *Common Ground* has as its focal point the mid-1970s crisis over busing and school integration, which had been brought about by a court decision to make Boston comply with the 1954 *Brown v. Board of Education* ruling, which Boston until then had not complied with. Like in the Yonkers case, the efforts to racially integrate Boston met massive white resistance (Teaford 2006, 152–156). Briefly alluding to this account of racial relations in Boston represents *Show Me a Hero*'s way of suggesting that the historical background portrayed in Lukas's book is a relevant context for understanding this miniseries' portrayal of the events in Yonkers. Indeed, when seeing *Show Me a Hero* as a long civil rights narrative, the reference to *Common Ground* looks like the miniseries' way of pointing out another northern civil rights struggle (here, in the 1970s) that gives further reason for extending the understanding of the civil rights narrative beyond the classical phase of the 1950s–1960s. But while *Show Me a Hero*'s shift in setting from the South in the 1950s and 1960s – known from, say, *Mississippi Burning* (1988), *The Rosa Parks Story* (2002), and *Selma* (2014) – is one thing, another is its focus on housing.

Show Me a Hero does not only extend the *duration* of the civil rights movement, it also looks to a theme that is rarely a focal point of pop-cultural depictions of the movement: housing. This also aligns *Show Me a Hero* with Hall's call to look beyond the limits of the 'dominant narrative.' Hall writes:

> By confining the civil rights struggle to the South, to bowdlerized heroes, to a single halcyon decade, and to limited, noneconomic objectives, the master narrative simultaneously elevates and diminishes the movement. It ensures the status of the classical phase as a triumphal moment in a larger American progress narrative, yet it undermines its gravitas. (Hall 2005, 1234)

The title of the 1963 "March on Washington for Jobs and Freedom" sums up how the civil rights movement has sought to address both

The Long Civil Rights Narrative: Show Me a Hero 125

substantive ("Jobs") and formal ("Freedom") inequalities. Or, to put it differently, the movement both has socio-economic and legal objectives. This dual ambition is overlooked when the struggle is memorialized as a fight for formal equality. While *Show Me a Hero* devotes considerable screen time to anti-integration activists, its depiction of pro-integrationists only rarely includes marches (*SMAH*, E4). By focusing on many meetings between public officials and politicians, the miniseries is mainly a legalist narrative. But this portrayal of attending to substantive inequality through the courts effectively *broadens* the civil rights narrative; the miniseries looks beyond the traditionalistic legislative narrative which tends to focus on formal equality. Instead, it focuses on socio-economic inequality related to housing policy.

Show Me a Hero challenges the classical narrative, which "simultaneously elevates and diminishes the movement." It rejects both the 1960s as a fully "triumphal moment" and the interpretation of the civil rights movement that has it focusing only on non-economic objectives. The miniseries' focus on Wasicsko as a tragic figure, however, also downplays the story of how it was the efforts of, for example, the NAACP that led to the media case, which spurred a somewhat wide coverage of the Yonkers story in the late 1980s. Unlike the narratives of what Hall labels the classical era, however, it is mainly a narrative told from a top-down perspective. According to Lisa Belkin, the NAACP's strategy was to "work the courts, not the streets," that is, they did not look to mobilize the citizens that would benefit from the victories they hoped to achieve: "It would not help the cause, they believed, to have angry black people confronting angry white people on the news every night" (Belkin 2015a, 136). In a sense, this background is a motivation for why so much of the drama in the miniseries focuses on the work by public officials and civil servants.

Interestingly, the focus on housing explores how formal inequality intersects with substantive inequality. Lipsitz notes that research shows that racial discrimination in relation to housing affects both health and wealth (Lipsitz 2011, 7), and this reflects how this *rights* violation affects substantive inequality. The presiding judge, Leonard Sand, found in his 1985 ruling in the case *United States v. Yonkers Board of Education* that the minority citizens of Yonkers had had their 14th Amendment rights violated, which had adversely affected education and living standards. This history of discrimination had led to a situation in the 1980s where 23 out of 34 Yonkers public schools were either 80 percent white or 80 percent minority. And nearly 98 percent of the city's public housing stock was located in the southwestern part of the city. That area housed 81 percent of the minority population, meaning that there was a large overlap between where public housing was located and where minority citizens lived (Belkin 2015a, 12).

The plaintiff, The United States, had filed its complaint against Yonkers in 1980 and in December 1987, the Court of Appeals for the Second Circuit affirmed Judge Sand's ruling on all counts and upheld the remedies he had called for (Moore 1992). The argument was that the city of Yonkers and its Board of Education had racially segregated the city both in housing and in schools for more than half a century. Since 1948 the city had "consistently failed to approve plans for subsidized low income housing units" except in the southwestern part of the city. The city had even created zoning regulations that prevented public housing from being built in areas where residents had protested such plans "and the integration it would bring" (Moore 1992, 597–598).

Since the post-war era all site proposals for low-income housing projects in the white areas of Yonkers were met with opposition, and, consequently, every time the proposed sites ended up being withdrawn or rejected (Moore 1992, 599). The plaintiffs further argued that the Yonkers Board of Education had contributed to segregation in schools by generally adhering to a school policy that meant that children would attend the schools that were closest to their homes. When housing was segregated, schools would also remain segregated. The court ended up emphasizing:

> that its finding of the City's segregative intent rested not on a failure to act, but on "a thirty-year practice of consistently rejecting the integrative alternative in favor of the segregative – a practice that had the unsurprising effect of perfectly preserving, and significantly exacerbating, existing patterns of racial segregation in Yonkers."
> (*United States v. Yonkers Board of Education* 1987, 65)

The court ruled that this practice violated the Fair Housing Act of 1968 and the Equal Protection Clause of the 14th Amendment (Moore 1992, 599). Judge Leonard Sand, found that there was:

no basis for doubt that City officials were aware that the course they were pursuing was one of segregation. ... It is, to say the least, highly unlikely that a pattern of subsidized housing which so perfectly preserved the overwhelmingly white character of East Yonkers came about for reasons unrelated to race. (Quoted in Belkin 2015a, 13)

The court found that residential segregation had been *intentional* in Yonkers. The vast majority of the minority population lived in public housing, and the city had made sure that public housing had been built almost exclusively in a single section of the city. This is problematic given the fact that that African Americans living in segregated metropolitan areas do less well in the educational system and earn less compared to African Americans living in more integrated areas (Boustan 2012, 318–319).

In the penultimate episode of the miniseries, the Schlobohm resident Carmen Febles comes home carrying a new set of pots but when her daughter Maria (Camilla Harden) moves to take the pots out of the box Carmen stops her:

CARMEN: No, no. Don't open these. They're for the new house. When we get the new house.
MARIA: Well, what's the point of a pot if you can't cook in it?
CARMEN: They're too good for this place. I dunno. I can't explain.
MARIA: They're like us. (*SMAH*, E5)

Their wish to settle in a home that is more appealing to them is fulfilled in *Show Me a Hero*'s last episode where we see Carmen symbolically unpacking that unopened set of pots (*SMAH*, E6). This minor plot point shows how this family's sense of self is tied into their sense of place. In Maria's eyes, their family is too good for the Schlobohm housing project. Like Gary's criticism of his fellow men and women, Maria's comment is motivated by her experience of living in the high-rises and not being able to get to her apartment without seeing people sell drugs. Drug dealing does not take up much screen time in this miniseries like it does in *The Wire*, but *Show Me a Hero*'s first episode shows Carmen's frustrations with the drug dealing she sees around her. Her children are still young, but she worries about where they will grow up.

The Wire's Blind Spot

One of *The Wire*'s qualities is its ability to tell how different facets of contemporary American society are linked to one another. Its dramatization of the interplay between deindustrialization, the war on drugs, and failing schools establishes a canvas big enough to claim American urbanity as its topic. This broad scope is integral to its urban portrait, but like *The Corner*'s zoomed-in focus on the humanization of people struggling with drug addiction, *Show Me a Hero* chooses a much narrower focus that its six-part miniseries format can handle. It takes a close look at the interrelated causes and detrimental effects of residential segregation in the contemporary American city. That is no small theme to take on, but its urban portrait is understandably more limited than the one offered by *The Wire*.

While lauding *The Wire* for its many accomplishments, Lipsitz laments the fact that it does not examine how the situation portrayed came about in the first place. Lipsitz points to concrete historical developments that made and kept Baltimore segregated throughout the twentieth century, and he criticizes the fact that "*The Wire* cannot tell us how white and black spaces in the city became separated." Pointing to the fact that Baltimore's housing stock was the third-worst of any city in America in the 1930s and referencing the NAACP's efforts to challenge the legality of restrictive covenants that kept African Americans confined to living in over-crowded areas with substandard housing, Lipsitz forwards a critique of *The Wire*'s portrayal of the segregated city (Lipsitz 2011, 103–105). He wants more historical background.

With the influence of such covenants continuing to make their influence felt even after the Supreme Court's *Shelley v. Kraemer* (1948) decision found that enforcing such covenants was unconstitutional, Lipsitz points out that blockbusting and white flight in the 1950s and 1960s furthered residential segregation and "White vigilante violence did the rest." In Lipsitz's words, this historical background created the "conditions that are taken for granted in *The Wire*" (Lipsitz 2011, 103–105). His criticism is interesting here because it almost foreshadows the way that *Show Me a Hero* later would contribute to the depiction of the American city in Simon's oeuvre. Unlike *The Wire* that portrayed the *consequences* of a

The Long Civil Rights Narrative: Show Me a Hero 129

segregated city, *Show Me a Hero* offers a look into the *causes* of residential segregation. *Show Me a Hero* offers its viewers a diachronic and complementary angle on some of the issues *The Wire* dealt with in a synchronic way. They are two sides of the same coin. *The Wire*'s synchronic urban portrait focuses on linking together different social phenomena while *Show Me a Hero*'s diachronic take on American urbanity is narrower by focusing only on housing.

One of the grimmer plot points of *The Wire* comes when the two gang members, Chris Partlow and Snoop, kill several people without leaving any bodies in the street, a fact that causes some confusion for the Major Crimes Unit. Partlow and Snoop use the many vacant houses in West Baltimore to hide the bodies, and in this way, the issue of housing is hinted at in *The Wire* but it never really takes center stage as, say, deindustrialization does.

With its focus on bricks and mortar and on how to create positive social change in urban neighborhoods, *Show Me a Hero* tackles the issue of housing head on. By doing this in a diachronic manner, Simon, Haggis, and Zorzi are able to tell a story about how the current state of the American metropolis came about. Lipsitz's criticism, however, is interesting because it draws on contextual insights about the historical roots of the situation that *The Wire* portrays. To Lipsitz, *The Wire* is guilty by omission for not including various facets of American and Baltimorean history, which he believes may lead certain viewers to "view *The Wire* as a record of increasing Black criminality that explains the poverty of Black communities" (Lipsitz 2011, 112). Here, I believe it is prudent to keep in mind Lavik's point that wanting more contextualization is asking a lot of *The Wire*, which, to him, represents "the most far-reaching and nuanced city portrait in the history of television" (Lavik 2014, 142). While Lipsitz lauds *The Wire* more than he criticizes it, I believe that his argument is interesting because it points to an issue where *The Wire* and *Show Me a Hero* converge.

Now, it may seem paradoxical to suggest that *The Wire* is synchronic in comparison to the diachronic angle of *Show Me a Hero* insofar as *The Wire*'s screen time amounts to approximately 60 hours, and *Show Me a Hero* clocks in at a mere six hours. But when one counts the final intertitles in *Show Me a Hero*, this miniseries spans 20 years of historical time. *The Wire*'s portrayal of social reproduction emphasizes that certain systemic, untoward conditions are perpetuated. It is a form of gridlocked present. Some characters in *The Wire*, like Bubbles and McNulty, do end up changing. The social structures that shape their lives, however, are reproduced. The systemic logic that *The Wire* forwards is one that transcends individuals. But where *The Wire* stresses continuity at the societal level, *Show Me a Hero* is marked by rupture, by change. It is more uplifting at a systemic level even though at the character level its 'hero,' Wasicsko, meets a tragic ending. Indeed, the title of the miniseries begs the viewer to consider what to make of Wasicsko's alleged heroism.

Wasicsko as Hero?

Though being a narrative of successful societal change, the miniseries subtly labels itself a tragedy. Like Lisa Belkin's book on which it is based, the title of the miniseries, *Show Me a Hero*, is but the first half of an old F. Scott Fitzgerald quote which continues "and I'll write you a tragedy" (*SMAH*, E4). Wasicsko is unsuccessful in seeking re-election as mayor and is not acknowledged for his efforts to make Yonkers comply with the court's decision to desegregate. This drives him to commit suicide, which is the tragedy of the miniseries. The title thus asks its viewer to consider the potential heroism of Wasicsko. He effects change, but is that enough to call him a hero?

In 1993, Wasicsko's assistant, James Surdoval, emphasized that Wasicsko was not "pro-desegregation" but rather "pro-compliance" (quoted in Berger 1993). Regardless of whether Surdoval's description is historically accurate, his distinction illustrates the issue at stake when considering whether Wasicsko should be viewed as a hero. If he is seen as a pro-compliance hero, it is because he champions the rule of law, and if he is a hero of desegregation, it is because he champions principles of anti-racism, fair housing, and desegregation. As one does not rule out the other he could be both, but there is nothing clear-cut about the alleged heroism of Wasicsko.

Show Me a Hero's paratextual thematization of heroism lies in the question of whether it is the effort that goes into the fight or the motivation for doing so that makes a hero? Wasicsko fights adamantly for the housing units against staunch opposition within

The Long Civil Rights Narrative: Show Me a Hero 131

city hall and from a very vocal grassroots campaign outside city hall. In two different discussions – one with his girlfriend Nay (Carla Quevedo) and one with the activist Mary Dorman (Catherine Keener) – he says that "the law is the law" (*SMAH*, E2), emphasizing a pro-compliance, rule-of-law standpoint that does not engage with racial issues. In the next episode, however, he has moved on from this pro-compliance standpoint. Looking at his dream house with Nay, Wasicsko ponders his situation, his stance, and his ambitions:

> You know, I was against the housing and I won? And now I'm for the housing, and I'm getting my ass kicked for it, so maybe I had it coming to me? But I think for the first time in my life, I am on the right side of something. And I am all alone. […] But the thing is, people just want a home, right? It's the same for everybody. This whole mess is over 200 homes in the city of tens of thousands of homes, and so what? I mean, we lost our fucking minds over this shit. We're about to bankrupt the city, and, I mean, at some point people come to their senses and I win. And I come out of this looking better than ever. Maybe I come out of this and give D'Amato a run for his money, you know? I don't know. Senate might be too big of a jump, but a congressional seat at least (*SMAH*, E3).

Here, Wasicsko has left behind compliance as his justification for his new stance on the housing units. Now he believes he is "on the right side" of the issue, citing the universal wish for people just wanting a home of their own. But Wasicsko ties this political standpoint to his wish for a swift ascendance in political life, which suggests that he is not an idealist through and through. His struggle to get the units built is considerable, and from a materialist position, his intentions are not relevant: he effects change, and therefore he is a hero. An idealist perspective, however, would consider his intentions to be central.

In his foreword to the 2015 edition of Belkin's book, David Simon stresses the importance of collaboration and of taking a pragmatic stance in politics and public governance, arguing that "Ideologues are useless in the middle, where people actually live" (Simon 2015, x). Wasicsko is in the middle, trying to reach a compromise that the city council can accept, and here, Simon paratextually endorses Wasicsko and his actions. Wasicsko's struggle has to do with making Yonkers comply with Judge Sand's decision, but his motivations change in the middle of the fight. He is no ideologue as is witnessed by how he is first introduced. About six minutes into the first episode Wasicsko – a council member at this point – is at a public city council meeting flirting with a young and attractive woman, telling her, "If your mother needs a handicap space just let me know," while Mayor Martinelli is trying to call a city hall meeting to order (*SMAH*, E1). Wasicsko is more preoccupied with chatting with an attractive woman than attending to political matters. This introduction certainly does not paint the picture of a zealot, suggesting that Wasicsko becomes more of an idealist during the course of the miniseries.

In the fourth episode, Wasicsko reckons with the fact he has changed his stance in the fight. Sitting at home with his, now, wife Nay watching anti-desegregation activist Jack O'Toole (Stephen Gevedon) being interviewed on TV, Wasicsko comments on how O'Toole avoids using racist slurs:

> You will never hear Jack O'Toole utter a racist phrase. 'Cause guys like that they learn how not to say the bad words. No more "coon," no more "nigger," nothing out of his mouth that'll give it away, you know. It's all property values and life and liberty, and people only living where they can afford and all that talk. But underneath it all, it's fear. The same as it ever was. I played into that fear too. When I got in for mayor, I did. It chewed me up. Man, what I would do with a second chance at that brass ring. (*SMAH*, E4)

This critique of O'Toole's dog whistle racism almost – but only almost – intimates that Wasicsko is to be seen as idealist at this point. Wasicsko acknowledges that he played into racist fears and how that "chewed him up." His last sentence, however, reveals that this insight becomes secondary to his personal ambitions: "Man, what I would do with a second chance at that brass ring." When Wasicsko had been out campaigning on the streets in his first mayoral campaign, a constituent had come up to him and said, "You'll go to the Supreme Court. That Jew judge ain't gonna build that garbage nohow. Not where I live! Tell that judge to go shove it." Wasicsko tries to argue with the agitated man, but is immediately cut off. Judging from his facial expressions, Wasicsko is clearly startled by the man's racist outburst and he afterwards remarks to his assistant that the housing issue "Kinda brings out the ugly in people" (*SMAH*, E1).

The Long Civil Rights Narrative: Show Me a Hero 133

Already at that point in time Wasicsko is aware that he is playing to racist sentiments, but it is only much later that he admits it to himself. When he finally does so, however, his final remark has more to do with his personal ambitions about being re-elected as mayor, than about admitting and regretting how he initially "played into that fear." He acknowledges his moral misstep but is more focused on being re-elected. Wasicsko's realization thus falls short of full anagnorisis; he acknowledges his past misdeeds, but the conclusion he draws from this insight has nothing to do with remedying his past wrongs – he is still fixated on "that brass ring."

The Politics of Storylines

There are two storylines at play in *Show Me a Hero*. One is Nick Wasicsko's tragic narrative that ends in his suicide and the other is a positive, societal storyline where residential integration ultimately becomes a success. The positive storyline of social change 'crosses' the downward trajectory of Wasicsko's character arc. As mentioned earlier, it is the Wasicsko story that affords *Show Me a Hero* with the opportunity of dramatizing housing issues. This would have been difficult to dramatize without Wasicsko's narrative arc with its clear rise and fall. Wasicsko's storyline, however, only rarely intersects with those of the tenants of the Schlobohm housing projects. In episode five, city official Robert Mayhawk (Clarke Peters) discusses a flyer with Yonkers Housing Authority director Peter Smith (Terry Kinney) and the subsequent scene shows Carmen Febles, Doreen Henderson (Natalie Paul), and Norma O'Neal receiving that flyer (*SMAH*, E5). But only very little screen time is devoted to showing such links between segregated social spaces.

The storylines of Simon's other series are more entwined. In *The Wire*, Bubbles' storyline offers a way of portraying the lives of Baltimore's most marginalized citizens. Through him, we get an extended tour through his social milieu, but his narrative arc also connects him with other settings, such as when he helps out detectives McNulty and Kima Greggs with their police investigations. Their storylines intersect. While the opening montage of *Show Me a Hero* is important in establishing the miniseries' tone and setting, its use of cross-cutting from the different social spaces helps the viewer understand these narratives as being intertwined even though the narrative only rarely lets the different storylines meet on screen. The miniseries portrays two dramas that are politically and thematically linked although they may not be very narrationally linked. This is where *Show Me a Hero* uses its narrative structure to stress a thematic point.

It is important for *Show Me a Hero* to present integration in a positive light. To be pessimistic would go against the miniseries' suggestion that successful desegregation is possible, so while *The Wire*'s narrative arc is 'pessimistic' insofar as it portrays a situation of social reproduction of an untoward state of affairs, *Show Me a Hero* resolves its central narrative conflict in a more positive way. As argued earlier, *The Wire*'s narrative of social reproduction is able to explain how the war on drugs has been allowed to continue as a permanent state of affairs for decades. *The Wire* shows how the situation it depicts can only be addressed by looking simultaneously at schools, the loss of jobs, political culture, and the war on drugs. So, while there is an argumentative purpose in *The Wire*'s bleakness, there is also a point in the positive outlook of *Show Me a Hero*; it needs to present desegregation as a positive story. In Simon's foreword to the 2015 reissue of Lisa Belkin's book, he argues for the continued relevance of discussing housing:

> Those houses are still there. People live in them, quietly, with others who live around the houses, just as quietly. But we are unwilling to take the lesson. In a clear and definitive arc that stretches from Yonkers to the present moment, we have learned so very little about balance, about the middle ground, about the compromise and tolerance that a viable democracy makes inevitable. ... Incredibly, the battle for Yonkers in 1987 is still the same argument, ongoing, today. (Simon 2015, xiii–xiv)

Simon is here extending his statement on residential segregation. The miniseries takes the discussion on desegregation a part of the way and this essay then elaborates Simon's critique. An 'against-the-grain' reading of *Show Me a Hero*, however, would argue that its narrative of successful desegregation in Yonkers suggests that the issues and problems the miniseries addresses have already been resolved; the viewer can be put at ease and not be troubled by its subject matter. That is not how I understand the miniseries, but this form of reading illustrates how the miniseries needs to perform a balancing act. It must show that desegregation can work in order to give a sense of optimism, but at the same time it must also show that many cities have not already attended to that issue. That explains why Simon's societal critique in the essay comes off a bit harsher than the miniseries itself. The real court case, as the intertitles tell us, did not end until 2007, when the last 800 houses were constructed. Considering that the complaint had originally been filed in 1980, during the last year of the Carter administration, the city effectively stalled its integration process for more than a quarter of a century. These are the waters that Simon must navigate in the miniseries and its paratexts: to be positive about the continued racial and social integration of America's cities without suggesting that the viewer should be complacent about it.

Though *Show Me a Hero* contains a personal tragedy in the form of Wasicsko's suicide, it also features more uplifting personal storylines regarding three of the four single mothers living in the Schlobohm public housing project. Through these characters, the miniseries illustrates some of the problems facing residents in impoverished neighborhoods while at the same time providing a positive depiction of people living in such neighborhoods.

Carmen Febles is a struggling mother who does her best for her children and the viewer understands how their lives will become easier when they move into their new townhouse. Carmen, however, does not behave in any way that viewers could potentially be critical of. In this sense, Doreen Henderson's storyline is a contrast to Carmen. At the start of the miniseries, the young Doreen, not yet a mother at this point, gets romantically involved with a young man, Skip (J. Mallory McCree), who lives and sells drugs in Schlobohm (*SMAH*, E1). Doreen has grown up in a suburban-style neighborhood and her parents are not happy with her going to see her sister and her friends in Schlobohm. Doreen, however, soon gets pregnant and moves in with Skip. But before their child is even born, Skip dies from an asthma attack (*SMAH*, E2). Unable to cope, Doreen ends up addicted to crack (*SMAH*, E4). This downfall is presented as an escapist move and she later gets clean and becomes a tenant representative in Schlobohm (*SMAH*, E5). However, because of her addiction, her storyline becomes very dark before ending up in a more positive place. In having her do drugs while home alone with her sleeping baby (*SMAH*, E4), *Show Me a Hero* does not show Doreen to be above reproach, but the miniseries also makes a point of showing how the task and responsibility of taking care of a baby on her own is completely overwhelming. This explains – but does not excuse – her way into drug abuse. The fact that she ends up being an active contributor to her new neighborhood, however, puts her in a more positive light.

Norma O'Neal, however, is more like Carmen in that she is not presented with any obvious flaws. Working as a personal care assistant for elderly citizens, Norma starts having trouble with her eyesight due to diabetes to the point that she is forced to stop working (*SMAH*, E2). Her condition means that she needs help from personal assistants, but because she lives in Schlobohm her helpers never show up (*SMAH*, E3). While Doreen ends up being a force for good in her community, her drug abuse as a mother may to some viewers suggest how social problems in this poor neighborhood are rooted in poor life choices made by specific individuals. *Show Me a Hero* does not pass such a harsh judgment on Doreen, but the miniseries almost needs to point out some of the negative consequences that can come from living in areas with many social problems. Indeed, if it did not point out some of the grave consequences of concentrated disadvantage, the miniseries would have little justification for making a case for the need to, in Simon's words, "integrate your poor into the rest of society" (Simon in Goodman 2015). Unlike Doreen's, Norma's difficult situation is in no way her own fault. This makes it harder for any viewer to dismiss her need to move into a better place in order to get adequate assistance in her daily life as anything but a reasonable and justified wish.

The fourth woman is the teenager Billie Rowan (Dominique Fishback) who gets involved with a young man, John Santos Jr. (Jeff Lima), gets pregnant, and has two children. Soon struggling to hang on, Billie faces more than her share of problems when John gets a jail sentence. Once he is released he decides to poke holes through his condoms so Billie will get pregnant again. He does not contribute to taking care of their children, yet when Billie tells him she cannot manage to have another child his only response is to malignantly ask her "What? You gonna have an abortion? You're gonna kill something we made?" (*SMAH*, E6). With such a malicious attitude even to the people closest to him, John is shown to have few redeeming qualities, and his effect on Billie and her life is for the worse. Given the fact that *Show Me a Hero* portrays Norma, Carmen, Doreen, and Billie as good people, the miniseries by no means vilifies the residents of the Schlobohm housing projects, but John nonetheless represents an unflattering form of youth culture found in this impoverished area. Through her involvement with John, Billie's storyline parallels Doreen's story by displaying some of the social problems that may arise in areas marked by concentrated disadvantage. This narrative element is important in terms of demonstrating why it is important to counter residential segregation.

The police eventually arrest John after he has committed a murder, which leads to the authorities finding out that John was living with Billie and their children. Because Billie had not listed John as living in her home means that she had effectively lied on her lease. She is therefore evicted from her townhouse and thus represents the single storyline of these women that does not have an uplifting ending. Considering the outcomes of the storylines focused on the three other Schlobohm residents, *Show Me a Hero* almost had to include a character who is ultimately not better off after moving into one of the townhouses. It would have seemed almost hyperbolic to suggest that the new townhouses would be the solution to all of the characters' housing problems (*SMAH*, E6). But though Billie's story does not end well, *Show Me a Hero* makes a point of showing that it is more John than Billie herself who is the cause of her troubles.

These storylines give screen time and voice to the tenants living in the Schlobohm area and – except for Billie – also offer a positive counterpoint to Wasicsko's tragedy. Their storylines give agency to the people living in public housing, which, in part, seems to be an overt evasion of the white savior trope on *Show Me a Hero*'s part. To law professor Osamudia R. James, a narrative like Harper Lee's classic *To Kill a Mockingbird* (1960) embodies how "America likes its stories about race: centered on innocent white protagonists benevolently exercising power, with black characters relegated to the margins even in stories about their own oppression" (James 2015). In other words, the white savior narrative suggests that when people of color achieve better living conditions it is through the benevolence of a white character.

As the trope of the white savior is prevalent in American media, it seems plausible that the creators of *Show Me a Hero* consciously deliberated the issue of agency in a story about a white mayor's fight for desegregation. With *Show Me a Hero* gaining its narrative coherence through Wasicsko's storyline, Simon and Zorzi had to balance the attention they gave Wasicsko with that given to other characters, particularly those living in public housing. In 2017, Simon even told Lee Gardner at the urban interest website *CityLab* that "one of the reasons I'm really proud of "Show Me a Hero" is the heroes were the bureaucrats. Not necessarily the politicians, and certainly not the demagogues" (Simon in Gardner 2017), which is a paratextual way of deemphasizing Wasicsko's agency in making the desegregation measures succeed. *Show Me a Hero*'s portrayal of the four women living in public housing is thus important in terms of being nuanced about the problems some people face in such areas, but the screen time given to these characters also counterbalances the emphasis on Wasicsko.

The closing onscreen texts at the end of the last episode tell us that Carmen Febles "moved into a townhouse in 1994. Now a grandmother of four, she still lives in Yonkers." The last intertitle reads: "Free of controversy, the 200 townhouses remain in use as public housing in East Yonkers," after which we see a brief shot of Mary Dorman and Doreen Henderson sitting beside each other on a townhouse porch talking amicably (*SMAH*, E6). Dorman is the critic who comes around to accept desegregation. Her initially staunch and vocal opposition to the new housing units and her subsequent acceptance of the housing units and of the new tenants is central to *Show Me a Hero*'s depiction of how desegregation can work. The real Dorman had indeed been very vocal in the case during the 1980s. She is an important part of Belkin's book and was also interviewed for the CBS program *48 Hours* did on the Yonkers case in September 1988.

It is interesting to note that when Belkin had finished writing her book on the Yonkers desegregation struggles, she asked Dorman to check what she had written about her. Dorman at first did not recognize herself in the way that Belkin presented her and sent Belkin a two-page letter, in the latter's paraphrase

> telling me [Belkin] how wrong, completely wrong, everything I wrote was. She didn't know who I was writing about but it couldn't have been her, and why am I saying these terrible things about her. So I went over and we spent half the day going through every single word that I had written about her, with all of my notes showing her I got

it from this conversation, this news clip. And at the end, she finally looked at me and said, "I owe you an apology. I didn't recognize the person I used to be, and I don't like her very much." (Belkin 2015b) Choosing to end *Show Me a Hero* with a shot of Dorman and Henderson gives the story a positive ending on a structural level, despite Wasicsko's sad ending and the melancholy music.

To historian Reinhart Koselleck, the concepts of *experience* and *expectation* are almost transhistorical categories. People have always had expectations that are informed by their experiences. These categories speak to "a general human condition" and they "claim a higher, or perhaps the highest, degree of generality" (Koselleck 2004, 257). Koselleck's point is that people's expectations of the future are rooted in some form of experience, which for him means that "there is no history which could be constituted independently of the experiences and expectations of active human agents" (256). Koselleck encapsulates these arguments in two concepts: the *space of experience* and the *horizon of expectation*. This dichotomy helps us understand why *Show Me a Hero* ends with the shot of Mary Dorman and Doreen Henderson chatting happily on a porch. The scene suggests that segregation worked in Yonkers. Viewers are given a televisual experience of successful residential desegregation that invites them to assume and expect that this can work in other instances as well.

This is important because Simon and Zorzi almost need to present the Yonkers case an example of successful segregation. They need to resolve the plot by offering the viewer a sense – a televisual *experience* – of successful desegregation if the miniseries is to live up to its overall goal. Only by presenting the Yonkers case in a positive manner can *Show Me a Hero* present the ideas of defensible space and scattered site housing as possible solutions to residential segregation. *Show Me a Hero* offers its viewers such an experience in order to establish a positive *horizon of expectation*. Though it centers on the battle for getting the new townhouses built, the miniseries gives its viewers a horizon of expectation that housing desegregation can work.

Summing Up

Three different types of public policies are able to attend to the issue of residential segregation: place-based policies, people-based policies, and indirect solutions. The first type of policy has to do with improving neighborhoods, either by attracting, for instance, affluent people to live in generally under-privileged neighborhoods, or by constructing – like in Yonkers – public housing units in predominantly more affluent neighborhoods that are affordable, for instance, to people of color with low incomes. The second strategy focuses on aiding, say, marginalized tenants and homeowners directly by providing better access to mortgage financing or housing vouchers. The third strategy is, for instance, to improve public transportation systems as way of making impoverished neighborhoods less isolated. This strategy, however, focuses on the symptoms rather than the causes of residential segregation (Boustan 2012, 319). This background shows how *Show Me a Hero*'s focus on remedying residential segregation proposes a place-based policy. The miniseries does not disparage other forms of integrationist housing policies, but these distinctions show us where *Show Me a Hero* is positioned in discussions on residential integration. This helps us identify the political identity of *Show Me a Hero*'s portrayal of the Yonkers case.

Housing is rarely examined in contemporary television, and the very fact that *Show Me a Hero* addresses this issue is an important part of its politics. Simon said on *Charlie Rose* that he thought that "there are arguments that we need to have in this country and they need to be brought forward and they need to progress as arguments" (Simon in Rose 2015). Simply trying to forward a discussion on housing and how it connects to segregated cities is thus a political act in itself to Simon. This focus on housing opens a discussion of the structural backgrounds and substantive inequalities that are hard to address in narrative form.

Through Wasicsko's character arc *Show Me a Hero* is able to dramatize changes in residential segregation, which, on a national scale, dropped by 32 percent from 1960 to 2000 (Boustan 2012, 320). The miniseries paints a positive portrait of this transition but it also shows how turbulent that transition was and can be. Indeed, when the miniseries first aired in August 2015, *New York Times* journalist Ginia Bellafante noted how it related directly to then-current events:

> The series arrives at a particularly relevant moment, not only because of the national conversation about race and criminal-justice reform

prompted by the loss of so many black lives at the hands of white law enforcers, but also because questions about the importance of economically integrating neighborhoods have become so central to urban planning in cities around the country, and crucially so in New York. (Bellafante 2015)

Such journalistic commentary on *Show Me a Hero* aligns well with how Simon stresses the relevance of producing historical dramas, arguing that "There's no point in doing period drama, if you're not reflecting on the world that currently exists" (Simon in Halskov 2019). Simultaneously downplaying and acknowledging *Show Me a Hero*'s status as a historical drama, Simon says "It's not a period piece. It is a period piece, but it just keeps going on, over and over. It's going on right now, two towns north of Yonkers in Tarrytown, in the same county with the same rhetoric and same demagoging" (Simon in Radish 2015). Saying that the miniseries is both a period piece and not a period piece comes from the fact that there is no doubt that it in a formal sense *is* a period piece, but it is important for Simon to stress that the miniseries engages with current issues.

To Simon, there is a clear and direct link from the Federal Housing Administration's racist practices in the 1930s, to the desegregation struggles in the 1980s–1990s, and to the 2010s. In Simon's view, "social engineering begins in the 1930s, with FHA mortgages and with the first public housing monies in the New Deal." His allusion to the concept of social engineering centers the discussion around the role of the American government in creating residential segregation. To him, it is important to contextualize discussions of residential segregation and social engineering in a long historical narrative: "The idea that the social engineering starts at the moment that somebody might want to restore somebody to their full civil rights, 40 years into the rigged game. And that's when you object? Sorry, that's racist to begin your argument there" (Simon in Rochabrun 2015). To Simon, this discussion hinges on where you start the narrative and to him one must go back, at least, to the New Deal era when discussing and dealing with residential segregation.

One example of how the American government played a part in funding and forwarding residential segregation is the Housing Act of 1949, which allowed cities to continue the practice of constructing segregated public housing projects (Rothstein 2017, 31). In 1949, Yonkers applied for funding to build 750 units of low-income housing and proposed a site in a predominantly white neighborhood in the northeastern part of the city. But activist groups fought these plans, arguing that the residents who would come to live in those units would be people coming from slums, and that the existing slums would stay slums. These activist groups argued that the City instead should clear the existing slum neighborhoods and then build the new housing units on the site where the slum used to be (*United States v. Yonkers Board of Education* 1987, 20–36). *Show Me a Hero*, in line with Simon's shorthand style of keeping exposition sparse, only alludes to this historical background in passing when lawyer Michael Sussman, at a meeting in Judge Sand's (Bob Balaban) chambers, says that "Yonkers intentionally segregated its housing and its schools for 40 years" (*SMAH*, E1).

While both Simon and Bellafante's comments stress the contemporaneity of *Show Me a Hero*, it is important to note here that Simon's view on this matter has to do with his understanding of American history. His view of American city is a historical one, a city that is only understood as the consequence of past actions and social conditions. I deliberately do not write that the city is *tied* to its past because such a phrasing establishes a distinction between the present and the past. The point is that, in Simon's oeuvre, the city is a historical phenomenon that cannot be understood by only looking at its state today. In his oeuvre, this is a big part of *Show Me a Hero* and *The Deuce*'s importance.

Show Me a Hero's prolongation of the traditionalist civil rights narrative serves two purposes. By emphasizing that the issue of residential segregation was never successfully resolved, the miniseries dramatizes one of the issues that the civil rights movement tried to attend to after the 1950s and 1960s. Since the publication of Hall's 2005 essay, historians have increasingly embraced the long civil rights narrative as the framework for understanding civil rights struggles in the U.S., but popular culture narratives on the civil rights movement still focus on the classical 1954–1968 era. As a rare exception to that general rule, *Show Me a Hero* brings the long civil rights narrative to the small screen, just like Destin Daniel Cretton's *Just Mercy*'s (2019) depiction of a civil rights case in the late 1980s brought the long civil rights narrative to the big screen. *Show Me a Hero* furthermore emphasizes how the issue of housing connects formal equality with substantive equality. This miniseries does not 'just' focus on the securing of *rights* of marginalized citizens, but puts a premium on connecting that to concrete standards of living. In my view, it is not a problem that *The Wire* did not portray the roots of residential segregation. It employed its synchronic perspective to address other important issues. But this also shows how *Show Me a Hero* adds an important historical dimension to the portrayal of The City in Simon's oeuvre. Simon's next project, co-created with long-time collaborator George Pelecanos, continues this historical interest in the city. But instead of housing and desegregation, *The Deuce* tackles a world of sex work and pornography in New York during the 1970s urban crisis.

5

Porn and Patriarchy: *The Deuce* (2017–2019)

In 1972, a *New York Times* editorial opined that "Few things make a New Yorker feel worse than watching American and foreign tourists walk past the Times Square porno-peepshows and dirty bookstores. The impulse is to shout, 'This is the underlife, not the real city'" (quoted in Teaford 2006, 129). This "underlife" is the setting of *The Deuce* and this old editorial thus speaks into the dynamics of how some people want to highlight some parts of their city to the outside world and have outsiders not take note of other parts of it. This perspective does not acknowledge that for the residents of such areas, this *is* the real city. This editorial marginalizes the underclass and adds to what sociologist Loïc Wacquant calls *territorial stigmatization*. Residents of such areas "bear the weight of the public scorn that is ... everywhere attached to living in locales widely labelled as 'no-go areas'" (Wacquant 2008, 29). It is not enough that the residents of such areas have to do without the amenities and privileges more prevalent in other areas, they also have to suffer this kind of discourse. This statement is, in an anachronistic way, reminiscent of how several Baltimoreans criticized *The Wire* for showcasing 'the wrong parts' of that city.

By always paying heed to the 'squalid' parts of the cities under scrutiny, Simon's work consistently counters this discourse. His series do not accept the premise of distinguishing between the 'underlife' and 'the real city,' so just as *The Wire* and *The Corner* told of parts of Baltimore that many citizens of that city maybe did not want to hear about, so too does *The Deuce* tackle the sordid parts of New York. The difference is that by now, New York – especially Manhattan – has become and is still becoming ever more gentrified.

But more than being a continuation of *The Wire*'s urban portrait, *The Deuce*'s take on the American city calls back to *The Corner*. Simon's first miniseries centered on the humanization of inner-city drug addicts, but it emphasized the urban setting as the relevant context of understanding Gary McCullough's life and world. The urban setting was not really the miniseries' main theme but served as an important context for its drama. *The Deuce* mirrors that take on the city. Its core themes are gender and capitalism, but it stresses the 1970s urban crisis as the relevant context for its depiction of these issues.

The Deuce's thematic focus thus sets this serial apart from much of Simon's work on the city, but it also distinguishes itself in its narrative structure. One of the features that makes *The Wire* cohere as a network narrative is how its characters' storylines are linked to each other. Sometimes Bubbles's storyline veers off on its own, but his role as a police informant always ties him back into the narrative arc revolving around the Major Crimes Unit. Baltimore is connected from high to low. *Show Me a Hero*'s storylines, on the other hand, do not really intersect in the same way. Only in a single scene does Wasicsko meet one of the women, Norma, who lives in public housing (*SMAH*, E6). By 'segregating' the politician's storyline from those of Norma, Carmen, Billie, and Doreen, the miniseries narrative structure imitates the segregated urban reality it addresses. Many of *The Deuce*'s storylines do not intersect very often but they all contribute to the serial's worldbuilding. Its different and often diverging storylines often speak to the same issues, thus creating a thematic unity even though its storylines veer off into different directions.

Co-created by Simon and Pelecanos, *The Deuce*'s multi-protagonist narrative traces how the parallel lives of a vast array of characters intersect and together constitute an interrelated community. One central plotline follows how twins Vincent and Frankie Martino (both James Franco) end up managing bars and 'massage parlors' as legitimate fronts for organized crime families. While Vincent is initially reluctant about partnering up with the mafia, his brother does not give a second thought about going into business with them and as the narrative progresses their storylines become more and more intertwined with the sex work industry, which, at the start of the serial, is located on the sidewalks of The Deuce, a strip of

Manhattan's 42nd Street. The sidewalks are where sex workers and pimps operate, and this storyline is woven ever closer to the story of Vincent and Frankie when the twins get involved with setting up massage parlors for the mafia.

The idea for the serial came from Marc Henry Johnson who had worked as an assistant locations manager on *Treme*'s pilot episode. Johnson had told Simon and Pelecanos of a man he knew who had been part of the burgeoning pornographic industry in the 1970s. By Pelecanos's account, he and Simon went up to talk to the man and soon realized that the stories he was telling them "touched on a lot of different themes" and "fit in to a lot of things that [they are] interested in like labor and gender politics" (Pelecanos in Rose 2017). After the release of its first season, Simon said on *Charlie Rose* that he saw the serial as a chance to "make an allegory about unencumbered capitalism" (Simon in Rose 2017). However, the serial ended up becoming more than an allegory of capitalism and, just as the story of Nick Wasicsko allowed Simon and Zorzi to tell a story of how Americas cities came to be segregated, the story of the Martino twins makes it possible for Simon and Pelecanos to tell a story of changing gender roles, a capitalism transformed, and urban problems.

Given how 1970s New York was and is the paradigmatic example of the America's ailing cities where especially "the Bronx came to symbolize the urban crisis nationally" (Bird 2019, 839), *The Deuce* constitutes yet another historical angle in Simon's depiction of America's societal problems. But as well as being the decade of the urban crisis, the 1970s were also a watershed in American cultural history. "Out of the 1970s," writes historian Thomas Borstelmann, "emerged the dominant contemporary American values of formal equality and free-market economics" (Borstelmann 2012, 312). Borstelmann's point is that this decade saw two major political and cultural shifts, one to the left and one to the right. To him, these two developments still frame American society today. The 1970s saw economic policies shift to the right, abandoning Keynesian economics in favor of a more fiscally conservative economic orientation all the while more left-leaning politics regarding gender, race, and sexuality gained a stronger hold in changing and setting the agenda on many cultural issues.

The Deuce drops in at start of this development and offers its take on this cultural watershed in American history. Though Simon had taken on several aspects of substantive inequality in American society, *The Deuce*'s approach to economic transactions represents a new element in his career. Its exploration of how representational gender issues in the media industry (arguably a form of cultural politics) connects to the economic exploitation of the women in the porn and sex trade industry (economics) stands as Simon and Pelecanos's way of zooming in on a paradigmatic shift in American history.

Economic Exploitation

In the storyworld of *The Deuce*, Eileen Merrell (Maggie Gyllenhaal) is an unusual sex worker on the sidewalks of 42nd Street. Going by the working name of Candy, her storyline embodies *The Deuce*'s exploration of economic exploitation and gender inequalities. Unlike the other sex workers out on The Deuce at the start of the serial, she is going it alone, refusing to have a pimp who will protect her in dangerous situations – and take the proceeds from *her* work. Due to a chance encounter with another sex worker, however, Eileen ends up making a pornographic movie, which becomes a transformative experience for her. She immediately knows she wants more of this industry to the point that before even leaving the set on her very first shoot, she is asking questions about the technical aspects of film making, learning about key lighting, fill lighting, and lighting screens (*TD*, S1E2). In this male-dominated environment, however, there is no shortage of roadblocks and obstacles barring Eileen from living out her dream to move behind the camera in this emerging pornographic industry.

Eileen's life around the Times Square of the early 1970s, however, is part of a larger economic story of sex work and porn where the women selling access – physical (sex work) or visual (pornography) – to their bodies do not reap the full profits of their work. The pimps and male pornographers reap much of that profit. An early scene shows photographer Bernie Wolf (Stephen Gevedon) taking erotic pictures of the sex worker Ashley (Jamie Neumann). Ashley thinks Bernie will show the pictures to people in the porn industry and that she will get to land future work. In a later scene, fellow sex worker Shay (Kim Director) assures Ashley that "Bernie'll get you work." However, the viewer is also told that the photographer was probably taking photographs of Ashley in order to sell them to porn stores on The Deuce. So Ashley pays Bernie $40 for taking the pictures even though there is a strong possibility that he will also profit from selling the pictures. This shows the exploitative nature of the nascent porn industry. Indeed, this theme of working conditions is sounded in the very beginning of the photoshoot scene where the radio is on in the background and the news announcer speaks of "a nationwide strike by air controllers in Canada" (*TD*, S1E2).

Given the fact that this storyline about erotic pictures opens with this scene focused on Ashley, the viewer is invited to see this transaction from her perspective. Eileen takes issue with this exploitative set-up (*TD*, S1E2). When Ashley talks to Shay and Darlene (Dominique Fishback) about how pictures of other sex workers are being sold in porn stores and that the profit goes to the photographers, Eileen enters the discussion to criticize the economic model that pornography is built on:

> EILEEN: But you only get paid once.
> SHAY: Same as a trick.
> EILEEN: No, every time some guy puts a coin in one of those machines, someone's making money off what you did and you're not making another dime. (*TD*, S1E2)

Eileen's problem with pornography is its economic model. Though the women are essential for producing pornography they are not the ones profiting from it. Eileen does not acknowledge that making pornography is the "same as a trick" (i.e. as having sex with a customer). The idea that a sex worker will earn a certain amount of money from "a trick" as from making a film does not make sense to Eileen because a film makes possible a whole range of subsequent economic transactions that the actor in the pornographic film will never benefit from. Darlene chimes in and says that her pimp, Larry (Gbenga Akinnagbe), once had asked her to make a movie for a man, but she thinks that "it was just for that man." Ashley, however, informs her that the reels at Fat Mooney's (E.J. Carroll) porn store are showing footage of her for paying customers.

The fact that Darlene has made porn without realizing how much she has been taken advantage of embodies Eileen's critique of porn. Darlene has not been economically compensated for her work and pornographic material of her has now been made public without her consent. Eileen's critique that the producers and not the performers profit from pornography is directly tied to how she does not want a pimp earning a profit from her work. Darlene is upset that Larry seems to have lied to her about making a movie, but when she later confronts him about this suspicion he shuts her down and her facial expression relays to us how disappointed she is by his response that he will just "look into it" (*TD*, S1E2).

This discussion of the economic aspects of sex work is elaborated in a scene where Lori (Emily Meade) has taken a ride with a john (John Cenatiempo) through the tunnel to New Jersey. Having been told that Lori needs to charge him an additional $10 because she has to get back to Manhattan after he lets her out of his car, the john becomes angry when he sees that she will also be able to make money off of her return trip to Manhattan:

JOHN: Hey, you charged me 30. Said you'd lose time on the return. But you work the trip both ways.
LORI: Yeah, it's busier on the inbound this time of night, especially on the weekend.
JOHN: So charge the inbound guy.
LORI: Hey, I just had your cock in my mouth, and you're gonna stand here and argue with me about 10 dollars?!
JOHN: No, just the principle of it, that's all.
LORI: Right. The principle.
[*Lori walks away*]
JOHN (*to himself*): Smart-mouthed little bitch. (*TD*, S1E3)

The fact that this episode is titled "The Principle is All" marks this scene as being thematically central. The tension here lies in the fact that the john opens a discussion of the "principles" about what they just did but he actually only discusses prices, not the fact that he paid Lori to perform oral sex on him. It is an economic logic that governs his thinking, and Lori's comment – "Right. The principle" – calls out the hypocrisy in that; he is not really interested in any principle. His insincere talk of principles and his outrage at paying an additional $10 for oral sex reveals his callousness and his skewed perspective on his own actions.

The scene ends on an ominous note after Lori walks away. The john says to himself that Lori is a "Smart-mouthed little bitch." He does not do anything more but it is clear that the john is physically much stronger than Lori and that he would be able to hurt her if he wanted to. Lori's discussion with this man thus serves as an ominous foreshadowing of how, in the last episode of the first season, the sex worker Ruby (Pernell Walker) – also known as Thunder Thighs – is killed by a customer just for insisting that he call her by her real name (*TD*, S1E8).

Ruby's insistence that the john acknowledges her by her name sounds a core theme in Eileen's storyline; being recognized as herself instead of the sex worker identity of being called "Thunder Thighs" or "Candy." Eileen's ambition about making it on her own and creating artistic pornographic films is a way for her to move on from doing sex work. But when she tries to raise money to fund her first film, the producer Alexander Pullman (Rick Holmes) demands that she does not just direct the film. He also wants her to have a role in it. "So what," Eileen replies "you're not gonna pony up unless I fuck on film?" She is already frustrated that she is not allowed to move behind the camera, but then Alexander even demands that Eileen fellates him if she wants him to help fund the film (*TD*, S2E3). Performing sexual acts for money is not a new experience for Eileen, but she loathes doing it here: both because it is sexual abuse but also because she does not want to earn her money as a sex worker anymore.

By using an over-the-shoulder shot, *The Deuce* makes sure that we get more or less the same view of Eileen that Alexander has when he makes his demand. That means that it is just as visible to him as it is to the audience how much Eileen hates what he is telling her to do. Also, by framing Eileen in a medium close-up where we only see the upper half of her body and her face (and not a close-up where we only see her face), the cinematography relies on Gyllenhaal's performance to show Eileen's disgust, frustration, and disappointment in this shot. Eileen hates his gaze but by not using a close-up on her face, *The Deuce* avoids shoving Eileen's reaction too much in the face of the audience. It does not become melodramatic in the old sense of the word. She feels that his view of her keeps her in a role that she wants to move beyond, and his demand reflects how her surroundings do not condone that move. To him, she is still

Figure 10 Eileen tries to hide her feelings.

'just' a sex worker and not an ambitious director with a creative vision for a film, and it frustrates Eileen that she is restricted from moving beyond that role.

The Deuce's second season elaborates this issue further. Having transitioned successfully from being a sex worker to working as a director of pornographic films, she is now metaphorically becoming more Eileen than Candy. Having become a notable player in the pornographic industry, the last episode of the season shows Eileen on a late-night talk show where her work is subject to the host's ridicule. But Eileen is okay with that because, in her mind, she is playing the long game. She believes that the publicity she will get from being on the talk show will eventually benefit her career, and she therefore puts up with the host's verbal abuse when he asks her about her own scenes in the film: "Did you make the cast do take after take until you were satisfied?" after which he invites the audience to laugh at the remark by turning his face towards the audience and smirking at them. In a similar vein, Eileen remains calm when her business partner Harvey Wasserman (David Krumholtz) is infuriated with the fact that the mob probably will take most of the profits from a film they are making. Eileen nonchalantly remarks that it "Looks like we're gonna make them some money, and they're gonna make me a name" (*TD*, S2E9). Eileen's central ambition with making the film is to shed her public identity as Candy and instead be known in the world as herself, as Eileen. Because even though she is now a film director, she knows that the media will not acknowledge her in the way that she desires. In the eyes of the world, she is an object of men's desires more than she is a person.

Season two's seventh episode, "The Feminism Part," features a scene that, somewhat self-reflexively, discusses Eileen's role in producing the pornographic feature film, *Red Hot*, an adaptation of *Little Red Riding Hood*. Lori plays the leading role, which speaks to a vision about making a film about female and not only male desire. It is not about what men like about women but about what women like. However, when Eileen and Harvey show the film to the moneymen, the mob boss Matty "The Horse" Ianniello (Garry Pastore) is not convinced about Eileen's visions for making "art porn." Marty Hodas (Saul Stein), however, weighs in to support Eileen's claim that there is indeed a market for more artistically ambitious porn films like *Red Hot*:

MARTY HODAS:	She is not wrong. We book it in theaters, it'll run for a while. Plus, Lori's hot as balls right now.
MATTY "THE HORSE":	There's no argument there.
HARVEY:	Don't forget about Candy.
MATTY:	She's still got a few moves.
EILEEN:	Hey. "She"? I'm right here. You can talk to me. I directed the film.
HARVEY:	I'm sorry. I'm sorry. I'm saying that Candy has made a name for herself behind the camera.
MATTY:	Hmm.
HARVEY:	And I think we put a lady director out in front of this. Cleans us up to people.
MARTY:	He's right, Matty. This one we can put the director out front, make her part of the package. It's good for the feminism part.
EILEEN:	"The feminism part"?
MARTY:	What I mean to say is you're a broad. It's a fuck film made by a broad. It's good for us. That's all I'm saying. Come on.
MATTY:	I'm sorry, Candy. Do me a favor. Give me a few minutes alone with the guys. OK? Thanks. (*TD*, S2E7)

At this point Eileen leaves the discussion. As one of the most important people funding the film, Matty "The Horse" Ianniello does not need to throw his weight around in the conversation to be heard. This exchange dramatizes the power relations at play here. Eileen, on the other hand, is losing control over her production, but her only possible course of action is to voice her objections in the conversation. Those objections, however, quickly lead to her being asked to leave the table.

When Harvey at the start of this extract interjects that Matty shouldn't "forget about Candy," Matty's acknowledgment of Eileen's contribution marginalizes her in two ways. His remark about her "still" having a "few moves" reveals that he thinks more about her attractiveness and her work as a performer in the film rather than her role as the film's director. His remark about her "still" having a "few moves" is a stab at her allegedly reduced value as a performer due to her age, but it also shows that he thinks more about her attractiveness and her work as a performer in the film than he thinks about her work as the film's director. His focus on her as a performer rather than a director also discursively reduces her agency in creating *Red Hot*. But more importantly, he refers to her in the third person and looks at Harvey when doing so. When Eileen sticks up for herself after Matty's remark, he merely looks at her.

The only response Matty offers Eileen is a skeptical facial expression that suggests that he is not at all interested in hearing her input. When Harvey interjects into Eileen and Matty's exchange saying "I'm sorry," it, at first, may seem somewhat unclear whether he is apologizing to Eileen or Matty about cutting in. If he is apologizing to Eileen it would be for not clarifying that Matty should not forget her contribution as a director rather than a performer. If he is apologizing to Matty, it is because he knows Matty does not want to discuss anything with Eileen. His body language, however, reveals how we are to understand his intentions. When he first hears Matty's reply about Eileen's "moves," he buries his face in his hands. He understands how insulting this is to Eileen and knows that she will not let this comment slide, and their discussion about the film will maybe be derailed as a result. This is not in Harvey's best interests.

His hand gesture, however, signals that he is apologizing more to Matty than to Eileen and his attempt to defuse the situation comes at Eileen's expense. Before the dialogue quoted above Harvey supports Eileen's argument that *Red Hot*'s status as an artistic porn film will help appeal to a female audience. Though he is friends with Eileen, Harvey tries to placate Matty and agrees to let the discussion proceed on Matty's terms. From that point on, Harvey and Marty Hodas discuss how they can use Eileen's role as the director as a rhetorical function in selling the film to a broader audience.

When Marty refers to this opportunity as "The feminism part," Eileen objects to this marketing-oriented (ab)use of a feminist sentiment. Eileen's two objections to Matty and Marty's statements, however, lead to Matty excluding her from the conversation. Marty's rhetorical question after she has left – "What the fuck's her problem?" – reveals how very little resistance Eileen can give before she is seen as a problem. The discursive room she has to operate within is so narrow that she is marginalized for even the most minor transgression of the rules governing this space.

Harvey and Marty Hodas's argument about presenting Eileen in relation to *Red Hot* speaks to the textual construction of agency and the packaging of media texts. They want to present *Red Hot* as a female-produced film and so does Eileen. She seems willing to take a few hits and unpleasant interviews in order for their film to be successful. But this dialogue all but spells out how different their motivations are in this matter. Matty "The Horse" and Marty Hodas only see upsides to her becoming a public figure, but Eileen and her family end up hurting from her publicity. In season two's finale Eileen goes to visit her parents in the suburbs who tell her that she cannot see her son anymore. The son has a bruised face, presumably for being beaten up at school due to his mother's work (*TD*, S2E9). The publicity Eileen gets seems to help her in some ways, but it comes at a cost for her and her family. For Matty "The Horse," however, there are only upsides to her becoming a public figure.

Mittell's distinction between *material* and *discursive* aspects of media authorship helps us identify how Eileen, while crucial in the production of the film as the director, is only foregrounded in order to legitimize the content of *Red Hot*. Mittell's notion of material authorship refers to who actually shapes the final outcome of a text, whereas his notion of discursive authorship has to do with how people discuss the creative origins of a media text (Mittell 2015, 87–105). Eileen is the creative architect of *Red Hot*, but it is for promotional and financial reasons that Matty and Marty want to forward her discursive authorship.

But Eileen is told to leave the table, showing that no matter how much she proves herself there is always a level of production she is barred from in this industry. Her agency is limited especially by Matty's influence. The self-reflexive part of this scene lies in the way it dramatizes how a female director can be foregrounded in the packaging of media texts even though a deeper layer of production is governed by money*men*. The producers on *The Deuce* made a point of including more women in the writers' room and of hiring more female directors (Velocci 2017). But this scene shows how such a practice can actually belie real-life agency in media productions. True to form, Simon and Pelecanos emphasize how economic power relations inform representational issues.

Lori offers a contrast here. She initially seems enthusiastic both about doing sex work and about doing porn. Soon after the pimp C.C. (Gary Carr) has first tried to hook her into sex work, Lori reveals that she all but had planned to become – actually continue as – a sex worker when arriving in New York from Minnesota. She talks about having worked as a sex worker since she was 16 years old and says that she needs to have a pimp if she is not to become lazy in her work (*TD*, S1E1). Emily Meade's interpretation of her character's arc is that when Lori arrives in New York City "she's pretending to be more innocent than she really is – but in truth, she really is more innocent than she thinks she is, and she's getting herself into more trouble than she realizes" (Meade in Sepinwall 2019). In many other situations, however, such a lack of personal insight would not come with such tragic repercussions. Her tragedy is explored in how she thinks she can enter the world of sex work and pornography and find what is missing in her inner life. Sadly, she never fills that hole inside of her and her character arc, which is interspersed with several junctures that leaves her and viewers with a hope that she will end up in a better place, is arguably one of the most tragic in *The Deuce*, probably in Simon's entire oeuvre.

After having filmed a few pornographic films, Lori goes to see one in rotation at Fat Mooney's porn shop and her face lights up when she sees herself on film. She even reaches out to the man standing right next to her, saying that he should instead watch the film being shown in her projector instead of the one he was otherwise watching. The man recognizes her and Lori walks out the store elated by a sense of satisfaction. Lori is beaming and Fat Mooney, with a smile on his face, yells at her, "Can I get your autograph, Miss Monroe?" underlining how clear it is that she feels like a star at this point (*TD*, S1E7). Lori uses porn to be seen in the world and it, in such a specific incident, boosts her sense of self.

Lori, however, eventually comes to feel trapped by C.C. and grows tired of being recognized by her fans. When she visits Eileen to audition for the lead role in *Red Hot* she confesses to Eileen how bad a situation she is in with C.C. Eileen asks Lori if it was C.C. who had been beaten her up and given her a black eye: "So, you need a different plan, don't you think?" Eileen asks Lori. Lori gets up to go to the bathroom but turns around to give Eileen her perspective on her situation:

LORI: You know what? It's easy for you to say shit like that. You don't have somebody breathing down your back. You have your own money. You can just come and go where ever you please.

EILEEN: You think somebody handed me this? This is the life I chose. You chose something different. Okay?

LORI: You think it's a choice, yeah? Okay, what am I supposed to do now? Just say "Oh! Hey C.C. Sorry. I changed my mind, catch you later." What the fuck kind of advice is that? Do you have any fucking idea what the fucking reality of this is? Everything I do, everywhere I go, every penny I spend, everything belongs to him. He is on me. He is in my head. He knows everything. What I wear, where I sleep, who I fuck. There is nothing about me that belongs to me. It all belongs to him. (*TD*, S2E5)

After Lori's outburst, Eileen hands Lori a tissue and pours both of them a drink. But she does not console Lori. She stares at her, making Lori ask: "Why are you looking at me like that?" Lori understands perfectly well that the way Eileen is looking at her is not rooted in empathy. Her visit to Eileen was meant to be an audition and in spite of Lori's pouring confession, Eileen is still thinking about their interaction in professional terms. Acting purely as a businesswoman, Eileen sees Lori's outburst as evidence that she will be a good casting choice for the movie, *Red Hot*, she is trying to make. In a sense, Eileen does help Lori by offering her a role in a film that might potentially boost her career. But she does not give her advice, she does not connect with her on an emotional level even though Lori sorely needs a sympathetic ear at this point. Lori hugs Eileen and Eileen gently strokes Lori's arm but that is all. Though Eileen is very much at a disadvantage in this very male-dominated industry, she is still better off than Lori at this point in time, but she does not use her resources to help the woman in need who is standing right in front of her.

Later on in season two, C.C. cannot handle the fact that Lori has become a successful performer in pornographic films. C.C. feels marginalized in the way her career is developing. The mob bosses Rudy and Matty "the Horse" make a business plan about signing Lori to an extended movie deal. The agent Kiki Rains (Alysia Reiner), however, tells them that C.C. will be a problem and they agree to buy him out, which he eventually agrees to. Filled with resentment, C.C. takes Lori out to dinner and tells her that he "Got [them] a room just like the old days. Gonna take a trip down memory lane. I'm gonna fuck you like you never been fucked tonight. I'm gonna fuck you like you never will be fucked again." Lori's new and greater level of agency in life is too much for C.C. and he decides to really injure her. His words reveal his aggression against her, but the severity of his malice is only revealed later when they get to the room where he rapes Lori in order to assert his dominance over her. When he leaves the hotel room, he calls her "Big movie star" and tosses $30 at her and "10 for the room," the amounts she used to charge when she started as a sex worker on Manhattan working for him (*TD*, S2E8).

In the subsequent episode, Lori is at the premiere of *Red Hot*, fearing that C.C. will show up. Later at Leon's diner, Frankie tells her that C.C. is dead and that she does not need to be afraid of him anymore. Overwhelmed by conflicting emotions of sadness and elation about finally being free, Lori simultaneously cries and laughs, signaling her mixed relationship with C.C. Season two concludes with Lori traveling to Los Angeles in order to promote *Red Hot*, which makes *The Deuce* able to connect its story of the emergence of porn with the emergence of the pornographic industry in the San Fernando Valley (*TD*, S2E9).

At the opening of season three, Lori is checking out of a rehab facility for the fifth time. Her boyfriend Greg Taylor (Ryan Farrell), however, wastes no time and wants her to meet with a porn producer in the San Fernando Valley right away. Greg is essentially a new C.C. and does not really care about her well-being (*TD*, S3E1). Lori's storyline in season three is suspended between her being continually mistreated in the porn industry and her attempts to find a new place in the world where she feels wanted. In the second episode of the season, Lori is caught off-guard when a male porn actor puts a gag in her mouth and tries to shove a corn on the cob up her ass. Lori is unprepared for that and wants to stop, but nobody stands up for her. Her agent Kiki tells her that she is "on [Lori's] side. Which is why I want you to go in there and say yes to everything" (*TD*, S3E2). Again and again Lori learns that neither Kiki nor Greg is really on her side. Later on, Kiki even persuades Lori to do a gangbang scene even though she is very uncomfortable and reluctant in the situation (*TD*, S3E6).

But there are also isolated drops of hope where Lori thinks – and maybe, by extension, the audience too – that she just might end up in a better place. She stars in a music video for a hair metal band, picks up playing the guitar, and wants to perform as singer at an open mic night (*TD*, S3E3 and 4). She also auditions for a role in a horror film but does not land the part. Greg is furious that an old acquaintance of his did not secure Lori the part but Lori does not want him to fight for her getting the role. To Lori, it is not about being in the film but about the filmmakers wanting Lori to be in it. Greg shouts at her: "I swear to Christ on the motherfucking cross, do you even know what you want?" and she finally reveals that the issue is that "They don't want me." She lets her guard down and for a second shows that her experience with being unwanted is a primary motivating factor for everything she does in *The Deuce* (*TD*, S3E4).

The roots of her emotional distress, however, are only hinted at when Lori, while traveling from city to city to get back to New York, passes through a residential neighborhood in Minnesota. From the backseat of a taxi, Lori stares at what we must assume is her childhood home. This scene suggests that Lori's emotional distress is rooted in her childhood and we thus understand her actions in the serial as somehow being fueled by emotional scars left by her upbringing. *The Deuce* invites us to hope for Lori and to root for her but we also see the ugliest side of the porn industry through Lori. After she has visited Vincent and Eileen to see if they could offer her help, she picks up a john on The Deuce. She seems to tell him her real name – Sarah – which she has not revealed to anybody before. After the john leaves the hotel room she abruptly commits suicide. This tragic end for Lori shows viewers the human costs that came with the emergence of the pornographic industry. Eileen's storyline shows the positive story that a few women experienced through the emergence of the pornographic industry and Lori shows the human suffering that was an integral part of that history.

Urban Change

At the start of *The Deuce*, the police routinely round up sex workers to arrest them for soliciting. Officer Chris Alston (Lawrence Gilliard Jr.) helps do this without any illusions that this practice will make any dent in the sex work industry in the city. It is more or less for show. The police require the sex workers to "show and prove," that is, show the police a document saying that they have been arrested within the last 48 hours. If they have been arrested in that period they are free to go, otherwise the police will arrest them. The sex workers thus face an unrelenting line of arrests while their pimps go free. One scene shows Alston rounding up a group of sex workers and the pimp Rodney (Method Man) taunts him, saying that what Alston is doing is "Like sweeping leaves on a windy day," reminiscent of how *The Wire* showed the police unable to affect the war on drugs in any way that made an impact (*TD*, S1E2).

Alston and his partner Danny Flanagan (Don Harvey) take the sex workers to their police station, let the women order takeout, and sit in the back lot of the police station and talk casually before they are taken back to the holding cells. The viewer sees how this form of policing has very little to do with enforcing the law and has nothing to do with investigating serious crimes. This situation thus lacks a compromise as in *The Wire* when Bunny Colvin speaks of how people carrying alcoholic drinks in brown paper bags allowed police officers to turn a blind eye on this minor offense. The situation portrayed on *The Deuce* needs a compromise that allows police officers to focus on more productive work than merely arresting the same sex workers time and time again. This practice echoes *The Wire*'s leading police officers' focus on clearance rates.

This is the state of affairs at the opening of *The Deuce*, but over the course of season one the police establish a no-go zone where they ferociously enforce anti-soliciting laws and the police thus play a part in changing the look of the area. Alston, however, has trouble figuring out what the police are actually trying to accomplish around the Deuce, "I mean other than the Deuce, where do they think all the dirt is gonna go?" he asks journalist Sandra Washington. He later realizes that the "no-go zone" for sex work the police have been tasked with setting up is, in fact, a politically sanctioned way of pushing sex work off the streets and into the parlors (*TD*, S1E6). As he explains to Washington in the subsequent episode, "We pushed them into the parlors. That's been the goddamn plan all along" (*TD*, S1E7).

The serial signals that it is the then-incumbent Mayor John Lindsay's (1966–1973) ambitions about improving his chances in seeking the nomination for the Democratic ticket for the 1972 presidential election that is behind the police focus on removing street sex work from plain sight (*TD*, S1E3). This plan, however, creates a profitable opportunity for organized crime to set up massage parlors as the new setting for the sex industry, which, in turn, will help fund their criminal activities in the city. Owing to Mayor Lindsay's political ambitions, law enforcement officers vehemently police sex workers soliciting in public, and *The Deuce* intimates that the under-policing of rapes and assaults and the over-policing of sex work are linked to City Hall's priorities.

The scene before Rodney says that Alston's work amounts to sweeping leaves on a windy day is a roll call at the police precinct where the desk sergeant, Rizzi (Michael Kostroff), tells the police officers about the crimes that have recently been committed in the precinct. Viewers have to connect these two scenes: they see the police officers not doing any work that actually affects their community in any positive way (i.e. they are metaphorically sweeping leaves on a windy day), and the roll call that tells viewers of the substantial crime problems this area faces. The juxtaposition of these two scenes dramatizes the misuse of police resources that go into incessantly arresting sex workers. Rizzi's body language reveals how mundane it is to list a number of rapes, murders, and robberies. Indeed, when he tells of a murder and several cases of aggravated assault, Alston asks if there are "Any descriptions?" to which Rizzi merely scoffs and says that there have been two rapes but that "One complainant [is a] known pros[titute], so who's to say?" which screams out of the second-class citizenship the sex workers have to suffer and how crimes against them are under-policed while the police are busy over-policing sex work. When Alston in the following scene is rounding up sex workers to take them to the precinct, the parallel with *The Wire* becomes very clear: police efforts are wasted on ineffectual work. Assaults and rapes are not policed because the police are busy rounding up sex workers that will be out in the streets again shortly.

In *The Corner*, the minor character Blue (Glenn Plummer) is arrested by the police in a way that seems meaningless to both the viewer and to Gary and Fran who watch the arrest taking place (*TC*, E4). This scene is a striking contrast to how other scenes show the police ignoring obvious offenses like when Gary and his acquaintance Tony (Ron Brice) have stolen a refrigerator from a home and are trundling it through the streets. The police drive right past them and Tony rhetorically asks whether Gary thinks the police are "worried about us?" and explains that the police will "rather snatch up some corner boy with a few rocks [i.e. drugs] in his pocket. Less work for 'em" (*TC*, E1). They steal a refrigerator with impunity while Blue, conversely, is arrested for a minor narcotics-related offense. *The Corner*'s way of showing the police focusing on one type of offense while disregarding others illustrates how some urban areas are both over-policed and under-policed at one and the same time. Obvious theft is ignored but Blue's possession of a small amount of drugs is policed vigorously. Jill Leovy concedes that "This is not an easy argument to make in these times" but maintains that the criminal justice system in this way "is at once oppressive and inadequate" (Leovy 2015, 8–9). This issue of simultaneous over-policing and under-policing is present in *The Corner*, *The Wire*, and *The Deuce*.

The Deuce's affinity with *The Wire* ties in with a more concrete echo of *The Wire* that is sounded when C.C. takes Lori to a movie theater to see a pornographic film. C.C. tells Lori that people "gotta go to one of them brown paper bag stores" if they want to see porn with, for instance, penetration. That kind of sexually explicit material is still illegal at this point in time (*TD*, S1E2). As critic Erik Adams notes in a review at *The AV Club*, the phrase "brown paper bag" in a David Simon serial invokes how Major Bunny Colvin in *The Wire* tried to create his "brown paper bag compromise" (Adams 2017). Colvin's point was that the brown paper bag that some people use to conceal alcoholic drinks "gave [the police] permission to go and do police work [...] that [was] actually worth the effort." Thanks to this compromise, the police were able to turn a blind eye to the minor offense of public drinking and could instead focus on more serious crimes. To Colvin, the use of the brown paper bag represents "a small moment of goddamn genius" which became "a great moment of civic compromise" (*TW*, S3E2). Adams argues that this over-policing is "their brown paper bag for prostitution" (Adams 2017), but seeing that *The Deuce* presents the police as wasting their time on "sweeping leaves on a windy day" it makes more sense to see this as *The Deuce*'s way of showing how this situation *needs* a brown paper bag compromise that could allow the police to focus on more pressing concerns such as violence and murder.

"New York, 1971" reads *The Deuce*'s opening intertitles though by its seventh episode, "Au Reservoir," we move into 1972 as witnessed by how that episode features the premiere of the classic pornographic film *Deep Throat*, which was released in June of that year. The second season is set in 1977 and the third season takes the story up to 1984. *The Deuce* is thus set at the high-water mark of the urban crisis. Jon Teaford writes that in this era downtown areas had gotten a reputation of being "off-limits after dark" due to the fact that surviving movie theaters now focused on showing pornography, coupled with the fact that more and more vacant stores were turned into porn stores and peepshows: "The once classy hubs of American entertainment were thus becoming the focus of a sleazy porn trade that offended and threatened many middle-class Americans" (Teaford 2006, 128).

Indeed, in 1975 New York City nearly filed for bankruptcy, which meant that New York State took over the city government's finances, and in 1977 economist Robert Zevin summed up the city's decrepit state in his declaration that "New York is not quite dead, but death is clearly inevitable" (quoted in Teaford 2006, 137). In Kosselleckian terms, the *space of experience* of New York City in the 1970s gave way to a *horizon of expectation* that was so bleak that to salvage the city was beyond Zevin's imagination.

While the quarter century after World War II was a period of prosperity for America as a whole, the era ultimately proved to be difficult for some of the country's central cities. That reality, however, did not become clear to the general public until the mid-1960s. In 1968, the mayor of St. Louis declared that "We just can't make it anymore," while the mayor of New Orleans believed that "The cities [were] going down the pipe." This discourse was common in the late 1960s and it continued throughout the 1970s when especially New York came to stand as the symbol of America's ailing cities. To one Atlanta mayoral candidate in 1973, New York was the specter that haunted his city's prospects for the future: "If nothing is done," he proclaimed, "Atlanta will be just another big city, a southern version of New York, a city where muggers and robbers control the streets and where downtown is a no-man's land, where the central city is a battleground where the average man dares not trod." In Teaford's words: "Just three decades before, New York City had been the hope of the world, the symbol of America's triumphant way of life. By 1975, however, some of its neighborhoods were being compared with the bombed-out Berlin of 1945, and commentators declared it no longer a place of opportunity" (Teaford 2006, 125, 136–138). Indeed, the 1970s can be seen as the pinnacle of the urban crisis, which Conn roughly confines to the period 1945–80 (Conn 2014, 9).

To many Americans, suburbia seemed more appealing and in 1970 the national census recorded a watershed shift in American social history. The nation had become a predominantly suburban nation with suburbanites now outnumbering people living in central cities: 54 percent in suburbia to 46 percent in the central cities out of all metropolitan residents. The often-affluent suburbanites were now out of reach for the central cities' tax coffers (Teaford 2006, 127). As people and businesses relocated to the suburbs, crime soared in inner cities, and the country at large bore witness to widely publicized urban riots that added to people's concerns about the city. The 1965 Watts riots in Los Angeles "brought the purported urban crisis to the forefront of the nation's consciousness" (Teaford 2006, 142). And with the news frequently telling stories about crime and violence many people came to see urban areas as dangerous.

By the end of the 1960s pollsters found that most people saw crime as the most pressing problem of the time (Teaford 2016, 139).

News coverage of the urban crisis meant that by the mid-1970s the American public had for a decade been shown images of an urban experience of hardship. As Teaford notes, "During the 1960s race riots had drawn the attention of television cameras to the social bankruptcy of the city" but in the 1970s, the major cities – key examples being New York City and Cleveland – experienced a financial crisis as they were facing insolvency. To Teaford, "the social conflicts of the 1960s and the funding problems of the 1970s leveled a telling blow at the nation's cities" (Teaford 2016, 150). Today, several cities have rebounded – a key example being New York – while other cities have never really recovered from the urban crisis. In 2015, Simon tried to dissuade people from participating in the riots that were happening in Baltimore and was subsequently met with criticism for that stance. Simon, however, rebutted:

> I live in a city [Baltimore] that hasn't recovered from the riots of 1968. L.A. can have a riot, New York can have a riot, London can have a riot, and they'll be fine in a year. Something bad happens in Crown Heights in New York? Eh, it's bad for Crown Heights, but New York's going to go right. It's the financial capital of the world. London, a world capital. Baltimore is a second-tier city. We just stopped losing population for the first time in 40 years three years ago, and you tell me that the riots are a good thing? Fuck you. Come to Baltimore and say that. I live there. […] You don't know what a riot is. You don't know what it could do to the civic firmament. (Simon in Saraiya 2015)

To Simon, the consequences of the riots of the urban troubles of the 1960s still loom large in Baltimore, which is not the case in the same way in New York City. His comment about what the consequences can be for the "civic firmament" speaks to how such events can affect the social make-up of a city in the long run. Though Simon said this in 2015 as part of the press cycle for *Show Me a Hero*, his point also applies to *The Deuce*'s depiction of New York during the urban crisis. The point is to historicize the American metropolis; its current state is a consequence of a historical past that, in Simon's view, is not something that is removed from the current state of the city.

The Deuce's historical moment is thus a time when America's urban cores in the Northeast were struggling, which was epitomized by New York and later especially the Bronx. There, partially as a consequence of the state closing down several fire stations as well as landlords paying young people to instigate fires in order to collect insurance money (Moskowitz 2017, 193–194), fires consumed many buildings in the borough. So where *Show Me a Hero* showed how the American metropolis became segregated and thus explored the blind spot that Lipsitz pointed out about *The Wire* (and, one could argue, *The Corner* too), *The Deuce* takes on yet another historical angle on the city. Set mostly in Manhattan, *The Deuce* only features a few scenes in the suburbs. The serial's portrayal of New York, however, provokes the thought of where was 'the good life' located at this point in time. Indeed, late in season two Vincent drives up to Vermont and ends up at a bar where he helps out a bartender who has too much work on his hands. That life appeals to Vincent, but when he gets back to New York and enthusiastically tells his girlfriend Abby (Margarita Levieva) about his trip, she reminds him that she is from Connecticut. That small-town life does not appeal to her, which disappoints the hopeful Vincent (*TD*, S2E7).

When Bubbles in *The Wire* says that "It's a thin line 'tween heaven and here" (*TW*, S1E4), he invokes the segregated reality of many American cities. *The Deuce* shows the 'seedy' underbelly of the city that many people sought to escape in the 1970s. Indeed, Eileen's suburban parents' condemnation of their daughter's work as a sex worker and pornographic filmmaker is a metaphor for suburban skepticism about the deteriorating urban core. As Teaford writes, many white Americans in that era left the city "to live, work, and play in the suburbs and abandon the central city to [what they saw as] troublesome blacks" (Teaford 2006, 146).

One of the ways that *The Deuce* explores such urban anxieties is through a key intertextual reference – in the shape of posters and billboards (*TD*, S1E1) – to Boris Sagal's *The Omega Man*, a 1971 post-apocalyptic film set in a world where most people have died due to a disease and where the vast majority of survivors have been reduced to zombie-like creatures. At the opening of the film, the protagonist Neville (Charlton Heston) is alone in a deserted, post-apocalyptic metropolis. Neville is quickly established as a confident and assertive character typical of a Heston protagonist, but he almost panics when he realizes, in an early scene in the film, that he is in the city center when the sun is going down. "In the late 1960s to the mid 1970s," film scholar Vivian Sobchack argues, "the science-fiction city has no positive values to sustain it – and so it falls down and apart" (Sobchack 1999, 134). *The Deuce* alludes to *The Omega Man*'s portrayal of the central city as a place of grave danger to invoke 1970s discourses about urban anxieties.

Neville was inoculated with a prototype drug just when the disease was killing everybody, which explains why he has not become a form of thinking zombie like most other survivors. A group of these survivors, led by Matthias (Anthony Zerbe) and collectively called "The Family", continually tries to break into Neville's house, which makes the viewer wonder why Neville does not abandon his urban home. This curiosity only becomes stronger when we later learn that a group of survivors is able to live relatively peacefully in the countryside. The character Dutch (Paul Koslo) explicitly asks Neville "what keeps you in the city?" to which Neville replies "that's where I live. That's where I used to live. That's where I'm going to live. And not Matthias or his Family or any other son of a bitch is gonna make me leave" (*The Omega Man*). Heston's character refuses to mimic the flight to the suburbs or to the country in the face of urban trials as was characteristic of that era. *The Omega Man* thus both reflects and engages with 1970s American urban anxieties, which were tied in with suburbanization and white flight from city centers. Though Neville has been able to maintain his home as a bastion of order in a setting of urban decay, he succumbs in the end. Befitting to its form as a cautionary tale, Neville's death at the end of *The Omega Man* suggests that the urban center has fallen and anyone wanting to survive needs to get out while they still have the chance. At the height of the urban crisis not even Charlton Heston can survive in the city. *The Deuce* subtly alludes to *The Omega Man* to invoke such 1970s urban anxieties.

The Deuce, however, not only invokes the urban crisis as a context for its portrayal of the pornographic industry. It also emphasizes the roots and causes of New York's transformation. At the opening of season three, Abby and Vincent are discussing why anyone would build a hotel like the New York Marriott Marquis on Times Square. "It's like building the Taj Mahal in the toilet," Vincent says, but

Porn and Patriarchy: The Deuce   167

Abby is confident that the people behind it know something they do not. Vincent, however, is adamant: "This is what I know. Deuce is like a cockroach. It was here before us. It's gonna be here long after you and me are gone" (*TD*, S3E1). Most viewers presumably know that the Manhattan of the 2010s is a far cry from its state in the early 1980s, and this dramatic irony shows how the Vincent and many people like him experienced the city from a perspective that was unaware of the efforts going into transforming New York City at that time.

In seasons two and three, Alston collaborates with Gene Goldman (Luke Kirby) to use police work to make owners of buildings that house sex work activities sell their real estate in order to gentrify Manhattan. One scene depicting their discussions about how to strategically use policing as a means to speed up New York's transformation symbolically features a plastic model of Manhattan in the foreground of this scene's establishing shot. The model of Manhattan suggests that the real issue at stake here is urban development and gentrification.

Throughout their efforts to change Manhattan Alston retains an idealist commitment to the project but he ends up disappointed when he notes how little he and Goldman have accomplished throughout their years working on changing Manhattan. He and Goldman pull

Figure 11 The model of New York City in the foreground suggests how urban transformation is pivotal to Alston's police work.

up to a curb and observe soliciting taking place out in the open, much like the situation looked on The Deuce in the earliest episodes of the serial. Alston concludes with disappointment: "We fixed nothing, Gene. All we did was push it," referencing how Abby at a town hall meeting was right in calling out what the gentrifiers were in the process of doing: "We never fix anyone. We never save anyone. All we do is push the shit to another corner of the room so people have space enough to build fresh shit and make money."

His commitment to their efforts was rooted in a belief that they were changing New York City for the better (*TD*, S3E8). Simon's long-running portrayal of urban issues in America retains its critical stance here. His and Pelecanos's point here is that dealing with the urban crisis can be done in the wrong way. Simon's vision for the American city is premised on attending the city's problems in a way that aligns more strongly with Alston's concern for the most marginalized citizens, which is not at the heart of what Goldman was tasked to do.

The Deuce ends with a scene showing Vincent returning to Manhattan in 2019 to attend a wedding. The scene dwells on Vincent's relationship with his surroundings and his relationships with his fellow men and women. But it also highlights that *The Deuce* claims the transformation of New York as a core theme. The closing shot emphasizes this point.

Vincent walks down a staircase to a subway station and the camera dollies laterally to show a bustling Times Square while the melancholy extradiegetic music rings out. The show ends with 50 seconds of footage of Times Square while the ambient sounds of the city are turned up. Film scholar Martin Lefebvre argues that landscapes – cityscapes is a better term here – in visual media sometimes come to take on a "contemplative autonomy" when they are more than just the background for actions and characters (Lefebvre 2011, 74). This extended shot of Manhattan embodies this form of contemplative autonomy. The shot emphasizes the importance of the city in Simon and Pelecanos's vision for the series. It has no clear semantic content but, while offering a narrative and emotional resolution to the serial, it offers viewers a moment to ponder the difference between the area in the 1970s and today. Had any viewers not understood that Pelecanos and Simon claim the city as a central topic, this scene underlines that ambition.

Exit

Central to Simon and Pelecanos's depiction of 1970s–1980s New York is the intersection between capitalism and gender in relation to sex work and pornography. Gearing up to its release, Pelecanos said that *The Deuce* would focus on "the remarkable paradigm of capitalism and labor" (Pelecanos in HBO 2017). Simon later said on *Charlie Rose* that writing and filming *The Deuce*'s first season during the 2016 presidential election campaign between Hillary Clinton and Donald Trump inspired the producers and writers to add to the original idea about economics and capitalism a stronger focus on what they saw as misogynist elements in American culture. With reference to the controversies surrounding Trump during that campaign, Simon said that he and his collaborators found that *The Deuce* also had to address the issue of "how men got to the point where they felt, even anonymously, they could talk about women this way. You can't tell me that that doesn't have something to do with the last 50 years of pornography becoming ubiquitous" (Simon in Rose 2017). In other words, the writers added to the original economic framing of their material a stronger focus on gender.

They started filming the pilot in October 2015 (Ivie 2015), and, according to Maggie Gyllenhaal, the first three teleplays had already been written when they started filming the first season of *The Deuce* (Gyllenhaal in Rose 2017). These facts are important to note. At the end of the first episode Ashley pleads with her pimp C.C. She does not want to work that night because it is raining outside and C.C. assures her that that is okay and they leave the bar to go spend time together. In the last scene of that episode, however, Vincent and Ellen (Amber Skye Noyes), a bartender at Vincent's bar, are just done having sex when they hear a woman scream and Ellen urges Vincent to go see where the scream came from. Vincent leaves their room and goes to the end of the hallway and sees through a window that C.C. has Ashley pinned up against a wall, cutting a knife into her armpit and threatening her that he will cut her in the face if she ever disobeys him like that again.

By ending its first episode with this scene, *The Deuce* emphasizes that this economy of sex work is based on misogynist violence and manipulative pimps, thus discouraging its viewers from being infatuated with C.C. or the other pimps from the very start. As mentioned earlier, Simon and the other writers and producers felt that they had to revise their depiction of Omar in *The Wire* as he was appearing as too much of a hero to some viewers. In this perspective, it seems that Simon and Pelecanos wanted to make sure that that did not happen to them again with the pimps in *The Deuce*. The end scene of the pilot thus stresses how sex work is embedded within a culture of violence against women, suggesting that *The Deuce*'s gender focus was there from the start, that is, before HBO asked Simon to go ahead and produce a full season. Its gender focus was thus 'only' strengthened while the first season was being produced. The scene, however, also foreshadows Vincent's storyline where he sees the misery around him but without ever doing anything about it. The fact that Vincent is looking through the window and watching how C.C. abuses Ashley without intervening later comes to stand as an emblematic moment for his way of (not) engaging with his surroundings.

But *The Deuce* does not in general portray women as agency-less victims that need to be saved by men. Eileen, especially, is able to make a career for herself as a director in spite of the roadblocks she constantly encounters. Indeed, it would have seemed very strange to make a serial about the rise of the pornographic industry without narratively acknowledging the agency of women. This emphasis on female agency in media depictions surely speak to and reflect contemporary discussions of representational politics in American popular culture, but it is also historically relevant in the sense that *The Deuce*'s first two seasons are set during a high point in the history of the American and international women's movements.

To Simon and Pelecanos, however, this narrative of gender inequalities is inextricably linked to an economic one. While the legacy of the second wave of the women's movement is manifold, *The Deuce* emphasizes its economic aspects. The marginalization of Eileen in the discussion about the promotion of *Red Hot* embodies the primacy of economic power. The fact that she is nonetheless used in the promotion of her film addresses this point: media representations of strong female agency is shown to be secondary to the economic power wielded by, especially, Matty "The Horse". This exploration of power relations ties in with Borstelmann's point about the dual ideational shifts that started in the 1970s: the economic swing to the right and the cultural swing to the left.

The Deuce emphasizes that female agency, at the end of the day, is fundamentally rooted in economic power. The serial thus suggests that while the 1970s saw some positive cultural victories for otherwise marginalized social groups in the U.S., these victories cannot make up for a change in the economy that continues to marginalize said groups regardless of the discursive victories they achieve. In this sense, *The Deuce* is a materialist television serial. Eileen makes a name for herself, which does wonders for her sense of self, but her career is less transformational for her economic situation and her role in promoting *Red Hot* dramatizes this point: a progressive media representation can belie the real (economic) power structures. *The Deuce* suggests that any discussion of media representations must also emphasize the economic transactions that are not visible on screen. Because Eileen is barred from sitting in at the table when the big decisions are made, *The Deuce* shows that that discursive element to female empowerment is secondary to economic power.

Conclusion

David Simon's continued dissection of the American city is critical but not despondent. Though he consistently zooms in on the challenges of American cities, he does not proclaim that the city is a lost cause. His exploration of urban problems is premised on the idea that the state and future of the city represent some of the most pressing issues facing America today, a stance that implicitly counters the American tradition of anti-urbanism (Conn 2014). As a contrast to the way that much cultural and political discourse is framed within, say, a national or racial lens, Simon's serials urge viewers to think about the future and society through the prism of the city.

Indeed, many of the titles of Simon's series point more to their urban setting than to themes or central characters: *The Corner* of an intersection, *The Wire* separating different Americas, the New Orleans neighborhood of *Treme*, and an old nickname for a section of Manhattan's 42nd Street, *The Deuce*. These spatial titles underscore Simon's interest in urban space. Unlike Simon's other productions, the title *Show Me a Hero* – adopted from Lisa Belkin's book on the Yonkers desegregation crisis – speaks more to theme than to place, yet the visual shape of the title in the miniseries is nevertheless spatial in a sense. The letters of the title in the opening sequence contain a roadmap, which indicates how the visual expression of the words "Show Me a Hero" stresses urban space even when the wording itself speaks more to theme (i.e. heroism) than to space. The titles of Simon's urban productions thus invite viewers to direct their attention to the urbanity they point to.

For the city is not just the setting of Simon's series, it is his central topic. The historical moment Simon says this in, however, is one framed by a decades-long tendency to overlook the city in political discourse. This loss of discursive prominence is surely linked to how cities are not central in federal elections and politics. Political scientists Dennis Judd and Annika Hinze talk of a "near-invisibility of cities in national politics" that is tied to the declining share of urban constituents and the rise in suburban electoral power. Since the Carter administration's unsuccessful bid towards building an urban policy agenda in the late 1970s, American federal politics has given less heed to urban problems, meaning that for "a long time, 'urban' has not been a category that the federal government cares very much about" (Judd and Hinze 2023, 260–274). This development followed in the wake of how, in the 1980s, the American federal government drastically reduced its financial support of the cities of America. In 1980, the federal government funded 12 percent of city budgets but by 1990 that number had plummeted to a mere 3 percent (Sugrue 2010, 70). The city's unenviable position extends right up to this day where, for instance, Sugrue laments the Obama administration's lack of a coherent urban policy (Sugrue 2018). This political neglect of urban problems is an underlying core grievance in Simon's work.

Given how William Julius Wilson's *When Work Disappears* served as an important inspiration for *The Wire*'s second season (Simon in Mills 2011), it seems prudent to consider how Wilson in this volume notes that discussions on social issues "that emphasize common solutions to commonly shared problems promote a sense of unity, regardless of the different degrees of severity to which these problems afflict certain groups" (Wilson 1997, xx). People's stake in attending to a social issue is influenced by whether or not they see themselves as part of a shared social entity. It is possible to "promote a sense of unity" by attending to specific social issues in ways that ultimately benefit several different social groups. Where do we draw the line between the 'us' we identify with and the 'others' who have 'their' set of problems? This is a central concern in Simon's oeuvre.

The Wire's second season emphasizes that the problems related to drug dealing and drug addiction are a "commonly shared problem" that requires a common solution. As mentioned earlier, a part of Simon's motivation for having a strong white storyline in season two came from a wish to avoid telling a story of drugs that focused exclusively on African Americans. In this perspective, *The Wire*'s way of not locating the drug problem *only* in Black inner-city communities opens for a different way of understanding the drug trade. *The Wire* shows both impoverished white and impoverished Black neighborhoods to be losing jobs or to have lost important jobs, and this is then shown to cause some people to turn to selling drugs. The serial therefore avoids suggesting that the problem it portrays is a problem for any 'others.' Simon invites his American viewers to acknowledge a need for a common solution to a shared social issue.

Indeed, Simon's serials make a point of not othering specific social groups, which is seen especially in how his serials grant an extensive amount of screen time to African American characters from different levels of society. To Michael B. Jordan, who played Wallace, *The Wire* was "one of the few shows ever, especially at that time, to have an eclectic group of characters being played by black actors" (Jordan in Abrams 2018, 308). Along with Simon's rejection of an anti-urbanist sentiment, this progressive representational politics is a hallmark of his productions. Making the charismatic Omar gay in *The Wire* is a key point but so is Simon's ambition about avoiding making *The Deuce* "the boys' version of the sex industry" as Simon told a reporter. Simon and his collaborators did not want to make *The Deuce* excessively explicit in its depiction of sex and sex work. But the serial could also go too far in the other direction, to a slippery slope that could have ended in borderline Puritan depictions of sexuality, or "*Pretty Woman* country" as Simon put it (Simon in Barry 2017). Pelecanos and Simon needed *The Deuce* to show what pornography is without the serial becoming a pornographic show itself. This ambition is, for instance, visible in some of the scenes focused on sex work or on filming pornography. *The Deuce* shows explicit sexual acts but it does not let the camera linger. But the serial also walks a fine line in not painting too positive a picture of its pimps. It could not deal with sexuality, sex work, and pornography without depicting these topics directly.

This is part of the representational high-wire act Simon has had to perform since *The Corner*, which wanted to rebut conservative victim blaming while showing its protagonists in all their too human struggles with drug addiction. But it also gave voice to Gary's disillusionment with what he saw as a lack of a sense of community among some of his peers. This representational issue was present even in Simon's initial talks with HBO. Later, Simon and Burns' representational politics also meant that *The Wire*'s portrayal of drug dealers and gangsters needed be sympathetic in order not to vilify criminals or show them as stereotypical 'bad guys.' Wallace, D'Angelo, and Bodie are central characters in this regard. Simon and Burns, however, also avoided glamorizing gangsters in a way that would make viewers gloss over the callous calculation of, say, Stringer Bell when he instructs Bodie to kill his friend Wallace (*TW*, S1E12). If some viewers had momentarily forgotten what sort of callousness goes into organized crime – maybe due to *The Wire*'s humanization of other West Baltimore criminals – the introduction of Marlo Stanfield in season three is a stark reminder of the grim realities of that part of the world.

A subtly self-reflexive scene in *Show Me a Hero* illustrates this point. A few anti-integrationists are driving around the Schlobohm housing projects taking pictures of the neighborhood. Only taking pictures of the controversial parts – such as drug dealing and a craps game – and choosing deliberately not to document the more ordinary aspects of life in the area, their actions address the issue of media misrepresentation of the underclass and media representation in general.

Figure 12 Two boys roughhousing are photographed at the exact moment where it might appear that they are fighting each other in the street and not just playing around. By switching to black and white and using a clicking camera sound, the episode signals what the anti-desegregation advocates choose to document.

The self-reflexive aspect of this scene lies in how the picture turns gray – signaling that a photograph is taken – only at some points and thus leaves other and more normal parts undocumented. The anti-desegregation advocates' deliberately biased depiction of the Schlobohm area is a reminder of how Simon's portrayal of the American city strives to also show the positive aspects of otherwise stigmatized areas, but not by excluding some of the problems that need attending to. Indeed, Simon's productions need to portray those untoward realities if viewers are to see a point in attending to urban marginalization. But they do so without vilifying these areas. This is Simon's balancing act.

Although Simon's serials sometimes become subtly self-reflexive as in the above shot, they all signal strongly that they depict real life in the American city. They are, in a word, realist. Film scholar Birger Langkjær constructively qualifies discussions of that slippery term by distinguishing between three forms of realism: social realism, psychological realism, and existential realism. The key difference between these subsets has to do with where the central narrative conflict is located. If it is a conflict in a broader societal sphere then we are dealing with social realism, if the conflict revolves around interpersonal relations then it is psychological realism, and if the conflict is an intrapersonal one revolving around, say, loneliness, death, or meaningfulness then it is a case of existential realism (Langkjær 2012, 21–24).

David Simon makes social-realist television series. His serials focus more on societal issues than on interpersonal themes or inner conflicts in their protagonists. His use of a multi-protagonist narrative structure often emphasizes a focus on some broader slice of urban American life rather stressing the inner lives of select characters (Fisher 2019, 18). *The Wire*'s exploration of multiple social arenas emphasize how connected people are in the American city and this focus shows how, say, *The Wire*, *Treme*, and *The Deuce* embrace the scope and approach of social realism.

However, that does not mean that *The Wire* does not contain elements of psychological or existential realism. When Beadie Russell, McNulty's girlfriend at the end of the show, learns that he has been forging evidence to get more funding for proper police work she scolds him, telling him "You had no fucking right. ... This is my life too" (*TW*, S5E8). McNulty knows she is right and he ultimately learns to accept another place in the world. He decides to leave behind those parts of his behavior that made him 'the vigilante cop.' The excruciatingly slow pace with which McNulty evolves as a character, however, gives him a psychological depth and makes him more human. The *Wire*'s elements of psychological realism and existential realism thus complement the social realism that is at the core of the serial.

The *Wire* here echoes a strong tradition in social-realist cinema. Langkjær argues that the protagonists of realist cinema do not face concrete problems that the protagonist can attend to through tangible actions as in, for instance, action films. The problems found in social realism are typically more structural than that: family relations, social conditions and so on. In *The Wire*, these problems are struggling schools, deindustrialization, the war on drugs, and institutional malfunction. McNulty's solution to such narrative conflict is therefore achieved not through this protagonist's actions but more through McNulty learning about himself. "The protagonists in realism cannot always do anything about the problem," Langkjær writes, "but they can deal with it in a more appropriate way" (Langkjær 2012, 87). McNulty's realization that he does not really change anything with the cases he builds against specific criminals, and that it is only in the closest personal relations that he really connects with people leads him to choosing a more constructive life, especially with regard to his relationship with Beadie.

In a similar vein, *The Deuce*'s core conflicts are about pornography, gender, and the city. It focuses on painting the bigger societal picture, but doing that requires creating believable and interesting characters. Television scholar Michael Z. Newman argues that getting to 'know' the characters in television serials requires a considerable investment of time, which means that viewers may well keep watching a series not just to follow the plot, but to learn how things are going to pan out for the characters that they sometimes watch for 30, 40, or 50 hours (Newman 2006, 23). Some scholars argue that viewers can even develop so-called parasocial relationships with characters in that they come to feel that they know the characters in a series and to enjoy 'spending time with them' (Mittell 2015, 127–128). In other words, many viewers probably see characters as a key point of interest in watching television series.

The Deuce invites viewers to root for Lori to land in a better place. However, for that character to work in a way that will serve Simon and Pelecanos's purpose, she needs to function in two different ways. First, she needs to work as a character in and of herself, and second, she also needs to function as a vehicle for making several points about society and pornography. Simon, however, insists that he is more interested in the latter function: "I have no interest in telling stories about characters. Characters are building blocks, and you have to write interesting characters, and you have to care about your characters as a writer, but characters are basically a tool in the tool box to tell a story about something larger" (Simon in Halskov 2019). There are two explanations for why Simon says this and I think that both of them are true. The first is that that Simon actually sees it in this way, that is, that he has little interest in "telling stories about characters." He is more interested in the bigger social issues that are so characteristic of social realism as opposed to the narrower focus that is the focus of psychological or existential realism.

The other reason could be motivated by Simon believing that some viewers focused too much on the characters of, especially, *The Wire*. Simon says that "if you ask me whether I should give a fuck about, in a fair fight, who'd win, Omar or Stringer, or who's cooler, my initial reaction and my second reaction and my fourth reaction is, 'Who gives a fuck?'" (Simon in Abrams 2018, 310). Simon wants viewers to think about the more political issues in his shows, and the notion that some viewers focus too much on the arguably charismatic characters that Simon has helped create to tell stories with political ambitions represents, to Simon, an unfortunate way of understanding his productions. Simon creates interesting characters to tell stories about specific themes and social realities, but these characters sometimes become so interesting in and of themselves that they, to some viewers, eclipse the topic that Simon and his collaborators want to highlight. That may be why Simon here wants to downplay the significance of characters in his serials. In his experience, this tension between keeping an eye on the overall themes and politics of a story while maintaining a focus on creating strong and believable characters is a key challenge in writing a show such as *The Deuce*:

> [S]ometimes we're in the writers room, and we're trying to say things with characters, and you can often get lost on the fact that the character has to occupy space that the character understands. All the didacticism

of, "Oh, we want to say this about sex work, we want to say this about misogyny, we want to say this about control," great. But on some level, Lori has to be explained to Lori. And there was a moment sometime in first season where [Emily] said, "She just really wants to be loved." And that cracked it. It was a bunch of writers sitting around with big schematics on the board, and we go, "Oh, yeah. That, too. Shit." (Simon in Sepinwall 2019)

Simon's description of how the writers' room try "to say [political] things with characters" shows a commitment to the broad societal perspective of social realism. Characters are here discussed as vehicles for exploring larger social phenomena. But just as McNulty needed to be developed to become a more human character, so too did Lori need to be developed in a way that was loyal to her own perspective. This is central because it is through characters that many viewers become invested in a serial, in its message, and in its political themes. This level is a *sine qua non* for the other political levels to work. This political level is almost always tied in some way to discussions of the American city, except for two miniseries that take on other themes, namely *Generation Kill* (2008) and *The Plot Against America* (2020).

Outside the City

With *Generation Kill*, Simon abandoned his focus on the American city but nonetheless returned to a key element that characterized *The Corner*; a miniseries adapted from a work of journalism. Based on *Rolling Stone* journalist Evan Wright's 2004 account of the 1st Reconnaissance Battalion's experiences in the first forty days of the 2003 invasion of Iraq, this miniseries was written by Simon, Wright, and Ed Burns and thematizes the Iraq War in a way that, in line with other portrayals of that war, sets it apart from depictions of, say, World War II or the Vietnam War. American Studies scholar Thomas Bjerre argues that World War II is often depicted in a tradition of moral certainty and nostalgia centered on honorable men. The Vietnam War, however, is depicted in very different way (Bjerre 2011, 224). Oliver Stone's Vietnam War film *Platoon* (1986), for instance, is a sort of morality play centered on a battle over the protagonist Chris Taylor's (Charlie Sheen) soul where Sergeant

Barnes (Tom Berenger) and Sergeant Elias (Willem Dafoe) stand as two diametrically opposed views on the war in Vietnam. Stone's sympathetic portrayal of the anti-authoritarian and counter-cultural Elias reveals the film's fundamentally moral angle on the war. This is quite the contrast to *Generation Kill* as it centers more on "depiction of adrenaline-seeking soldiers ... who, having grown up on violent films and video games, are frustrated by the reality of war" (Bjerre 2011, 229–230). This miniseries has a less clear-cut moral angle, if any.

The show's title points out how it depicts this generation of soldiers to embrace warfare in a different way than we see in films about World War II and the Vietnam War. The marines are enthusiastic about their work when they feel they get to do what they have been trained to do, like when Sergeant Brad "Iceman" Colbert (Alexander Skarsgård) grinningly assesses their efforts, saying "Gentlemen, we just seized an airfield. That was pretty fucking ninja" (*GK*, E3). In his book, Evan Wright makes a point of arguing that the marines of the 2000s were shaped by a different historical era than their predecessors in the American military, which Simon himself argues is translated into the miniseries in a somewhat non-direct way: "Does anyone stand up and say, "Hey, we're different from the guys in *Band of Brothers*?" No. But when marines are going into battle rapping Eminem and talking about warfare in the context of a video game, or clearing a village and referencing the show *Cops*, those things are in and of themselves indicative of a generational change" (Simon in Beck 2008, 45). Implicit in Simon's words is an argument that says that the American public's understanding of warfare should match what war looks like in the twenty-first century. Viewers cannot get any useful understanding of how war is fought in this century by watching historical WWII films. The marines embrace the fundamentally violent nature of their work and the miniseries does not vilify them for doing so. And though some marines and officers are more competent and ethical than others in *Generation Kill*, it is more shades of gray than, for instance, in Stone's war film.

A major theme in *Generation Kill* is the marines' frustrations with the incompetence of their superior officers. This miniseries embraces the same mid-level perspective that Simon and Burns used in *The Wire*, which focalized its narrative through detectives, not through commanding officers. *Generation Kill* depicts especially

Sergeant Colbert and Lieutenant Nathaniel Fick (Stark Sands) as voices of reason compared to some of their superior officers whose actions and priorities, time and time again, strike the viewer as strange and sometimes even as evidence of incompetence. In the third episode, the 1st Reconnaissance Battalion is patiently surveilling a small village when another unit swoops in and attacks, presumably killing several women and children off-screen. The attack ends dramatically when a missile destroys the hamlet. Seeing this attack from Colbert's perspective, the decision to attack and destroy this non-military location makes no sense. But this scene is not included to sound any anti-war sentiment. Colbert is not in opposition to the culture and organization of the marine corps. He embraces it fully, but he nonetheless feels that the way that the war is conducted by his senior officers borders on incompetence. War is not portrayed as unjust as such, but *Generation Kill* voices a critique that the Iraq War resulted in casualties that could and should have been avoided.

The miniseries activates several perspectives on warfare; that of the marines and that of the outsider represented by the embedded *Rolling Stone* reporter referred to mainly as Scribe (Lee Tergesen). Scribe, for instance, says that if the Americans were to encounter a gas attack that "would justify the invasion," to which Corporal Josh Person (James Ransone) immediately replies that "There's no doubt Saddam's got chemicals. It's just you liberal dicksucks who try to pick everything apart" (*GK*, E2). The marines fully believe that the invasion is justified and Simon, Burns, and Wright do not really sound any reservations about the justness of Operation Iraqi Freedom. Even though *Generation Kill* casts Colbert as its voice of reason, the miniseries does not use him as a mouthpiece for the leftist politics that Simon and Burns represent. When an Iraqi man proclaims his fondness for America as the marines drive by him – "We love you, Americans. We love you!" – Colbert flippantly yells back "Thank you! Vote Republican!" (*GK*, E2). The favorable depiction of Colbert comes from his competence and conscientious behavior in the war.

Neither Burns nor Simon have probably ever suggested that more people should vote for the GOP. Their politics probably do not align all that much with Colbert's political views, but *Generation Kill* nonetheless invites viewers to sympathize with Person and Colbert given how they both, along with Nate Fick, are portrayed as competent, ethical, and professional marines. Some viewers might frown at some of the more politically incorrect utterances that especially Person delights in cascading, but the reconnaissance marines are not presented as morally dubious. *Generation Kill* does not take sides here, which is also seen in some scenes where the more ethical characters disagree with each other. When Colbert takes issue with how they assaulted a hamlet a few minutes earlier in episode 3, he is in a complete minority and Lieutenant Fick shuts the discussion down quickly (*GK*, E3). Characters that *Generation Kill* portrays as intelligent and conscientious are not on the same page, which shows just how much the miniseries embraces a tone of ambiguity in its portrayal of the invasion of Iraq.

One of the last tragic events in *Generation Kill* occurs when Captain Bryan Patterson (Michael Kelly) is ordered to help two engineers mark a minefield at night. Refusing to accept the idea that this mission must be carried out at night in direct violation of standard practice, Patterson disobeys orders in order to protect his men, believing that this is not a necessary risk to take. Captain America (Eric Nenninger), however, immediately accepts the order, which results in an engineer stepping on a landmine, causing that engineer to lose his leg and another man to lose one of his eyes. The subsequent day Patterson hits Captain Craig "Encino Man" Schwetje (Brian Patrick Wade) for handing down the order that got those two men hurt (*GK*, E7). This is as close to poetic justice *Generation Kill* ever gets.

Television scholar Deborah L. Jaramillo argues that *Generation Kill* shows competent officers to be marginalized in the marine corps while "dangerous officers like Encino Man and Captain America are rewarded, pointing to systemic problems that are glossed over in sanitized portraits of the military" (Jaramillo 2016, 316). But it is not only the officers that *Generation Kill* shows as problematic. Colbert, Person, and Scribe all ride in the same Humvee as the inexperienced and young Lance Corporal Harold James Trombley (Billy Lush), one of the most trigger-happy marines in the show. At the end of episode two, he excitedly exclaims "Hey, I fucking got one!" when he has killed an Iraqi, and in the next episode we see him shooting and – it turns out later – fatally wounding a young boy. Having just fired, Trombley shouts that he is "Shooting motherfuckers like it's cool" (*GK*, E3). It is a little later in the episode that a woman carries a young boy to the marines hoping for help.

Only then do we understand the consequences of Trombley's actions. This scene underlines the tragic consequences of what Trombley did, but is also important in relation to our understanding of his character. His facial expression reveals no remorse or distress, calling on viewers to look critically at him. The next episode, however, shows Trombley to be selfless and brave when the marines are attacked. He does not seek cover like his fellow marines but instead stays on the road and soon spots where the enemy fire is coming from, and afterwards he gets a smile of approval from Colbert (*GK*, E4). Trombley is not without qualities as a marine.

Generation Kill does not really tell us in any clear way if we are to conclude that Trombley is just morally dubious and let that be our conclusion, or if *Generation Kill* is rather blaming the officers responsible for assigning Trombley to take part in the invasion of Iraq. Do we look at the individual only or do we also consider the institutional context that has included Trombley in this mission? If we look at *Generation Kill* in a way that is informed by how Simon and Burns portrayed institutions in *The Wire*, we are probably inclined to see the contours of a finger blaming the institution. A crucial point lies in the fact that Trombley is revealed to not have gone through basic reconnaissance training, which means that he is on a mission that he is less prepared for than his fellow marines (*GK*, E1). Though Trombley is morally immature, it is important that *Generation Kill* shows him to be the exception to the rule. The vast majority of the marines are portrayed as skilled professionals.

Most of Simon's serials primarily take issue with specific socio-economic realities in the American city. It is true that *The Corner* takes an intertextual grievance with the hood film's way of portraying American inner-city neighborhoods, and that *The Deuce* features elements of self-reflection in how it portrays female agency in the nascent porn industry in the 1970s, but Simon's serials point more to the real world than it raises textual grievances. It is somewhat different with *Generation Kill*. This miniseries is less focused on taking issues with the historical realities of the invasion of Iraq and more interested in intertextually pointing its finger against other war narratives that, in the eyes of *Generation Kill*, do not aspire to the same form of truthfulness and realism that it does itself.

Ed Burns emphasizes that it was important to him that *Generation Kill* was authentic and real to the point that marines watching it would feel that the miniseries gave an accurate depiction of their experiences. This ambition followed in the heels of *The Wire*: "The obligation of the storytellers is to write for the characters ... So that when the cop and the longshoreman or the addict or the Marine sees it, if they can authenticate it, then you've done your job" (Burns in Weiss 2008). For Simon, Burns, and Wright, there was an ambition about relaying to the American public an accurate depiction of the war. *Generation Kill*'s implicit intertextual grievance is with depictions of modern warfare that are less accurate. A main point for Simon about making *Generation Kill* into a miniseries was his belief that Wright's narrative was important enough to reach a broader audience than the people who would read Wright's book. Speculating about how many people would watch the show over five years, Simon argued

> That's twenty million people who now have a sense of modern warfare, who go into their daily lives and their roles as citizens more fully aware of what it means to engage in modern state-sponsored war-fare. If they're in favor of it, they know what the truth is, and they know it's not going to be clean. If they're opposed to it, they know what the truth is. (Simon in Beck 2008, 46)

Implicit in Simon's words is the claim that this show is more truthful than many other screenbased depictions of modern warfare. Evan Wright's experience as an embedded reporter during the invasion and Ed Burns's experience as a soldier in the Vietnam War (Wollaston 2009) give *Generation Kill* strong paratextual claims about being able to depict what warfare is. The marine Rudy Reyes played himself in *Generation Kill* and also participated in interviews in connection with the release of the miniseries (Chadwick and Cohen 2008; NPR 2008; Wollaston 2009). His presence in the show itself and in such paratexts also adds to the miniseries' claim to realism. Indeed, the last scene of *Generation Kill* points to the potentially problematic relationship between what war is and how it is depicted in the media. Corporal Jason Lilley (Kellan Lutz) has made a video diary set to Johnny Cash's song "The Man Comes Around." The first clips show the marines horsing around, explosions going off, and the men acting funny in front of the camera. These clips emphasize fun and camaraderie and the men all watch the video smiling. But then the film switches to also showing dead Iraqis lying in the roadside – interspersed with clips of marines having fun. This juxtaposition of death and joy disturbs the marines and one by one they all walk away, with only Trombley watching the video until its end. Jaramillo argues that the video "functions not as a celebration of spectacular violence but as an archive of everyday violence that implicates the men in destructive routines" and that it consequently "repels just about everyone" (Jaramillo 2016, 317). The men embrace warfare as a part of their job, but they are disturbed when they see their horsing around juxtaposed with dead bodies. They know what their work entails but they do not like to see this sort of portrayal of war, with machismo, camaraderie, and fun featured in a montage next to a graphic documentation of violence and death. This is *Generation Kill*'s self-reflexive critique of other war depictions in film and television, and maybe also a critique of itself. As mentioned, Trombley is the only man that watches the entire video and even says to Person that "It's fucking beautiful" when they see an Iraqi soldier is killed. Person looks at him, half with concern and half in disbelief.

Film scholar Monica Michlin notes that *Generation Kill* distinguishes between two ways of being a good soldier. The qualities at stake are professionalism and morality (Michlin 2016, 44). Trombley's desensitized words depict him as lacking empathy and his earlier actions show him to be less competent that the other marines in the 1st Reconnaissance Battalion. He is not portrayed as a good soldier in either sense of the word. But it is important that he is alone in watching the video until its end. He is the exception to the rule in a marine unit that *Generation Kill* has no interest in vilifying. The core ambition is to depict war in a way that is off the beaten path of American television and film history. This portrayal of the invasion of Iraq was Simon's first and most definitive 'detour' away from depicting American urbanity. The second time he would turn to another topic than the American city came twelve years later with *The Plot Against America*.

Based on Philip Roth's 2004 alternate history about what might have happened if the aviator Charles Lindbergh had run as the Republican candidate against, and defeated, then-incumbent Franklin D. Roosevelt in the 1940 presidential election, David Simon and Ed Burns's 2020 adapted miniseries is a vocal critique of the political order under Donald Trump's presidency. Simon said that HBO and his production company, Blown Deadline Productions, made a point of airing the six-part miniseries early on in 2020 so that it would not be "devoured by daily headlines" as the presidential election in November drew closer. Simon himself sees the miniseries as "a political piece" and, for instance, argues that its depiction of a Democratic rally attacked by racist protestors and Lindbergh supporters without the police interfering (*Plot*, E5) addresses the events in 2017 Charlottesville (Simon in Bilmes 2020), where a white supremacist drove his car into a crowd killing one person and injuring 35 others (Duggan 2017).

During the 2015–2016 presidential election cycle there was some discussion about whether or not proto-fascist discourses were emerging in America. In the words of historian Gavriel Rosenfeld, several people "contended that Trump's political triumph [bore] a worrisome resemblance to interwar European fascism" (Rosenfeld 2019, 555). While that issue is a matter of debate, it is important to note that Simon believes that Roth's novel explores "the dynamic that led to Donald Trump" (Simon in Golub 2020). In another interview, Simon said that "The intriguing part of this for me is that it's not 1944 or 1942, to use the historical allegory. It's 1932, 1933 in America, to use the Nazi allegory. This is the moment where somebody seizes upon 'the other' as being everyone's problem" (Simon in Folkenflik and Waller 2020). Given the fact that Hitler seized power in January 1933, Simon is not saying that the situation in America in the 2010s is comparable to what happened later in the 1930s and 1940s, but that the *early* 1930s is a relevant point of comparison.

The fact that Simon utters these statements in connection with the release of the miniseries suggests that this discourse represents a central political context in terms of understanding *The Plot Against America* as an interlocutor in public conversations in America. The show centers on the Levin family in which the mother and father represent two different outlooks on the emergent fascist and antisemitic discourse in this alternate reality. The father is the strong-minded Roosevelt supporter – and former supporter of the populist/socialist Eugene Debs (*Plot*, E3) – Herman Levin (Morgan Spector) who never backs down from an argument. The mother is Elizabeth "Bess" Levin (Zoe Kazan) whose experiences growing up as the only Jewish child in her neighborhood makes her more fearful of what might happen to American Jews in the future. "You don't know. Not like I know," Bess tells her husband, "You grew up in the Third Ward around Jews. You never had to think twice" (*Plot*, E1). This line resonates throughout the series as Herman constantly stands his ground in all ideological discussions – seemingly without acknowledging how bad things might get – all the while Bess's view of the changing political climate makes her more fearful of what might happen in the future. Elizabeth's sister, Evelyn Finkel (Winona Ryder), fears growing old alone and ends up in a relationship with Rabbi Lionel Bengelsdorf (John Turturro) who, as the plot develops, becomes a staunch supporter of Lindbergh. The family thus represents a microcosm for the different stances this minority can take as their country turns against them.

Like Simon's other productions, *The Plot Against America* strikes a balancing act in how it depicts its milieu. An important part of this balance comes from how it portrays the family's identity in terms of being both American and Jewish. One interviewer asked Simon how he saw his own identity in relation to those two categories to which Simon replied that the issue "was resolved in Roth's mind and it's resolved in my mind. I'm an American. The hyphenate doesn't make me any less American. It doesn't make anybody who's a Muslim-American or a Mexican-American or a Brazilian-American or a Chinese-American, less American" (Simon in Bilmes 2020). Simon's argument about his hyphenated identity not making him "any less American" tacitly rejects Theodore Roosevelt's famous rejection of 'hyphenate identities' in 1915: "There is no such thing as a hyphenated American who is a good American. The only man who is a good American is the man who is an American and nothing else" (Roosevelt in Link and Link 2012/1915, 166). Simon rejects that belief and so does the miniseries.

In the opening episode, Herman is listening to Charles Lindbergh (Ben Cole) on the radio saying that while the Jewish people are looking out for their best interest when they allegedly want America to enter the war in Europe, so too are Americans right in protecting *their* own interests. Herman is upset saying, "Other people, us and them, our interests. We're Americans, you fascist son of a bitch!" (*Plot*, E1). Having fully embraced his American identity, Herman calls out Lindbergh's somewhat subtle strategy of othering Jewish Americans. The miniseries aligns with Herman's perspective through how the family speaks American English. Their dialect seems to be more of a regional New Jersey dialect rather than any foreign accent. Bess and Evelyn's mother, Dora Finkel (Eleanor Reissa), does have a foreign accent and there seems to be a point in having her die and be buried half-way through the show (*Plot*, E4). When she dies the *entire* family speaks American English, which implies a wholehearted embrace of their American identity.

Lindbergh's words foreshadow an oncoming and gradually more divisive discourse of othering that only grows stronger as the miniseries progresses. Burns and Simon are suggesting that this discourse – which is less extreme than other forms of more direct racist and xenophobic discourse shown later in the series – is dangerous in itself and that it can lead to, for instance, xenophobic violence. When the miniseries shows how strongly American Jews become persecuted in later episodes (*Plot*, E5–E6), Burns and Simon are suggesting that Lindbergh's words in this radio broadcast speech need to be interpreted as a dangerous and potential precursor to, or foreshadowing of, later and more violent forms of othering and persecution.

When the Levins, who live in a predominantly Jewish neighborhood in New Jersey, are out looking at a new house in another neighborhood Bess looks more at the neighborhood than she looks at the house. A man washing his car a few houses away stares at them. The family clearly sees themselves as American but Bess is more concerned than Morgan is about how much other social groups will ostracize them in this potentially new neighborhood (*Plot*, E1). Two episodes later, the family is on a sightseeing trip, driving around Washington when they lose their orientation in traffic and Herman tries to change lanes. A police officer (Dean Neistat) pulls over to ask "What's going on, Jersey?" The son Sandy tells the officer the name of the hotel they are staying at and the officer tells them to follow him. While Herman is thrilled they are "getting the royal treatment," Bess is absolutely terrified though she tries to hide her emotions in order not to scare their children in the backseat. Not only does this scene illustrate an important difference in Bess and Herman's perceptions of antisemitism and their vulnerability to it, it also underlines fear as an omnipresent fact of life for Jews in Lindbergh's America. Bess almost rhetorically asks Herman where the police officer is really leading them. "Bess, he's taking us to our hotel. What's wrong?" Herman responds, illustrating that not only is he less fearful than Bess, but also that her reaction is beyond his imagination (*Plot*, E3).

It makes perfect sense that Bess is scared here. She understands better than Herman the ascendant antisemitism in America in this storyworld, but it is also crucial that the officer says "What's going on, Jersey?" The police officer could, surely, just be showing that he looked at their license plate, but, as evidenced by a 1948 survey of the American Jewish population, New Jersey in the 1940s had a relatively high number of Jewish citizens and had the highest number of communities housing more than 1,000 Jews (Seligman and Swados 1948–1949, 665–672). And Herman is repeatedly recognized as being Jewish throughout the course of the miniseries.

After the Levins have looked at their potential new home, the family drives by a German beer garden where several men yell antisemitic slurs at them (*Plot*, E1). When Herman is changing a flat tire on the roadside on his way back to New Jersey from visiting his nephew Alvin (Anthony Boyle) in Canada, an Orthodox Jewish driver stops next to him and asks him if he is a "Landsman" which Herman acknowledges (*Plot*, E4). Bess knows that people sometimes correctly identify them as being Jewish and that adds to her fear. That means that when the police officer addresses Herman as "Jersey" she fears that that is a form of malignant othering of her family. Nothing, however, happens to the Levins here, and the police officer does actually help them, but the scene shows how an altered social and political context causes Bess to look for any sign that potentially represents danger to her and to her family. This portrayal of Bess's fear is central to *The Plot Against America*'s critique of what discourses of othering can mean for people's way of living their lives.

By relating what might have happened in American history if Lindbergh had become president, *The Plot Against America* represents a form of counterfactual history. Historians disagree over the scholarly merits of trying to figure out what might have happened if some events had turned out differently. Legal scholar Cass Sunstein articulates the classical positive take on what counterfactual history is able to do when writing that "counterfactual history is inevitable, because any causal claim is an exercise of counterfactual history" (Sunstein 2016, 434). This is the premise of counterfactual history. 'If *this* had not happened, then things would have turned out very differently,' the argument goes. Only through such imagined courses of events do we see the importance of the way things *did* turn out at different junctures in history.

The Plot Against America uses its counterfactual form to emphasize the importance of what indeed did happen during FDR's presidency in the 1940s. After the Japanese attack on Pearl Harbor and the German declaration of war in December 1941, America entered World War II. But Burns and Simon's miniseries only intermittently touches on the war. Simon's three multi-season dramas – *The Wire*, *Treme*, and *The Deuce* – all have opening credits sequences but most of his miniseries do not: *The Corner*, *Generation Kill*, and *Show Me a Hero*. Because *The Plot Against America* is told through the Levin family it only touches on the war in those scenes when, especially, Herman goes to see newsreels in a cinema in Newark. The miniseries also touches somewhat directly on the war when Herman's nephew Alvin enrolls in the Canadian army "to kill Nazis" (*Plot*, E3). Unlike Simon's other miniseries, *The Plot Against America* does feature an opening credits sequence, which it uses to situate its family-focused drama in the broader social events of this alternate historical trajectory. This sequence features archival footage of Charles Lindbergh, Franklin Roosevelt, Adolf Hitler, antisemitic propaganda, and much more set to the 1933 song "The Road is Open Again." This footage contextualizes the events in the miniseries and broadens the show's canvas in terms of portraying this alternative reality. Though it focuses on the Levin family, *The Plot Against America* insists that its audience understands this 'narrow' scope of the show to engage with larger themes in American history and society.

"The Road is Open Again" was originally written to promote the National Recovery Administration, a government agency created as part of Roosevelt's New Deal program. The song used in the miniseries, however, was re-recorded with Michael Kostroff singing the lead (Dessem 2020). Seen in relation to the alternate history that the miniseries portrays, a few of the song's lines come to take on a new meaning: "All the world's on the way/ To a sunnier day/ For the road is open again." When used in *The Plot Against America*, the line that "the road is open again" becomes a way to emphasize the contingency of historical developments.

A teleological view of history is premised on the idea that when you look at the past you look at, or look for, the reasons why things turned the way they did. In other words, the fact that Roosevelt was elected for a third term in the 1940 presidential election can come to appear, in hindsight, to be the only way that that election could have turned out. But it is the skewed perspective of teleological thinking that makes it look like that. When we start thinking that the "road [of historical development] is open again," we get to see how things looked in the summer of 1940, but not from the perspective of our point in history. *The Plot Against America* uses "The Road is Open Again" to invoke the usefulness of looking at the past through such a non-teleological lens.

Roth's novel ends with the course of history returning to the 'normality' of history. Thanks to the efforts of a resistance movement of which Alvin is a part, Charles Lindbergh's plane disappears while he is out flying and Roosevelt is re-elected as President. The U.S. enters the war and the world returns to normal. Burns and Simon's ending is more ambiguous. A presidential election is held in November 1942 but we see ballots being stolen and burned. The show ends with a shot of a radio broadcasting election coverage into the Levin household. According to Simon, it was HBO executive Kary Antholis who had suggested ending the show with a very open ending (Simon in Sagal 2020, E6), without revealing who ultimately wins the election (*Plot*, E6). *The Plot Against America* avoids consoling the viewer into thinking that everything turned out the way it should, and, to Simon, there was a very specific reason for chosing this open ending.

One British interviewer asked Simon if the miniseries was not a case of preaching to the choir, to which Simon replied, "You win elections in my country not by trying to convince the other guy's base to vote for you. You win elections by getting your base to the polls. Hence where we ended this miniseries" (Simon in Bilmes 2020). In Simon's view, *The Plot Against America*'s alternate history was thus, in one way, an invitation for especially Democratic voters to show up on election day in 2020. It is for this reason that the miniseries does not want to suggest that viewers can rest assured that the normal state of things will, inevitably, be restored, thus recalling how *The Wire* did not want to suggest that the situation it portrays will fix itself. The political thrust in Simon's career has rarely been more explicit than the ending of *The Plot Against America*.

Simon's Political Statement

The realist drive and the progressive representational politics are important parts of Simon's aesthetics and cultural politics, but there is also a strong left-leaning current in Simon's work with regards to socio-economic questions. By his own account, his "politics are to the left of the Democratic Party. I'm probably in Europe what would be called a democratic socialist" (Simon in Baldwin 2013), explaining, in another context, that he believes that "unrestrained capitalism, while an effective tool for generating short-term profit, proves itself a useless metric for calibrating a just and inclusive society" (Simon 2012). Democratic socialism is in itself is a very diverse political tradition (e.g. Dybdal 2014), but it is also very much a minority standpoint in American political history. Arguably, Simon's democratic socialist view about capitalism's inability to create "a just and inclusive society" ties in with his argument about whether or not to think of America as a single or several entities, as I discussed in the introduction. This egalitarian politics, generally speaking, seeks to expand democratic principles to economic life and is committed to serving the interests of the working class and the underclass. The way that this politics translates into Simon's serials, however, is especially seen in their exploration of certain structural inequalities.

My argument is that David Simon's twenty-first century televisual democratic socialism is best understood through how he links a central concern for structural and economic issues with a strong progressive representational practice. While Simon's serials are generally very progressive in how they depict, say, African Americans and sexual minorities, they nonetheless emphasize atextual issues like residential segregation, deindustrialization, drug policing, and gentrification as their core concerns. The most central example of Simon's exploration of structural issues is *The Wire*'s portrayal of how different social issues are interlinked. In a related fashion, *The Deuce* emphasizes how urban transformation is the structural background that fundamentally shapes the emergence of the pornographic industry.

Some of the structural issues that Simon's serials engage with, however, are somewhat difficult to dramatize, such as the demographic consequences of the marginalization of African Americans in New Orleans in the wake of Katrina and what that may do to the future make-up of Louisiana's political life. At one point, Davis McAlary talks to real-life political strategist Jacques Morial (Jacques Morial) who argues that "if New Orleans gets whiter the state slides from purple to red," that is, Louisiana will go from being a swing state

Conclusion   193

to becoming a safe state for Republicans in political elections. Morial qualifies his argument by saying: "The culture of New Orleans, that's what's at risk. If they knock out the infrastructure that sustains the culture, then it's gone forever." Davis starts riffing, wanting to write a song that speaks to the issue Morial is talking about, but he soon gets to meets a creative roadblock: "So, um, nothing really rhymes with infrastructure" (*Treme*, S1E7). This comic remark comes from the fact that Davis cannot find the creative entry point that will allow him to write a song about post-Katrina gentrification. *Treme* is here alluding to how some political issues are difficult to address in a specific art form.

The *Corner*'s six-part structure, for instance, barred Simon and Mills from speaking to the big societal issues like the war on drugs that were part of Burns and Simon's book. It could only speak to a narrower agenda about the humanization of inner-city residents struggling with drug addiction. This meant deemphasizing important societal issues regarding, for instance, policing. When Simon got the chance to produce *The Wire*, he foregrounded these broader social issues, which is seen especially in how season three's storyline about Major Colvin's Hamsterdam project focuses on policing in a way that *The Corner* only voiced rather subtly. Residential segregation is arguably also difficult to dramatize and it was only Nick Wasicsko's life story that offered *Show Me a Hero* a coherent character arc that allowed Simon, Zorzi, and Haggis to dramatize this facet of American urbanity.

Despite the narrative challenges inherent in dramatizing some structural realities in American society, Simon's serials nevertheless emphasize these greater structural issues like gentrification and the war on drugs. The serial's progressive representational politics are embedded in those interests. This way of linking a structural-economic leftist position with a cultural leftist sentiment is interesting insofar as it places Simon's politics as a bridge-builder between several left-leaning positions going back at least to the 1970s. To appreciate the contours of the politics in Simon's work thus requires a bit of context.

As mentioned, some historians argue that the 1970s–1980s saw both a strengthening of liberal cultural politics in relation to embracing formal equality and a greater degree of inclusivity, just as these decades also saw a swing to the right in economic thought. Historian Robert Collins argues that this shift happened in the 1980s (Collins

2009, 5 and 244). Borstelmann embraces Collins's argument but argues that its relevance "holds true for the sweep of American life since the 1970s" to when Borstelmann published his work in 2012. Borstelmann notes how wealth and income disparities have grown in that period, making class differences widen. But this disparity has not been attended to and so "Rather than addressing growing economic inequality, Americans tended instead to celebrate racial and ethnic diversity" (Borstelmann 2012, 280).

Simon counters this discursive dismissal of economic inequality in American society and politics. The boys in season four of *The Wire* are shown to be good children in a bad situation. Young Randy's (Maestro Harrell) storyline is especially interesting here. Randy has a very constructive attitude about how to approach life and has the strongest support system at home in the shape of his foster mother Miss Anna (Denise Hart), who tries her best to keep Randy out of trouble. But due to events out of his control, Randy is ultimately targeted by other children and his life trajectory is changed permanently. *The Wire* shows Randy's life to be fundamentally shaped by his impoverished environment in a way that is hard to evade.

Namond Brice (Julito McCullum) is the son of Wee-Bey Brice, who is part of Avon Barksdale's criminal organization. His mother embraces her husband's criminal life and berates her son for not being hard enough or not being careful enough when selling drugs (*TW*, S4E8 and S4E10). This style of child rearing is surely problematic and Namond's behavior is, of course, informed by his parents' lives and their way of seeing the world. He behaves poorly in school, but is pulled out of a bad situation when Bunny Colvin offers to adopt him (*TW*, S4E13). Randy, conversely, is the more well-behaved child, but he ends up in a boys' home. By showing how Namond's and Randy's life trajectories are ultimately shaped by their social contexts, *The Wire* emphasizes the importance of social circumstances for life opportunities. With implicit reference to the boys' storylines in season four, George Pelecanos later said that

> We answered the scurrilous claim and lie I've heard all my life, "Why can't those kids just work hard and get out of the ghetto?" We showed people why things are the way they are in an East Coast urban environment like that. Achieving that alone was something major and made me proud to be involved. (Pelecanos in HBO 2017)

This storyline embodies *The Wire*'s structural view on social ills and shows how this impoverished neighborhood restricts these boys' life opportunities.

The Deuce also portrays the consequences of social marginalization through several women's storylines that explore how sex work and the pornographic industry chew some women up. This theme is sounded from the earliest expository dialogue in season one's opening episodes all through several of the female storylines: Ruby, Lori, and also Eileen. In *Show Me a Hero* economic inequality is explored through how people living in marginalized neighborhoods are confronted with social problems, like Norma O'Neal who cannot get the help she needs in her own home because healthcare assistants are afraid to come to Schlobohm. This focus on structural inequalities, however, does not mean that Simon shies away from tackling cultural politics in relation to representational and diversity issues.

Indeed, Simon sees *Treme* as an argument for the viability of a multicultural city. The serial holds that New Orleans demonstrates how a very diverse city can work. For Simon it is not one issue over the other. But his serials' focus on, for example, housing and economic marginalization surely does not fit into that cultural liberal position that abandons a focus on economic equality for the sake of celebrating 'diversity.' Historian Thomas Frank takes this issue into the realm of politics at the federal level when he rhetorically asks "What ails the Democrats? So bravely forthright on cultural issues, their leaders fold with matters of basic economic democracy" (Frank 2016, 15). To Frank, dominant voices within the Democratic Party have abandoned the formerly strong links to the working class and as a result "issues of work and income inequality [has faded] from its list of concerns" (Frank 2016, 29–30). Frank's critique is part of a larger trend where, as Sugrue points out, several Democrats have been critical about how their party came to prioritize "cultural issues over economic concerns" (Sugrue 2010, 83). Simon's serials do emphasize progressive cultural politics, but socio-economic inequality is more central in his oeuvre.

In other words, Simon's oeuvre emphasizes both questions relating to the distribution of wealth and resources as well as to the (lack of) recognition of marginalized groups. But while his works offer 'solutions' in relation to the latter issue they more often point out problems in relation to the former. Simon's way of having representational issues oriented towards offering solutions includes *The Corner*'s and *The Wire*'s sympathetic portrayal of people struggling with addiction and *The Deuce*'s way of focalizing its story of the pornographic industry through sympathetic female porn actors and sex workers. It is, in general, another story when it comes to Simon's way of attending to issues about socio-economic injustices like, say, deindustrialization or a malfunctioning media culture in *The Wire* or the marginalization of sex workers in *The Deuce*. Here Simon's productions more often point out problems than voice solutions.

One aspect of cultural politics that has accompanied Simon throughout his career as a showrunner pertains to his portrayal of especially African American characters. In hindsight, it seems telling that the first article on Simon's career as a showrunner was titled "Who Gets to Tell a Black Story?" (Scott 2000), seeing as some critics have voiced concerns over how he depicts people from other walks of life than his own. The issue of whether *The Wire* was a case of white middle-class writers and producers unfairly depicting the African American underclass was raised already when the serial was still being produced. While screenwriter David Mills was working on *The Wire*, he responded to such objections that he was "somewhat sympathetic to the racialist critique of white middle-class writers presuming to tell black ghetto stories. But in the end, good art trumps everything" (Mills 2006). Mills and Simon had been friends since writing for the *The Diamondback* at the University of Maryland in their college days, and Mills is thus both guarding his old friend as well as his boss in the writers' room on *The Wire*. That, however, does not mean that his opinion is a mere consequence of those circumstances. To Mills, the ability to tell such stories comes not from a person's background but from having a particular skillset.

Simon does not accept that it is impossible for him to portray people from other walks of life than his own and this position seems inspired by his journalistic background. When Simon was promoting *The Plot Against America*, he argued in one interview that:

> I think you have to be Jewish-American or you at least have to be familiar with that milieu. It's not like you can't acquire it. You can. Nobody has to be something to write about it. I don't have to be an Irish cop or a black guy from West Baltimore to write *The Wire*. But you have to do the work. (Simon in Bilmes 2020)

Simon's position could be viewed as him making a virtue of out of necessity, that is, in order to tell the stories he produces he needs a form of justification that allows him to do so. His view could, however, be just as much informed by his journalistic experience as a reporter at *The Baltimore Sun*. It could also come from his experiences from when he spent a year in the Baltimore Police Department's homicide unit and then wrote a book on that, and later he and Ed Burns spent a year in West Baltimore which resulted in a second book of journalism that they then wrote together.

Simon has since explained his stance, saying that "I know my skillset. My skillset is I can acquire information. I have a good ear. I can listen to the way people talk and reproduce it. ... What I can't do is know a story before I acquire it. For that, I need to attend to other people and their realities" (Simon in Antholis 2019, episode 4). Simon is arguing that it is possible to know 'the other' and that he (and people in general) are able "to attend to other people and their realities" in a meaningful way. That position is foundational for his career as a storyteller. Pelecanos and Simon nonetheless charged screenwriter Will Ralston, a transgender man, with "help[ing] shepherd the gay story lines along through season one" of *The Deuce* as Ralston told a reporter after the first season's run (Ralston in Gould 2017). Simon and Pelecanos oversee the storylines but they use different outlooks represented in the writers' room to qualify their depictions of various social arenas.

Simon did concede, however, in a 2015 interview that he thinks he "did a poorer job in [his] earlier projects of writing women" (Simon in Clayton and Nigatu 2015), which some critics have also touched on. Lavik, for instance, notes how Marlo Stanfield's two enforcers in *The Wire*, Chris Partlow and Felicia "Snoop" Pearson, both are capable of murdering people in cold blood. However, when Chris violently beats young Michael Lee's father to death we learn that Chris – like Michael – was probably sexually abused as a child (*The Wire*, S4E10). *The Wire* reveals no such background information about Snoop and it is therefore unclear why she seems so emotionally detached from violence. The male murderer is humanized to a degree while the female one is not. Lavik similarly notes that characters like Rhonda Pearlman (Deirdre Lovejoy) and Theresa D'Agostino (Brandy Burre) are underdeveloped to a fault. Their personal lives are only explored through their relationships with McNulty. We never learn why Pearlman remains interested in a dysfunctional relationship with the wayward police detective. And while D'Agostino's purely sexual interest in McNulty makes *him* realize that he wants more out of a relationship than just sex, it never becomes clear why *she* acts in this way. In Lavik's assessment, D'Agostino is "one part male fantasy and one part storytelling prop" that can help further McNulty's character arc (Lavik 2014, 143–146).

Given the criticism *The Wire* faced with regards to its gender politics, it seemed obvious that more above-the-line women had to brought aboard when Simon and Pelecanos had gotten the go-ahead for *The Deuce*. This gender focus is, for instance, reflected in how 15 out of 25 its episodes are directed by women, though most writing credits go to men. Cognizant of how an all-male writers' room telling a story with substantial elements of gender inequalities may result in a skewed portrayal of especially female characters, Simon tells how he and the other producers were also "including several other women, a black writer and a transgender man" in order to discuss the writing so that it would not only be "the boy's version of the rise of pornography" as Simon put it (Simon, 2017). Michelle MacLaren directed the pilot and thus laid down the visual template that subsequent directors had to follow. Simon said on *Charlie Rose* that "*The Deuce* is an opportunity to discuss gender politics which we've done very little of" (Simon in Rose 2017). Simon seems perfectly aware that his earlier productions did not attend to gender issues, but HBO's decision to produce *The Deuce* gave him and Pelecanos a chance to explore this issue in relation to urban developments.

Despite such shortcomings, the way that Simon's serials broach both economic and cultural inequalities represents a counterargument of a position that philosopher Richard Rorty took issue with in the 1990s. Rorty lamented what he saw as the *cultural* Left's retreat from discussing economic issues to focus only on discussions about a "mind-set":

> When the Right proclaims that socialism has failed, and that capitalism is the only alternative, the cultural Left has little to say in reply. For it prefers not to talk about money. Its principal enemy is a mind-set rather than a set of economic arrangements – a way of thinking which is, supposedly, at the root of both selfishness and sadism. (Rorty 1999, 79)

Simon's way of showing African Americans in many walks of life is surely nuanced, demonstrating that he embraces one of the more prevalent issues that the cultural Left focuses on: media representation. But Simon's focus on economic issues surely places his politics outside the category of left-leaning thinkers than the ones Rorty criticizes in the above quote. Simon does not fit the description of a cultural Leftist whose "principal enemy is a mind-set rather than a set of economic arrangements." He emphasizes economics but not at the expense of *representational issues* regarding race or gender. This is not to argue that inequalities relating to gender and race are not related to economic issues. They most certainly are, but my argument is that the way Simon explores especially racial issues, and in *The Deuce* also gender issues, puts a premium on seeing race in relation to the economic realities of housing, which is seen in *Show Me a Hero* and *Treme*. This, then, ties into how Simon does not see *The Wire* as being principally about race, though some viewers may see it that way. He says that he has "always been fascinated that some people thought *The Wire* was about race. Race comes up for the characters. They talk about it. But the show was about how power and money route themselves and why we're no longer able to solve our problems as a society. It's a critique of that" (Simon in Dreifus 2018).

The Corner's humanization of people struggling with drug addiction takes issue with predominant discourses about inner cities and this miniseries thus counters this mind-set about these issues, but it also calls, somewhat discreetly, attention to the structural realities – that is "a set of economic arrangements" – that have informed the situation the miniseries portrays. And while *Show Me a Hero* shows how racist discourse plays on dog-whistle politics like when a very agitated woman at a town hall meeting talks of "these public housing people" (SMAH, E2), its main agenda is to show how American cities have remained segregated. It stresses the hard facts of bricks and mortar and does not focus on the more symbolic inequalities related to media representation.

Film scholar Richard Dyer argues that "Struggling over words is one of the most immediate, practical, day-to-day forms of what may be broadly characterized as left cultural politics" (Dyer 2000, 6). Struggles over words may come in the form of discussions about how a specific minority is portrayed in the media, but it can also focus on how specific *places* are depicted in various ways. Simon suggests that his serials can be seen "as travelogues of a kind. Here's a chance for you to go to a drug corner in West Baltimore. I know you're never going on your own" (Simon 2008). Cultural studies scholar Raymond Williams would agree, arguing that "watching dramatic simulation of a wide range of experiences is now an essential part of our modern cultural pattern" (Williams 2003, 56). Simon's point is that many people only encounter many areas of their society in mediated form. This means that there can be social ramifications to what audiences 'learn' about people, neighborhoods, and ways of life that they rarely, if ever, experience firsthand. This implicitly calls for a fair depiction of the neighborhoods that televisual productions show.

Simon's focus on structural realities like housing, deindustrialization, the war on drugs that has led to the incarceration of several hundred thousand African American men, gentrification, and suburbanization is a rebuttal of the tendency to *over*emphasize the celebration of "racial and ethnic diversity," in Borstelmann's words. He argues that this "de facto alliance [between cultural liberalism and economic conservatism] ... had become the contemporary American condition, the ground on which the vaunted American middle class continued to shrink" (Borstelmann 2012, 280). Literary critic Walter Benn Michaels argues that a too strong focus on how America attended to some inequalities in relation to racial and gender has obscured a sense of the growing economic inequalities in the U.S.:

> In 1947 – seven years before the Supreme Court decision in *Brown v. Board of Education*, sixteen years before the publication of Betty Friedan's *The Feminine Mystique* – the top fifth of American wage-earners made 43 per cent of the money earned in the US. Today that same quintile gets 50.5 per cent. In 1947, the bottom fifth of wage-earners got 5 per cent of total income; today it gets 3.4 per cent. After half a century of anti-racism and feminism, the US today is a less equal society than was the racist, sexist society of Jim Crow. (Michaels 2008, 33)

Michaels complicates an otherwise triumphalist narrative of post-war American history. For while both the civil rights and the women's movements have done important work in correcting many inequalities in American society, the wealth gap is increasing.

One part of this development is in part the result of deindustrialization, which Simon has often discussed in lectures and interviews. In *The Wire*'s second season, Nick Sobotka cannot get enough hours at the docks to earn enough money to buy a house that he can move into with his girlfriend Aimee and their young daughter. Nick lives in his parents' basement, which is a cause of conflict for the young couple, and Nick's first experience with crime is when he and his cousin Ziggy Sobotka steal a container full of cameras in order to sell them off to the criminal organization headed by The Greek (*TW*, S2E3). From that point Nick enters the drug trade, initially to help his cousin who has gotten himself into problems. The point is that Nick has very few outs in terms of providing for his family. Season two of *The Wire* thus has two functions in its elaboration of the drug trade plot from season one. One function is to show that the drug trade is not only an African American phenomenon. In Simon's eyes, *The Wire* had to change its core setting in order not to suggest that drug crime can be located only in poor African American communities. The other function of season two is to show how the world of the drug trade can represent one of the few sources of income in a world where skilled and unskilled laborers have an increasingly hard time finding work. In a 2011 PBS interview Simon said that

> Telling kids they shouldn't go sell drugs in Baltimore is like telling somebody they shouldn't be a coal miner in 1930 in West Virginia. What other jobs are there? […] The postindustrial economy doesn't need mass labor and factories. It doesn't need manufacturing. It needs information systems job. Jobs that are not here and aren't coming back to Baltimore. (Simon in Simon 2011)

Simon's point about the drug world here reads like a rebuttal of the "just say no" discourse associated with Nancy Reagan in the 1980s, which arguably framed wide-reaching societal issues as individual problems. The deindustrialization of America marginalized many people from the job market, a situation that has endured for decades (Linkon 2018) and Simon's way of connecting these two phenomena is very much in line with how *The Wire* depicted this connection. As the formalized and legal economy does not need or have room for them, some people have few opportunities. But turning to the illegitimate economy of the drug trade can help them sustain themselves and their families. Simon, speaking in 2011, furthered his argument by saying that "There is one America that is functional still even though it's in a recession. And there is another America that hasn't been functional for a long time and the two of them are going their separate ways" (Simon in Simon 2011).

Simon's project thus veers more towards discussions of class and structural inequalities regarding housing and deindustrialization rather than focusing on representational politics. His works are attentive to both structural and symbolic inequalities. This connects to his argument about envisioning America as a collected whole rather than as a scattered archipelago marked by residential segregation, concentrated poverty, and social marginalization. This stance is also a critique of negative discourses against the underclass as embodied by Ramona McAlary in *Treme*, the radio caller in *The Corner*, the dog-whistling anti-desegregationist Jack O'Toole in *Show Me a Hero*, and New York's political leadership's belief in gentrification as an adequate response to the 1970s urban crisis in *The Deuce*.

Simon and his creative team have been able to produce a range of serials with a distinct through-line over a twenty-year span. These stories all reach out into the world and take issue with specific social-historical issues. *The Corner* tackles the realities of the crack epidemic, emphasizing the need to humanize the people it afflicted. It takes on conservative discourses on inner-city problems, while also showing that Simon does not fit the bill of the liberal that evades discussions of problematic social behavior in inner-city neighborhoods. *The Wire*'s 60-episode run engages with a range of issues like deindustrialization, a troubled school system, and the war on drugs. Crucially, this serial emphasizes how these social issues need to be understood in relation to each other. "All the pieces matter," Lester Freamon says in one of the most thematically central lines in the serial (*TW*, S1E6). *The Wire*'s intricately networked narrative structure enables its sociological gaze in which everything is contextualized in relation to other social phenomena. *Treme*'s similarly intersecting storylines continue this gaze, but does so to explore the challenges brought about by Hurricane Katrina. This portrayal of New Orleans proclaims that the city as such is the place of the future while it also rebuts negative discourses about New Orleans after Katrina and anti-urbanism more broadly. *Show Me a Hero* zooms in on the consequences of residential segregation and suggests that the narrative of civil rights struggles needs to attend to the issue of housing, just as it needs to extend beyond the 1960s and beyond the South. Finally, *The Deuce* zooms in on economic marginalization of especially women during the urban crisis, and the pornographic industry here functions as a prism through which Simon and Pelecanos explore gender inequalities. By looking at all of Simon's serials together, we come to understand his take on the American city in a more elaborate way and we see how each production adds new nuances to his urban portrait. Simon's vision of American urbanity always looks at the problems the city faces, but maintains that the future of the city itself should be a core concern in American society in the twenty-first century.

References

Abrams, Jonathan (2018) *All the Pieces Matter: The Inside Story of The Wire*. New York: Crown Archetype.

Adams, Erik (2017) "This Week on The Deuce: A Dozen Characters in Search of a Brown Paper Bag." *The AV Club*, September 17. www.avclub.com/this-week-on-the-deuce-a-dozen-characters-in-search-of-1818496361

Akass, Kim (2015) "The Show that Refused to Die: The Rise and Fall of AMC's *The Killing*." *Continuum: Journal of Media & Cultural Studies* 29, no. 5: 743–754.

Alexander, Michelle (2010) *The New Jim Crow*. New York: The New Press.

Alvarez, Rafael, ed. (2010) *The Wire: Truth be Told*. Edinburgh: Canongate Books.

Andersen, Robin (2018) *HBO's Treme and the Stories of the Storm: From New Orleans as Disaster Myth to Groundbreaking Television*. New York: Lexington Books.

Anderson, Elijah (1999) *Code of the Street: Decency, Violence, and the Moral Life of the Inner City*. New York: W.W. Norton & Company.

Andreeva, Nellie (2014) "EMMYS: HBO's Michael Lombardo On The Decision To Enter 'True Detective' As Drama." *Deadline*, April 3. https://deadline.com/2014/04/true-detective-hbo-michael-lombardo-emmys-drama-709357/

Antholis, Kary (2019) "David Simon, *The Wire*, *The Corner* and *Homicide*." *The Crime Story Podcast with Kary Antholis*, episodes 24–27, September 23–26.

Azcona, María del Mar (2010) *The Multi-Protagonist Film*. Oxford: Wiley-Blackwell.

Badger, Emily (2015) "Obama Administration to Unveil Major New Rules Targeting Segregation across U.S." *Washington Post*, July 8.

Baldwin, Alec (2013) "David Simon." *Here's the Thing*, WNYC, June 10.

Beck, Richard (2008) "Beyond the Choir: An Interview with David Simon." *Film Quarterly* 62, no. 2: 44–49.

Beiser, Vince (2011) "An Interview with David Simon." *The Progressive*, February 28.
Belkin, Lisa (2015a) *Show Me a Hero*. London: Pan Books.
Belkin, Lisa (2015b) "'Show Me a Hero' Is 'More Resonant Today Than When I Wrote It.'" Interview by Vicky Gan. *CityLab*. August 17.
Bellafante, Ginia (2015) "Lessons of Yonkers From David Simon's 'Show Me a Hero'." *New York Times*. August 5.
Bennett, Tara (2014) *Showrunners: The Art of Running a TV Show*. London: Titan Books.
Berger, Joseph (1993) "Bafflement at Yonkers Official's Death." *New York Times*. October 31.
Bilmes, Alex (2020) "David Simon: 'There's Nothing To Do But Have The Fight.'" *Esquire*, July 11.
Bird, Jess (2020) "Fire in the Bronx: Austerity, Quality of Life, and Nightlife Regulation in New York City Post-1975." *Journal of Urban History* 46, no. 4: 836–853.
Bjerre, Thomas Ærvold (2011) "Authenticity and War Junkies: Making the Iraq War Real in Films and TV Series." *Journal of War and Culture Studies* 4, no. 2: 223–234.
Bluestone, Barry, and Bennett Harrison (1982) *The Deindustrialization of America*. New York: Basic Books.
Blum, Lawrence (2011). "'B5–it got all the Dinks': Schools and Education on 'The Wire'." *Darkmatter* 4.
Bordwell, David (2006) *The Way Hollywood Tells It. Story and Style in Modern Movies*. Berkeley, CA: University of California Press.
Bordwell, David (2011) "Alignment, Allegiance, and Murder." *Observations on Film Art* (blog). May 16.
Borstelmann, Thomas (2012) *The 1970s: A New Global History from Civil Rights to Economic Inequality*. Princeton, NJ: Princeton University Press.
Boustan, Leah Platt (2012) "Racial Residential Segregation in American Cities." In *The Oxford Handbook of Urban Economics and Planning*, edited by Nancy Brooks, Kieran Donaghy, and Gerrit-Jan Knaap, 318–339. Oxford: Oxford University Press.
Brøndal, Jørn (2016) *Det sorte USA*. Copenhagen: Gads Forlag.
Burns, Ed, and David Simon (1998) *The Corner: A Year in the Life of an Inner-City Neighborhood*. New York: Broadway Books.
Campbell, Donald (1976) *Assessing the Impact of Planned Social Change*. Hanover, NH: Public Affairs Center, Dartmouth College.
Carranza, Ashley Jae (2018) "The Rebirth of King's Children." In *Uncovering Stranger Things: Essays on Eighties Nostalgia, Cynicism and Innocence in the Series*, edited by Kevin J. Wetmore Jr., 8–19. McFarland & Company Inc.

CBS This Morning (2015) Hosted by Gayle King and Charlie Rose. August 13. www.youtube.com/watch?v=Y5uirvsPZ44

Chadda, Anmol, and William Julius Wilson (2011) "'Way Down in the Hole': Systemic Urban Inequality and *The Wire*." *Critical Inquiry* 38: 164–188.

Chadwick, Alex, and Alex Cohen (2008) "'Generation Kill' Ready to Deploy on HBO." *Day to Day*, NPR, March 19. www.npr.org/templates/story/story.php?storyId=92452344

Clayton, Tracy, and Heben Nigatu (2015) "Episode 23: The Audacity of Despair." *Another Round*, Buzzfeed, September 1.

Collins, Robert (2009) *Transforming America Politics and Culture During the Reagan Years*. New York: Columbia University Press.

Conn, Steven (2014) *Americans Against the City: Anti-Urbanism in the Twentieth Century*. New York: Oxford University Press.

Corkin, Stanley (2017) *Connecting The Wire: Race, Space, and Postindustrial Baltimore*. Austin, TX: University of Texas Press.

Cowie, Jefferson, and Joseph Heathcott (2003) "Introduction. The Meanings of Deindustrialization." In *Beyond the Ruins: The Meanings of Deindustrialization*, edited by Jefferson Cowie and Joseph Heathcott, 1–15. Ithaca, NY: ILR Press.

Crosby, Joanna (2013) "This Ain't Aruba, Bitch." In *The Wire and Philosophy: This America, Man*, edited by David Bzdak, Joanna Crosby, and Seth Vannatta, 3–11. Chicago: Open Court.

Crutcher, Jr., Michael (2010) *Tremé: Race and Place in a New Orleans Neighborhood*. Athens, GA: The University of Georgia Press.

Dessem, Matthew (2020) "What's the Deal With the Theme Song for *The Plot Against America*?" *Slate*, March 29. https://slate.com/culture/2020/03/plot-against-america-road-open-again-credits-theme-song-dick-powell-fdr-wilson-washington.html

deWaard, Andrew (2008) "The Geography of Melodrama, The Melodrama of Geography: The 'Hood Film's Spatial Pathos." *Cinephile* 4, no. 1: 58–65.

deWaard, Andrew (2012) "The Hood is Where the Heart Is: Melodrama, Habitus, and the Hood Film." In *Habitus of the Hood*, edited by Chris Richardson and Hans A. Skott-Myhre, 254–270. Bristol: Intellect.

Diawara, Manthia (1993) "Black American Cinema: The New Realism." In *Black American Cinema*, edited by Manthia Diawara, 3–26. New York: Routledge.

Dowler, Kenneth (2002) "Media Influence on Citizen Attitudes toward Police Effectiveness." *Policing and Society* 12, no. 3: 227–238.

Dreier, Peter, and John Atlas (2009) "*The Wire* – Bush-Era Fable about America's Urban Poor?" *City & Community* 8, no. 3: 329–340.

Dreifus, Claudia (2018) "The Guy Who Wouldn't Write a Hit: An Interview with David Simon." *New York Review of Books*, August 22.

DuBois, W.E.B. (2007/1903) *The Souls of Black Folk*. Oxford: Oxford University Press.

Duggan, Paul (2017) "Charge Upgraded to First-degree Murder for Driver Accused of Ramming Charlottesville Crowd." *Washington Post*, December 14.

Dunleavy, Trisha (2018) *Complex Serial Drama and Multiplatform Television*. London: Routledge.

Dybdal, Anders, ed. (2014) *Socialdemokratiske tænkere*. Copenhagen: Informations forlag.

Dyer, Richard (2000) *The Matter of Images: Essays on Representation*. New York: Routledge.

Etheridge, Blake D. (2008) "Baltimore on The Wire: The Tragic Moralism of David Simon." In *It's Not TV: Watching HBO in the Post-Television Era*, edited by Marc Leverette, Brian L. Ott, and Cara-Louise Buckley, 152–164. New York: Routledge.

Fisher, Jaimey (2019) *Treme*. Detroit, MI: Wayne State University Press.

Floto, Inga (2007) *Historie – en videnskabshistorisk undersøgelse*. Copenhagen: Museum Tusculanum Press.

Folkenflik, David, and Adam Waller (2020) "'The Plot Against America': HBO Series Imagines A Charles Lindbergh Presidency." *On Point*, WBUR, March 13. www.wbur.org/onpoint/2020/03/13/plot-against-america-hbo-series

Franich, Darren (2012) "David Simon Talks 'Treme,' America, and a Possible End to his TV Career: 'Maybe I'm in the Wrong Line of Work.'" *Entertainment Weekly*, September 23. https://ew.com/article/2012/09/23/david-simon-treme/

Frank, Thomas (2016) *Listen, Liberal*. New York: Metropolitan Books.

Friedman, Tami (2003) "'A Trail of Ghost Towns across Our Land': The Decline of Manufacturing in Yonkers, New York." In *Beyond the Ruins. The Meanings of Deindustrialization*, edited by Jefferson Cowie and Joseph Heathcott, 19–43. Ithaca, NY: ILR Press.

Fuqua, Joy V. (2012) "'In New Orleans, We Might Say It Like This ...' Authenticity, Place, and HBO's *Treme*." *Television & New Media* 13, no. 3: 235–242.

Gardner, Lee (2017) "David Simon Does Not Miss the Sleaziness." *CityLab*, October 16.

Gebauer, Matthias (2005) "Will the Big Easy Become White, Rich and Republican?" *Der Spiegel*, September 20. www.spiegel.de/international/new-orleans-after-katrina-will-the-big-easy-become-white-rich-and-republican-a-375496.html

George, Courtney (2012) "Keeping It "Reals": Narratives of New Orleans Jazz History as Represented in HBO's *Treme*." *Television & New Media* 13, no. 3: 225–234.

Glaeser, Edward, and Jacob Vigdor (2012) "The End of the Segregated Century: Racial Separation in America's Neighborhoods, 1890–2010." *Civic Report* 66: 1–28.

Golub, Mark (2020) "David Simon." *L'Chayim*. Jewish Broadcasting Service, June 18. https://jbspodcasts.podbean.com/e/lchayim-david-simon/

Goodman, Amy (2015) "Two Separate Americas: David Simon's New Mini-Series Looks at "Hypersegregation" in Public Housing." *Democracy Now!* August 26.

Gould, Richard (2017) "Spanning Pre to Post Across Coast to Coast – An Interview with Will Ralston." *Designing Sound*, December 22. https://designingsound.org/2017/12/22/spanning-pre-to-post-across-coast-to-coast-an-interview-with-will-ralston/

Gura, David (2015) "'Show Me A Hero' Creator David Simon on Yonkers, HBO, Race." *Bloomberg Television*. Interview with David Simon. August 15. www.youtube.com/watch?v=MqwOSv-o6mM

Haastrup, Helle Kannik (2006) "Den funktionelle intertekstualitet i mainstreamfilmen: Fordobling, distinktion og forklaring." *Norsk Medietidsskrift* 13, no. 1: 8–27.

Haastrup, Helle Kannik (2011) "Grænseoverskridende multi-protagonist-fortællinger: fra kunstfilm til Hollywood." *Akademik Quarter* 3: 269–280.

Hale, Grace Elizabeth (2011) *A Nation of Outsiders*. New York: Oxford University Press.

Hall, Jacqueline Dowd (2005) "The Long Civil Rights Movement and the Political Uses of the Past." *Journal of American History* 91, no. 4: 1233–1263.

Halskov, Andreas (2019) "When Television Grew Up: David Simon, Modern America and the Maturing of the TV Landscape." Interview with David Simon. *16:9*, October 25. www.16-9.dk/2019/10/david-simon/

Hartnell, Anna (2017) *After Katrina: Race, Neoliberalism, and the End of the American Century*. Albany, NY: State University of New York Press.

HBO (2015) "Miniseries Show Me a Hero Inside the Series Parts One and Two." November 22. www.youtube.com/watch?v=3fWlr3w0wxE

HBO (2017) "What David Simon and George Pelecanos Want You to Know About Their Shows." *hbo.com*. June 1. www.hbo.com/the-deuce/article/what-david-simon-and-george-pelecanos-want-you-to-know-about-their-shows

High, Steven (2013) "'The Wounds of Class': A Historiographical Reflection on the Study of Deindustrialization, 1973–2013." *History Compass* 11, no. 11: 994–1007.

Hindman, Douglas Blanks, and Kenneth Wiegand (2008) "The Big Three's Prime-Time Decline: A Technological and Social Context." *Journal of Broadcasting & Electronic Media* 52, no. 1: 119–135.
Inskeep, Steve (2008) "'Glory,' 'Wild Bunch' Among David Simon's DVD Picks." *Morning Edition*, National Public Radio, December 19. www.npr.org/templates/story/story.php?storyId=98494970
Ivie, Devon (2015) "The Set for David Simon's New Show Is Loaded With Some Pretty Snazzy '70s-Era Cars." *Vulture*, October 16.
Jackson, Kenneth T. (1985) *Crabgrass Frontier: The Suburbanization of the United States*. New York: Oxford University Press.
James, Osamudia R. (2015) "Now We Can Finally Say Goodbye to the White Savior Myth of Atticus." *New York Times*, July 15. www.nytimes.com/roomfordebate/2015/07/15/how-should-schools-deal-with-the-new-atticus-finch/now-we-can-finally-say-goodbye-to-the-white-savior-myth-of-atticus
Jaramillo, Deborah L. (2016) "*Generation Kill*: The Invasion of Iraq As Seen on HBO." *A Companion to the War Film*, edited by Douglas A. Cunningham and John C. Nelson, 305–319. Malden, MA: Wiley-Blackwell.
Jefferson, Thomas (1787) "Letter to James Madison." December 20. https://founders.archives.gov/documents/Madison/01-10-02-0210
Jensen, Eric L., Jurg Gerber, and Clayton Mosher (2004) "Social Consequences of the War on Drugs: the Legacy of Failed Policy." *Criminal Justice Policy Review* 15, no. 1: 100–121.
Jensen, Mikkel (2017) "'From the Mind of David Simon': A Case for the Showrunner Approach." *Series – International Journal of TV Serial Narratives* 3, no. 2: 31–42.
Jensen, Mikkel (2021) "Textual Agency: Quentin Skinner and Popular Media." *Series – International Journal of TV Serial Narratives* 7, no. 1: 19–29.
Johnson, Steven (2006) *Everything Bad is Good for You*. London: Penguin Books.
Kallas, Christina (2014a) *Inside the Writers' Room: Conversations with American TV Writers*. London: Palgrave Macmillan.
Kallas, Christina (2014b) "Inside the Writers' Room: Post #8: The Real Secret of Success of American TV, Part I." *Hope for Film* (blog), July 30. http://trulyfreefilm.hopeforfilm.com/2014/07/inside-the-writers-room-post-8-the-real-secret-of-success-of-american-tv-part-i.html
Kinder, Marsha (2008) "Re-Wiring Baltimore: The Emotive Power of Systemics, Seriality, and the City." *Film Quarterly* 62, no. 2: 50–57.
King, Jr., Martin Luther (1963) "March on Washington 'I Have a Dream' Speech." Speech given on August 28. In Richard D. Heffner and Alexander

B. Heffner, eds. (2018), *A Documentary History of the United States*, 409–412. New York, NY: Signet Classics.

Kois, Dan (2010) "Treme Recap: What You Need." *Vulture*, April 19. www.vulture.com/2010/04/treme_recap_what_you_need.html

Kollmeyer, Christopher (2018) "Trade Union Decline, Deindustrialization, and Rising Income Inequality in the United States, 1947 to 2015." *Research in Social Stratification and Mobility* 57: 1–10.

Koselleck, Reinhart (2004) *Futures Past: On the Semantics of Historical Time*. New York: Columbia University Press.

Langkjær, Birger (2012) *Realismen i dansk film*. Frederiksberg: Samfundslitteratur.

Lassen, Frank Beck, and Mikkel Thorup (2009) "Introduktion til Quentin Skinner og intellektuel historie." In *Quentin Skinner. Politik og historie*, edited by Frank Beck Lassen and Mikkel Thorup, 7–45. Copenhagen: Hans Reitzel.

Lavik, Erlend (2012a) "The Poetics and Rhetorics of *The Wire*'s Intertextuality." *Critical Studies in Television: The International Journal of Television Studies* 6, no. 1: 52–71.

Lavik, Erlend (2012b) "Style in The Wire." *Vimeo*. https://vimeo.com/39768998

Lavik, Erlend (2014) *Tv-serier: The Wire og den tredje gullalderen*. Oslo: Universitetsforlaget.

Lavik, Erlend (2015) *Forfatterskap i TV-drama: Showrunnermodellen, one vision – og Kampen for tilværelsen*. Oslo: Universitetsforlaget.

Lefebvre, Martin (2011) "On Landscape in Narrative Cinema." *Canadian Journal of Film Studies* 20, no. 1: 61–78.

Leovy, Jill (2015) *Ghettoside. A True Story of Murder in America*. New York: Spiegel & Grau.

Linkon, Sherry Lee (2018) *The Half-Life of Deindustrialization: Working-Class Writing about Economic Restructuring*. Ann Arbor, MI: The University of Michigan Press.

Lipsitz, George (2011) *How Racism Takes Place*. Philadelphia: Temple University Press.

Lister, Michael (2015) "'It's all in the Game': Citizenship as the 'Missing Middle.'" In *The Wire and America's Dark Corners: Critical Essays*, edited by Arin Keeble and Ivan Stacy, 67–80. Jefferson, NC: McFarland & Company, Inc.

Loury, Glenn C (1998) "Discrimination in the Post-Civil Rights Era: Beyond Market Interactions." *The Journal of Economic Perspectives* 12, no. 2: 117–126.

Love, Chris (2010) "Greek Gods in Baltimore: Greek Tragedy and *The Wire*." *Criticism* 52, nos. 3 & 4: 487–507.

Lynskey, Dorian (2018) "The Wire, 10 Years On: 'We Tore the Cover off a City and Showed the American Dream was Dead.'" *The Guardian*. March 6.

Madden, Caroline (2020) *Springsteen as Soundtrack: The Sound of the Boss in Film and Television*. Jefferson, NC: McFarland & Company Inc.

Mason, Wyatt (2010) "The HBO Auteur." *New York Times*, March 17.

McCabe, Janet, and Kim Akass (2008) "It's Not TV, it's HBO Original Programming." In *It's Not TV: Watching HBO in the Post-Television Era*, edited by Marc Leverette, Brian L. Ott, and Cara Louise Buckley, 83–93. London: Routledge.

McGuire, Patrick A. (2012) "A Conversation with David Simon, Creator of *The Wire*." In *Tapping into The Wire*, edited by Peter L. Beilenson and Patrick A. McGuire, ix–xviii. Baltimore, MD: Johns Hopkins University Press.

McMillan, Alasdair (2009) "Heroism, Institutions, and the Police Procedural." In *The Wire: Urban Decay and American Television*, edited by C.W. Marshall and Tiffany Potter, 50–63. London: Continuum.

Michaels, Walter Benn (2008) "Against Diversity." *New Left Review* 52, July/August: 33–36.

Michlin, Monica (2016) "Between Unsanitized Depiction and 'Sensory Overload': The Deliberate Ambiguities of *Generation Kill* (HBO, 2008)." *TV/Series* 9.

Mills, David (2006) "The Writer Speaks." *Slate*, October 9. https://slate.com/culture/2006/10/the-writer-speaks.html

Mills, David (2007) "Q&A: David Simon." *Undercover Black Man* (blog), January 22. http://undercoverblackman.blogspot.com/2007/01/q-david-simon-pt-1.html

Mills, Joel (2011) "WSU Honors Creator of The Wire on HBO." *The Lewison Tribune Online*, September 23.

Mittell, Jason (2015) *Complex TV: The Poetics of Contemporary Television Storytelling*. New York: New York University Press.

Moore, Edward E. (1992) "United States v. Yonkers Board of Education, 837 F.2d 1181 (2d Cir. 1987)." *The Urban Lawyer* 24, no. 3: 597–601.

Moskowitz, Peter (2017) *How To Kill a City. Gentrification, Inequality, and the Fight for the Neighborhood*. New York: Nation Books.

Newman, Michael Z (2006) "From Beats to Arcs: Toward a Poetics of Television Narrative." *The Velvet Light Trap* 58: 16–28.

Newman, Oscar (1996) *Creating Defensible Space*. Washington DC: Office of Policy Development and Research.

Nicolaides, Becky, and Andrew Wiese (2017) "Suburbanization in the United States after 1945." In *Oxford Research Encyclopedia, American History*, edited by Jon Butler, 1–53. Oxford: Oxford University Press.

O'Rourke, Meghan (2006) "Behind The Wire." *Slate*, December 1. https://slate.com/news-and-politics/2006/12/interviewing-the-man-behind-the-wire.html

Pallares-Burke, Maria Lúcia (2002) "Quentin Skinner." *The New History*, edited by Maria Lúcia Pallares-Burke, 212–240. Cambridge: Polity Press.

Pastore, Jr., Joseph M. (2007) "In Yonkers We Trust." *New York Times*. May 20. www.nytimes.com/2007/05/20/opinion/nyregionopinions/20WEpastore.html

Pearson, Jesse (2009) "David Simon." *Vice Magazine*, December 2.

Pearson, Roberta (2007) "Anatomising Gilbert Grissom. The Structure and Function of the Televisual Character." In *Reading CSI: Crime TV Under the Microscope*, edited by Michael Allen, 39–56. London: I.B. Tauris.

Pedersen, Carl (2016) "Martin Luther King, Jr." In *Amerikanske tænkere*, edited by Astrid Nonbo Andersen and Christian Olaf Christiansen, 299–319. Copenhagen: Informations Forlag.

Postlewait, Thomas (1996) "From Melodrama to Realism: The Suspect History of American Drama." In *Melodrama: The Cultural Emergence of a Genre*, edited by Michael Hays and Anastasia Nikolopoulou, 39–60. New York: St. Martin's Press.

Potts, Rolf (2013) "Treme's Big Problem: Authenticity." *The Atlantic*, November 27. www.theatlantic.com/entertainment/archive/2013/11/-em-treme-em-s-big-problem-authenticity/281857/

Quigley, William P. (2006) "Boating Out of New Orleans: Who Was Left Behind in Katrina and Who Is Left Behind Now?" *Clearinghouse Review. Journal of Poverty Law and Policy*: 149–158.

Radish, Christina (2015) "'Show Me a Hero' Writers David Simon and William F. Zorzi on Lengthy Development, HBO, and More." *Collider*, August 15.

Richman, Alan (2006) "Yes, We're Open." GQ, November 3. www.gq.com/story/katrina-new-orleans-food

Rochabrun, Marcelo (2015) "Show Me a Hero: a Q&A With David Simon." *Propublica*, August 21.

Roosevelt, Theodore (2012) "Hyphenated Americanism." In *The Gilded Age and Progressive Era: A Documentary Reader*, edited by William A. Link and Susannah J. Link, 165–169. Oxford: Wiley-Blackwell.

Rorty, Richard (1999) *Achieving Our Country: Leftist Thought in Twentieth-Century America*. Cambridge, MA: Harvard University Press.

Rose, Charlie (2015) *Charlie Rose*, August 12. Interview with David Simon and Oscar Isaac.

Rose, Charlie (2017) *Charlie Rose*, September 8. Interview with David Simon, George Pelecanos, Maggie Gyllenhaal, and James Franco.

Rose, Cynthia (1999) "The Originator of TV's 'Homicide' Remains Close to his Police-reporter Roots." *Seattle Times*, February 18. https://archive.seattletimes.com/archive/?date=19990218&slug=2944857

Rosenberg, Alyssa (2016) "'The Wire's' David Simon on the Drug War and Why he Hates 'Cops' and 'Law & Order'." *Washington Post*, October 24.

Rosenstone, Robert (2000) "Oliver Stone as Historian." In *Oliver Stone's USA*, edited by Robert Toplin, 26–39. Lawrence: University of Kansas.

Rosenstone, Robert (2001) "The Historical Film: Looking at the Past in a Postliterate Age." In *The Historical Film: History and Memory in Media*, edited by Marcia Landy, 50–66. New Brunswick, NJ: Rutgers University Press.

Rothstein, Richard (2017) *The Color of Law*. New York: Liveright Publishing Corporation.

Rowe, Mike (2014) "After, After 'The Wire.'" *Mikerowe.com*, November 10. http://mikerowe.com/2014/11/after-after-the-wire/

Rowthorn, Robert, and Ramana Ramaswamy (1997) "Deindustrialization – Its Causes and Implications." *Economic Issues* 10, Washington DC: International Monetary Fund.

Sagal, Peter (2017–2021) *The Plot Against America Podcast*. Interviews with David Simon. HBO.

Saraiya, Sonia (2015) "'You Tell Me That the Riots are a Good Thing? F*ck You. Come to Baltimore and Say That': David Simon on Police Brutality, the Legacy of 'The Wire' and the Future of American Cities." *Salon*, August 5. www.salon.com/2015/08/04/you_tell_me_that_the_riots_are_a_good_thing_fck_you_come_to_baltimore_and_say_that_david_simon_on_police_brutality_the_legacy_of_the_wire_and_the_future_of_american_cities/

Schelstraete, Jasper, and Gert Buelens (2013) "'This Game is Rigged': Dickens, *The Wire* and Money." *Dickens Quarterly* 30, no. 4: 288–298.

Scherstuhl, Alan (2016) "Stranger Things Is the Best-Ever Miniseries Adaptation of a Horror Novel (Even If That Novel Doesn't Exist)." *LA Weekly*, July 20. www.laweekly.com/film/stranger-things-is-the-best-ever-miniseries-adaptation-of-a-horror-novel-even-if-that-novel-doesn-t-exist-7154087

Scott, Janny (2000) "Who Gets to Tell a Black Story?" *New York Times*, June 11. www.nytimes.com/2000/06/11/us/who-gets-to-tell-a-black-story.html

Seligman, Ben B., and Harvey Swados (1948–1949) "Jewish Population in the United States." *The American Jewish Year Book* vol. 50: 651–690.

Sheehan, Helena, and Sheamus Sweeney (2009) "*The Wire* and the World: Narrative and Metanarrative." *Jump Cut* 51.

Siff, Stephen (2018) "'Why Do You Think They Call It Dope?': Richard Nixon's National Mass Media Campaign Against Drug Abuse." *Journalism & Communication Monographs* 20, no. 3: 172–247.

Simon, David (2008) *The Audacity of Despair*. Lecture at The Doreen B. Townsend Center for the Humanities, September 10. www.youtube.com/watch?v=nRt46W3k-qw

Simon, David (2009) "Introduction." In *The Wire: Truth Be Told*, edited by Rafael Alvarez, 1–36. New York: Grove Press.

Simon, David (2012) "Commencement Address, Georgetown University." *The Audacity of Despair*, May 12.

Simon, David (2014a) "Robin Williams: A Brief Encounter." *The Audacity of Despair*. August 12.

Simon, David (2014b) "The Wire and Baltimore." *The Audacity of Despair*. November 11.

Simon, David (2015) "Foreword." ix–xiv. In Lisa Belkin's *Show Me a Hero*.

Simon, David (2018) "Tony." *The Audacity of Despair*, June 11.

Smith, David (2017) "David Simon: 'If you're not Consuming Porn, you're Still Consuming its Logic'." *The Guardian*, September 10.

Simon, Scott (2011) *Need to Know*. PBS, October 6. www.pbs.org/video/need-to-know-the-corner/

Smith, Murray (1995) *Engaging Characters: Fiction, Emotion, and the Cinema*. Oxford: Clarendon Press.

Sobchack, Vivian (1999) "Cities on the Edge of Time: The Urban Science Fiction Film." In *Alien Zone II: The Spaces of Science Fiction Cinema*, edited by Annette Kuhn, 123–143. London: Verso.

Sugrue, Thomas (2009) *Sweet Land of Liberty*. New York: Random House.

Sugrue, Thomas (2010) *Not Even Past: Barack Obama and the Burden of Race*. Princeton, NJ: Princeton University Press.

Sugrue, Thomas (2014) *The Origins of the Urban Crisis*. Princeton: Princeton University Press.

Sugrue, Thomas (2018) "A Decent-Sized Foundation: Obama's Urban Policy." In *The Presidency of Barack Obama: A First Historical Assessment*, edited by Julian E. Zelizer, 144–161. Princeton, NJ: Princeton University Press.

Sunstein, Cass (2016) "Historical Explanations Always Involve Counterfactual History." *Journal of the Philosophy of History* 10, vol. 3: 433–440.

Sweeney, Sheamus (2013) "From Here to the Rest of the World": Crime, Class and Labour in David Simon's Baltimore." PhD dissertation, Dublin: Dublin City University.

Talbot, Margaret (2007) "Stealing Life. The Crusader Behind 'The Wire'." *The New Yorker*. October 22.

Taylor, J.D. (2015) "The Paper Bag Compromise: Hiding the Problem of Drug Dependency in Hamsterdam." In *The Wire and America's Dark Corners: Critical Essays*, edited by Arin Keeble and Ivan Stacy, 95–113. Jefferson, NC: MacFarland & Company, Inc.

Teaford, Jon C. (2006) *The Metropolitan Revolution: The Rise of Post-Urban America*. New York: Columbia University Press.

Teaford, Jon C. (2016) *The Twentieth-Century American City*, 3rd edition. Baltimore, MD: Johns Hopkins University Press.

Thompson, E.P. (1966) *The Making of the English Working Class*. New York: Vintage Books.

Thompson, Kristin (2003) *Storytelling in Film and Television*. Harvard, MA; Harvard University Press.

Trifun, Natasha M. (2009) "Residential Segregation after the Fair Housing Act." *Human Rights Magazine* 36, no. 4: 14–19.

Trotta, Joe, and Oleg Blyahher (2011) "Game Done Changed: A Look at Selected AAVE Features in the TV Series *The Wire*." *Moderna Språk* 105, no. 1: 15–42.

Tuck, Stephen (2012) *We Ain't What We Used To Be*. Cambridge, MA: Belknap Press.

Turner, Frederik Jackson (1998) *Rereading Frederick Jackson Turner*. New Haven, CT: Yale University Press.

United States Census (2010) "Census Urban and Rural Classification and Urban Area Criteria." www.census.gov/geo/reference/ua/urban-rural-2010.html

Velocci, Carli (2017) "How HBO's 'The Deuce' Avoids Crossing the Line Into Sexual Exploitation." *The Wrap*, September 12. www.thewrap.com/how-the-deuce-works-not-to-cross-the-sexually-exploitive-line/

Vest, Jason P. (2011) *The Wire, Deadwood, Homicide, and NYPD Blue: Violence is Power*. Santa Barbara, CA: Praeger.

Vint, Sherryl (2013) *The Wire*. Detroit, MI: Wayne State University Press.

Vito, John De, and Frank Tropea (2010) *Epic Television Miniseries: A Critical History*. Jefferson, NC: MacFarland & Company, Inc.

Wacquant, Loïc (2008) *Urban Outcasts. A Comparative Sociology of Advanced Marginality*. Cambridge: Polity Press.

Ward, Brian (2006) "People Get Ready": Music and the Civil Rights Movement of the 1950s and 1960s." *History Now* 8 (June).

Weingarten, Christopher R. (2016) "'Stranger Things': Meet the Band Behind Show's Creepy, Nostalgic Score." *Rolling Stone*, August 1. www.rollingstone.com/music/music-features/stranger-things-meet-the-band-behind-shows-creepy-nostalgic-score-247138/

Weiss, Joanna (2008) "Baltimore to Baghdad." *Boston.com*, July 6. http://archive.boston.com/ae/tv/articles/2008/07/05/baltimore_to_baghdad/

White, Morton, and Lucia White (1962) *The Intellectual Versus the City*. Harvard University Press and MIT Press.

Williams, Linda (1998) "Melodrama Revised." In *Refiguring American Film Genres*, edited by Nick Browne, 42–88. Berkeley: University of California Press.

Williams, Linda (2014) *On The Wire*. Durham, NC: Duke University Press.
Williams, Raymond (2003) *Television: Technology and Cultural Form*. London: Routledge.
Wilson, William Julius (1997) *When Work Disappears*. New York: Vintage Books.
Wilson, William Julius (2012) *The Truly Disadvantaged*, 2nd edition. New York: Vintage Books.
Wollaston, Sam (2009) "It Looks More Real Than Anything I've Ever Seen." *The Guardian*, January 14. www.theguardian.com/world/2009/jan/14/generation-kill-the-wire
Woods, Sean (2015) "'Show Me a Hero': David Simon Is Still Mad as Hell." *Rolling Stone*, August 11. www.rollingstone.com/politics/politics-news/show-me-a-hero-david-simon-is-still-mad-as-hell-36834/

Television Series

Daredevil (2015–2018) Directed by Phil Abraham, Stephen Surjik, Peter Hoar et al. and written by Drew Goddard, Luke Kalteux et al. Netflix.
Generation Kill (2008) Directed by Susanna White and Simon Cellan Jones and written by David Simon, Ed Burns, and Evan Wright. HBO.
GLOW (2017–2019) Directed by Jesse Peretz, Lynn Shelton et al. and written by Liz Flahive and Carly Mensch. Netflix.
Homicide: Life on the Street (1993–1999) Directed by Kenneth Fink, Alan Taylor, Barry Levinson et al. and written by Tom Fontana, James Yoshimura, Anya Epstein et al. NBC.
Iron Fist (2017–2018) Directed by John Dahl, Stephen Surjik et al. and written by Scott Buck, M. Raven Metzner et al. Netflix.
Jessica Jones (2015–2019) Directed by Stephen Surjik, Jennifer Getzinger, Uta Briesewitz et al. and written by Melissa Rosenberg, Hilly Hicks Jr., Jamie King et al. Netflix.
Luke Cage (2016–2018) Directed by Andy Goddard, Marc Jobst, Clark Johnson et al. and written by Cheo Hodari Coker, Akela Cooper, Aïda Mashaka Croal et al. Netflix.
Roots (1977) Directed by Marvin J. Chomsky, David Greene et al. and written by Alex Haley, James Lee et al. ABC.
Show Me a Hero (2015) Directed by Paul Haggis and written by William F. Zorzi and David Simon. HBO.
The Corner (2000) Directed by Charles S. Dutton and written by David Simon and David Mills. HBO.
The Defenders (2017) Directed by S. J. Clarkson et al. and written by Douglas Petrie and Marco Ramirez et al. Netflix.

The Deuce (2017–2019) Directed by Michelle and MacLaren, James Franco et al. and written by George Pelecanos, David Simon et al. HBO.

The Plot Against America (2020) Directed by Thomas Schlamme and Minkie Spiro and written by David Simon, Ed Burns, and Reena Rexrode. HBO.

The Sophisticated Gents (1981) Directed by Harry Falk and written by Phyllis Minoff, Melvin Van Peebles. NBC.

The Walking Dead (2010–2022) Episodes 1–177. Directed by Greg Nicotero, Michael E. Satrazemis, Ernest R. Dickerson and written by Frank Darabont, Robert Kirkman, Scott M. Gimple et al. AMC.

The West Wing (1999–2006) Directed by Christopher Misiano, Alex Graves, Thomas Schlamme et al. and written by Aaron Sorkin, Debora Cahnm, Eli Attie et al. NBC.

The Wire (2002–2008) Directed by Clark Johnson, Ed Bianchi et al. and written by David Simon, Ed Burns, George Pelecanos et al. HBO.

Treme (2010–2013) Directed by Agnieszka Holland, Anthony Hemingway, Ernest Dickerson et al. and written by David Simon, Eric Overmyer, David Mills, George Pelecanos et al. HBO.

When the Levees Broke (2006–2007) Directed by Spike Lee.

Films

Adaptation (2002) Directed by Spike Jonze. Screenplay by Charlie Kaufman. Sony Pictures Releasing.

Blue Collar (1978) Directed by Paul Schrader. Screenplay by Paul and Leonard Schrader. Universal Pictures.

Boyz n the Hood (1991) Written and directed by John Singleton. Columbia Pictures.

Clockers (1995) Directed by Spike Lee. Screenplay by Richard Price and Spike Lee. Universal Pictures.

Deep Throat (1972) Directed and written by Gerard Damiano. Bryanston Distributing Company.

Dirty Harry (1971) Directed by Don Siegel. Written by Harry Julian Fink, R.M. Fink, and Dean Riesner. Warner Bros.

Just Mercy (2019) Directed by Destin Daniel Cretton. Screenplay by Destin Daniel Cretton and Andrew Lanham. Warner Bros.

Menace II Society (1993) Directed by the Hughes Brothers. Screenplay by Tyger Williams. New Line Cinema.

Platoon (1986) Directed and written by Oliver Stone. Orion Pictures.

Schindler's List (1993) Directed by Steven Spielberg. Written by Steven Zaillian. Universal Pictures.

Selma (2014) Directed by Ava DuVernay. Screenplay by Paul Webb. Paramount Pictures.

The Omega Man (1971) Directed by Boris Sagal. Screenplay by John and Joyce Corrington. Warner Bros.

The Rosa Parks Story (2002) Directed by Julie Dash. Screenplay by Paris Qualles. CBS.

The Searchers (1956) Directed by John Ford. Screenplay by Frank S. Nugent. Warner Bros.

The Wild Bunch (1969) Directed by Sam Peckinpah. Screenplay by Walon Green and Sam Peckinpah. Warner Bros.-Seven Arts.

United States v. Yonkers Board of Education (1987) 837 F. 2d 1181. December 28. https://openjurist.org/837/f2d/1181/united-states-v-yonkers-board-of-education

48 Hours (1988) "Not on My Street." Directed by Eric Shapiro. Written by Thomas Flynn. CBS. September 29.

Index

1st Reconnaissance Battalion 179, 181, 185
14th Amendment 125–126

Abby *see* Parker, Abigail "Abby"
Adams, Erik 162
Adaptation 95
Aimee (character on *The Wire*) 77–78, 201
Akass, Kim 51
Albrecht, Chris 50
Alexander, Michelle 81, 85
Alston, Chris (character on *The Deuce*) 159–161, 167–168
Alvarez, Rafael 7
Andersen, Robin 11, 91, 109
Anderson, Elijah 77
Anderson, Paul Thomas 96
Annie (character on *Treme*) 95, 98, 107
antisemitism 188–190
anti-urbanism 111–114, 172, 174, 202
Arnie (character on *Treme*) 103
Ashley *see* Spina, Dorothy "Ashley"
Atlanta 163
Atlas, John 28, 81, 84
Azcona, María del Mar 52, 96

Baker, Darrin "Doughboy" (character in *Boyz n the Hood*) 29
Baltimore 1–2, 9, 13–14, 17, 19–20, 28, 30, 32, 40, 42, 48, 52, 56, 60, 63–65, 69, 72, 74–75, 77, 79, 83–84, 94, 100, 110, 128–129, 133, 144–145, 164, 175, 197, 201
Barksdale, Avon (character on *The Wire*) 52, 93, 96, 194
Barksdale, D'Angelo (character on *The Wire*) 54, 81
Batiste, Antoine (character on *Treme*) 97, 109–110, 114
Batiste-Williams, LaDonna (character on *Treme*) 92–93, 97, 104–105, 111
Belkin, Lisa 115, 125, 130–131, 134, 138, 172
Bell, Stringer (character on *The Wire*) 62, 96, 175, 178
Bellafante, Ginia 140–141
Bengelsdorf, Lionel (character on *The Plot Against America*) 187
Bernette, Creighton (character on *Treme*) 11, 87–89, 92, 95, 97, 107
Bernette, Sofia (character on *Treme*) 97
Bernette, Toni (character on *Treme*) 89, 92–95, 97
Bernstein, Carl 6

Betts, Omar Isaiah "Snot Boogie" (character on *The Wire*) 47, 91
Bjerre, Thomas 179–180
Blown Deadline Productions 186
Blue (character on *The Corner*) 161
Blue Collar (film) 76
Bluestone, Barry 73
Boice, Veronica "Ronnie" (character on *The Corner*) 21, 35–37
Bordwell, David 34, 54
Borstelmann, Thomas 146, 170, 194, 200
Boyd, Francine (character on *The Corner*) 18, 23, 31–32, 34–35, 37, 44, 161
Boyz n the Hood (film) 25–29, 46
Brice, Namond (character on *The Wire*) 194
Brice, Roland "Wee-Bey" (character on *The Wire*) 93, 194
Broadus, Preston "Bodie" (character on *The Wire*) 40–41, 55–56, 93, 175
the Bronx 146, 165
Brooks, David "Daymo" (character on *Treme*) 92–93, 97
Brother Mouzone (character on *The Wire*) 62
Brown v. Board of Education 119–120, 124, 200
Brown, Larry (character on *The Deuce*) 148–149
Bubbles *see* Cousins, Reginald
Burns, Ed 5–6, 8, 26, 37–39, 41, 45, 60, 82, 174–175, 179–181, 183–185, 188, 190–191, 193, 197

Campbell, Donald T. 58–60
Candy *see* Merrell, Eileen "Candy"
capitalism 2, 103, 145–146, 169, 192, 198
Captain America *see* McGraw, Dave "Captain America"
Carcetti, Thomas (character on *The Wire*) 52, 72
Carter, Jimmy 135, 173
Carver, Ellis (character on *The Wire*) 53, 81–82
Cash, Johnny 184
C.C. (character on *The Deuce*) 155–158, 161, 169, 170
Chadda, Anmol 61
Charlie Rose (TV show) 140, 146, 169, 198
Charlottesville 186
Chase, David 49, 51
Chopin, Kate 95
Civil Rights Act of 1964 119–121
civil rights movement 22, 119–121, 123–125, 142
clearance rates 56–59, 160
Clinton, Hillary 169
Colbert, Brad "Iceman" (character on *Generation Kill*) 180–183
Collins, Robert 193–194
Colson, Terry (character on *Treme*) 92–94
Colvin, Howard "Bunny" (character on *The Wire*) 52–53, 62, 81–83, 159, 162, 193–194
Common Ground (book) 124
concentrated disadvantage 42–44, 75, 136–137
Conn, Steven 3–4, 111–113, 163
Corkin, Stanley 40–41
counterfactual history 189–190
Cousins, Reginald "Bubbles" (character on *The Wire*) 13–15, 40, 45, 53, 65, 74, 80, 94, 130, 133, 145, 165
cowboy 62–69
Cowie, Jefferson 71

Index

Coxson, Nat (character on *The Wire*) 71
crack epidemic 18, 85, 202
Crenshaw Mafia Brothers 25–27
Crutcher, Michael 87
Cutty *see* Wise, Dennis "Cutty"

D'Agostino, Theresa (character on *The Wire*) 197–198
Daniels, Cedric (character on *The Wire*) 64, 66
Darlene *see* Pickett, Donna "Darlene"
Davis, Clay (character on *The Wire*) 74, 80
Dawson, Zenobia (character on *The Wire*) 61
de jure and *de facto* segregation 121, 123
Debs, Eugene 186
defensible space 139
deindustrialization 1, 17, 57, 69–80, 128–129, 177, 192, 196, 200–202
Democratic Party 191, 192, 195
Desautel, Janette (character on *Treme*) 95, 97, 109–110, 114
Detroit 78
Diawara, Manthia 26
DiBiago, Bruce (character on *The Wire*) 74–76
Dickens, Charles 83–84
Digable Planets 122
Diggins, Claude (character on *The Wire*) 69–70
Dirty Harry (film) 63
Dominican Republic 120
Dorman, Mary (character on *Show Me a Hero*) 131, 138–139
Dowler, Kenneth 89
Downey, Chris 8
Dreier, Peter 28, 81, 84
DuBois, W.E.B. 4
Dunleavy, Trisha 9, 62

Dutton, Charles S. 17, 20, 25, 29–32, 35–36, 38, 41, 45
Dyer, Richard 199

Edward Tilghman Middle School 59

Fair Housing Act of 1968 121, 126
Fat Curt (character on *The Corner*) 32
Fat Mooney (character on *The Deuce*) 148, 155–156
Febles, Carmen (character on *Show Me a Hero*) 120, 127, 133, 135–138, 145
Federal Housing Administration 121, 141
feminism 152–154
Fick, Nathaniel (character on *Generation Kill*) 181–182
Finkel, Dora (character on *The Plot Against America*) 187–188
Finkel, Evelyn (character on *The Plot Against America*) 187
Fitzgerald, F. Scott 130
Flanagan, Danny (character on *The Deuce*) 159
Flashback 19–22, 24, 34, 86, 100
Fontana, Tom 9–10, 49
Forster, E.M. 61
Frank, Thomas 195
Freamon, Lester (character on *The Wire*) 55, 63–64, 69, 74, 202
Freamon, Tyreeka (character on *The Corner*) 18, 25, 35
Frog (character on *The Wire*) 77
Fuqua, Joy 109–110

gender representation
  in *The Deuce* 147, 155, 170–171, 198–199
  in *The Wire* 197–198
Generation Kill (TV series) 8, 16, 23, 98, 179–185, 190

gentrification 200
  in *The Deuce* 144, 167–168, 202
  in *The Wire* 72
  in *Treme* 91–92, 99, 103, 193
George, Courtney 108
Goldman, Gene (character on *The Deuce*) 167–168
Greek mythology 66, 86
Greggs, Kima (character on *The Wire*) 55, 57, 60, 81, 83, 133

Haastrup, Helle Kannik 53, 64
Haggis, Paul 10–11, 129, 193
Hale, Grace 63, 69
Hall, Jacqueline Dowd 119–120, 124–125, 142
Hamsterdam 53, 193
Harrison, Bennett 73
Hartnell, Anna 103
Hauk, Thomas (character on *The Wire*) 81–82
HBO 6–7, 10, 11, 23, 38, 41, 48–51, 85, 170, 174, 185–186, 191, 198
Heathcott, Joseph 71
Henderson, Doreen (character on *Show Me a Hero*) 133, 135–139, 145
Henry (character on *Treme*) 108
Hidalgo, Nelson (character on *Treme*) 102–105, 114
Hill Street Blues 53
Hinze, Annika 173
Hitler, Adolf 186, 190
Hodas, Marty 152, 154–155
Homicide: A Year on the Killing Streets (book) 9
Homicide: Life on the Street (TV series) 9–10, 17, 33, 44–45, 110
Hood films 27, 29, 46
Hooks, Benjamin (character on *Show Me a Hero*) 118

Horseface (character on *The Wire*) 80
Housing Act of 1949 141–42
humanization and dehumanization
  in *The Corner* 12, 18–19, 29, 31–35, 44–46, 56, 86, 128, 145, 193, 197, 199, 202
  in *The Wire* 175, 197
Hurricane Katrina 11, 12, 88, 90–92, 94, 97–99, 101–105, 107, 111, 113, 192–193, 202

Ianniello, Matty "The Horse" (character on *The Deuce*) 152–155, 157, 170
Ifill, Sherrilyn 120
Innes, Shardene (character on *The Wire*) 69
intertextuality
  in *Generation Kill* 180, 183–184
  in *The Corner* 24–29, 32, 183
  in *The Deuce* 165
  in *The Wire* 63–65, 86, 89
  in *Treme* 95

Jackson, Kenneth 121–122
James, Osamudia R. 137
Jaramillo, Deborah L. 182, 185
jazz funeral 87
Jefferson, Thomas 112
Jeffries, Anna (character on *The Wire*) 194
Jethro Tull 122
joblessness 75
Johnson, Marc Henry 146
Jordan, Michael B. 174
Judaism 32, 35, 45, 186–189, 196–197
Judd, Dennis 173
Just Mercy (film) 142

Kallas, Christina 9
Kinder, Marsha 57, 84
King, Gayle 10

King Jr., Martin Luther 14, 29
Kois, Dan 107
Kollmeyer, Christopher 71
Koselleck, Reinhart 139, 162–163
Krawczyk, Andy (character on *The Wire*) 72–73
Lambreaux, Albert (character on *Treme*) 90, 96–101, 104–107, 110–112, 114
Lambreaux, Davina (character on *Treme*) 90, 112
Lambreaux, Delmond (character on *Treme*) 97–98, 108
Landsman, Jay (character on *The Wire*) 64
Langkjær, Birger 176–177
Lassen, Frank Beck 25
Lavik, Erlend 33, 51, 54, 55–56, 60–61, 63–64, 85, 86, 96, 129, 197–198
Lee, Harper 137
Lee, Michael (character on *The Wire*) 80, 197
Lefebvre, Martin 168
Legacy of Ashes 6
Leovy, Jill 28, 58, 161
Letort, Delphine 118
Levin, Alvin (character on *The Plot Against America*) 189–191
Levin, Elizabeth "Bess" (character on *The Plot Against America*) 186–189
Levin, Herman (character on *The Plot Against America*) 186–190
Levittowns 122
Lewandowski, Jerome (character on *The Wire*) 74
Liguori, C.J. (character on *Treme*) 103–104
Lil Calliope (character on *Treme*) 98
Lilley, Jason (character on *Generation Kill*) 184

Lindbergh, Charles (character on *The Plot Against America*) 185–191
Lindsay, John 160
Lipsitz, George 28, 125, 128–129, 165
Little, Omar (character on *The Wire*) 62, 80, 170, 178
Loury, Glenn 121
Luddites 71, 73

MacLaren, Michelle 198
Madden, Caroline 117
Madison, James 112
Madison, Lori (character on *The Deuce*) 149–150, 152, 155–159, 161, 177, 179, 195
Major Crimes Unit 48, 57–58, 60, 64, 66–68, 72, 74, 80, 89, 96, 100, 129, 145
Manhattan 144, 146, 149, 157, 165, 167–168, 172
March on Washington for Jobs and Freedom 29, 124
Mardi Gras Indians 87, 96, 104
Martin, Brett 49–50
Martinelli, Angelo (character on *Show Me a Hero*) 115, 132
Martino, Frankie (character on *The Deuce*) 145–146, 157
Martino, Vincent (character on *The Deuce*) 145–146, 159, 165–170
Mayfield, Curtis 22
Mayhawk, Robert (character on *Show Me a Hero*) 133
McAlary, Davis (character on *Treme*) 96, 97–100, 108, 111, 192–193
McAlary, Ramona (character on *Treme*) 98–99, 202
McCabe, Janet 51
McCullough, DeAndre (character on *The Corner*) 18, 21, 25–32, 34–35, 44

McCullough, Gary (character on *The Corner*) 18–25, 30–39, 41–42, 44–45, 56, 65, 100, 127, 145, 161, 174
McCullough, Ricardo (character on *The Corner*) 36–37
McGraw, Dave "Captain America" (character on *Generation Kill*) 182
McKee, Robert (character in *Adaptation*) 95
McMillan, Alasdair 85
McNulty, Jimmy (character on *The Wire*) 13, 22, 47, 55, 57–60, 62–70, 93, 130, 133, 176–177, 179, 197–198
Mello, Dennis (character on *The Wire*) 64
melodrama 30–32, 65, 102
Merrell, Eileen "Candy" (character on *The Deuce*) 22, 147–157, 159, 165, 170–171, 195
Michaels, Walter Benn 200
Michlin, Monica 185
Mills, David 8–10, 22, 38, 41–42, 45, 193, 196
Miss Anna *see* Jeffries, Anna
Miss Ella *see* Thompson, Ella
Mississippi Burning (film) 118, 124
Mittell, Jason 20, 22–23, 49, 53, 56, 60, 104, 154
Moreland, Bunk (character on *The Wire*) 55, 67–68, 83
Moskowitz, Peter 72, 91, 99
multi-protagonist narratives 176
 in *The Deuce* 145
 in *The Wire* 52–53
 in *Treme* 97
 in *Show Me a Hero* 122

NBC 9, 10, 17, 48, 49
New Deal 141, 190
New Jersey 149, 187–189
New Orleans 11, 87–114, 163, 172, 192–193, 195, 202
New York City 2, 46, 109, 115, 143, 144, 146, 155, 158, 162–169, 202
New York Times 35, 140, 144
Newman, Michael Z. 177
Newman, Oscar (character on *Show Me a Hero*) 42–43, 118
Nixon, Richard 89
Noble, Nina Kostroff 5
NYPD Blue (TV series) 10

O'Neal, Norma (character on *Show Me a Hero*) 15, 133, 136–137, 145, 195
O'Toole, Jack (character on *Show Me a Hero*) 132, 202
opening credits 190
Operation Iraqi Freedom 181
Orlean, Susan 95
Overmyer, Eric 51, 87, 90, 92, 103, 105, 110, 113–114
over-policing and under-policing 159–162
Oz (TV series) 48–50

Parker, Abigail "Abby" (character on *The Deuce*) 165–168
Partlow, Chris (character on *The Wire*) 100, 129, 197
Patterson, Bryan (character on *Generation Kill*) 182
Pearl Harbor 190
Pearlman, Rhonda (character on *The Wire*) 197–198
Pearson, Felicia "Snoop" (character on *The Wire*) 100, 129, 197
Pearson, Roberta 22
Peckinpah, Sam 63
Pedersen, Carl 119
Pelecanos, George 5, 7–8, 143, 145–147, 168–170, 174, 177, 194, 197–198, 203

Person, Josh (character on *Generation Kill*) 181–182, 185
Pickett, Donna "Darlene" (character on *The Deuce*) 148–149
Platoon (film) 179–180
Polan, Dana 50
policing 58, 81–82, 86, 159–162, 167, 192–193
pornography 1–2, 143, 146–152, 155, 157, 159, 161–162, 165–166, 169–170, 174, 177–178, 192, 195–196, 198, 203
Postlewait, Thomas 30
Potts, Rolf 102–103, 107
Pretty Woman (film) 174
Price, Richard 7
progressives 3–4, 113
Proposition Joe *see* Stewart, Joseph "Proposition Joe"
prostitution *see* sex work
Pruitt-Igoe 42
Pryzbylewski, Roland (character on *The Wire*) 59
Public Enemy 122
Pullman, Alexander (character on *The Deuce*) 150–151
Pulp Fiction (film) 96

Quigley, Bill 104

Rains, Kiki (character on *The Deuce*) 157–158
Ralston, Will 197
rape 48, 82, 111, 157, 160–61
Rawls, Bill (character on *The Wire*) 57–61, 64, 102
R.C. (character on *The Corner*) 21
realism 5, 18, 30–32, 54, 64–65, 95, 176–179, 183–184, 191
representational politics 174–176, 191–193, 195–196, 199, 202
in *The Corner* 27–28, 35, 199
in *The Deuce* 147, 155, 170–171
in *The Wire* 78
in *Treme* 88
in *Show Me a Hero* 133–139, 199
residential segregation 192, 202
in *Show Me a Hero* 1, 3, 44, 97, 114, 115–116, 118, 120–124, 127–129, 134, 137–143, 192–193
Rexrode, Reena 8
Reyes, Rudy 184
Rich Man, Poor Man (TV series) 23
Ricky (character in *Boyz n the Hood*) 28–20
Ringo (character on *The Wire*) 78
Rita (character on *The Corner*) 32
Rizzi (character on *The Deuce*) 160–161
Rodney (character on *The Deuce*) 159–160
Ronnie *see* Boice, Veronica "Ronnie"
Roosevelt, Franklin 185–186, 190–191
Roosevelt, Theodore 187
Roots (TV series) 25
Rorty, Richard 198–199
Rosenfeld, Gavriel 186
Rosenstone, Robert 52, 61
Roth, Philip 185–187, 191
Rothstein, Richard 122–123, 141
Rowan, Billie (character on *Show Me a Hero*) 136–137, 145
Rowe, Mike 17
Ruby "Thunder Thighs" (character on *The Deuce*) 150, 195
Russell, Beadie (character on *The Wire*) 68, 176–177

San Fernando Valley 157–158
Sand, Judge Leonard (character on *Show Me a Hero*) 116, 125–127, 131, 142
Santos Jr., John (character on *Show Me a Hero*) 136–137

Scalio (character on *The Corner*) 38
Schelstraete, Jasper 68
Schindler's List (film) 32, 45
Schlobohm 15, 43, 120, 122, 127, 133, 135–137, 175–176, 195
Schwetje, Craig "Encino Man" (character on *Generation Kill*) 182
Scoogie (character on *The Corner*) 37
Scott, Janny 35–38, 41, 196
Scribe (character on *Generation Kill*) 181–182
second-lining 87
self-reflexivity
　in *Generation Kill* 185
　in *Show Me a Hero* 175–176
　in *The Corner* 30–31
　in *The Deuce* 2, 152, 155, 183
　in *The Wire* 64–65
　in *Treme* 95
Selma (film) 124
sex work 1–2, 80, 143, 145–151, 151, 155, 157, 159–162, 165, 167–170, 174, 179, 195–196
sexual abuse 150, 170, 197
Shay (character on *The Deuce*) 148
Shelley v. Kraemer 128
Show Me a Hero (book) 14, 115, 130–131, 134, 138–139, 172
Show Me a Hero (TV series) 1,3, 6, 8, 10, 12, 14–16, 22–23, 42–44, 97, 100–101, 114, 115–143, 145, 164–165, 172, 175, 190, 193, 195, 199, 202
showrunner 5–10, 49, 196
Simon, David 1, 4, 12, 13, 16, 23, 24, 44, 46, 53–54, 70, 82, 86, 88–90, 92–94, 97–98, 100, 102, 103, 105, 110, 113, 115, 122, 128–129, 133, 139, 142–143, 144–147, 155, 162, 168–170, 172–177, 181, 183–185, 187–188, 190–191, 193–197, 200–203
　as journalist 9–10, 26, 37, 39, 41–42, 45
　as showrunner 5–10, 38, 48, 49
　on branding 51
　on characters 178–179
　on cities 4–5, 11, 48, 110–112, 134–135, 164, 201
　on democratic socialism 192, 199
　on *Generation Kill* 180, 184
　on policing 82
　on politics 14–15, 131, 136, 140, 191, 202
　on representation 17, 174, 196–199
　on *Show Me a Hero* 3
　on social engineering 141
　on *The Wire* 1, 12, 62–67, 76, 78, 83–84, 86, 110–111, 169–170, 200–201
　on *The Deuce* 2–3, 146, 169, 174, 198
　on *The Plot Against America* 186, 191
　on *Treme* 87, 110–111
　on writing 15, 22, 41, 45, 49, 114, 138, 141, 178–179
Singleton, John 25–26, 29
Skinner, Quentin 10–12, 25
Skip (character on *Show Me a Hero*) 135
Smith, Murray 33–34, 56, 102
Smith, Peter (character on *Show Me a Hero*) 133
Sobotka, Frank (character on *The Corner*) 69–80
Sobotka, Nick (character on *The Wire*) 72–73, 76–80, 85, 201
Sobotka, Ziggy (character on *The Wire*) 77–80, 201
social engineering 141
social reproduction 54–55, 74–75, 80–81, 83, 89, 92, 129, 134

Son, Diana 7
Sonny (character on *Treme*) 107–110
South Central 26, 28
Spallone, Hank (character on *Show Me a Hero*) 116
Spina, Dorothy "Ashley" (character on *The Deuce*) 147–148, 169–170
Springsteen, Bruce 116–117, 122
St. Louis 42, 163
Stagecoach (film) 96
Stanfield, Marlo (character on *The Wire*) 81, 100, 104, 175, 197
Stevedores 70–75, 80
Stewart, Joseph "Proposition Joe" (character on *The Wire*) 77
Stranger Things (TV series) 23
Strong, Josiah 4
Styles, Tre (character in *Boyz n the Hood*) 29
suburbanization 13, 166, 200
Sugrue, Thomas 71, 78, 119, 173, 195
Sunstein, Cass 189
Surdoval, James 130
Sussman, Michael (character on *Show Me a Hero*) 42–43, 118, 142
Sweeney, Sheamus 33

Tae (character on *The Corner*) 27
Taylor, Greg (character on *The Deuce*) 158
Taylor, J.D. 62
Teaford, Jon C. 4, 162–165
teleology 54, 95–96, 114, 190–191
territorial stigmatization 144
The Awakening (novel) 95
The Baltimore Sun 9–10, 52, 197
The Corner (book) 26, 37, 39, 45, 82
The Corner (TV series) 1, 6, 8, 12, 15–16, 17–46, 56, 65, 76, 86, 87, 94, 95, 100, 110, 115, 128, 144–145, 161, 165, 172, 174, 179, 183, 190, 193, 196, 199, 202
The Deuce (TV series) 1–2, 6, 8, 16, 22, 53, 87, 142–43, 144–171, 172, 174, 176–178, 183, 190, 192, 195–199, 202–203
The Diamondback (student newspaper) 9, 196
The Impressions 21–22
The Long Walk Home (film) 118
The O'Jays 32
The Omega Man (film) 165–166
The Orchid Thief 95
The Plot Against America (TV series) 8, 16, 23, 98, 179, 185–191, 196
The Rosa Parks Story (film) 124
The Searchers (film) 64
the Seventh Ward 112
The Sophisticated Gents 25
The Sopranos 49, 51
The Wild Bunch (film) 63–64
The Wire (TV series) 1–2, 6–8, 12–13, 16, 17–18, 22, 27–28, 33, 38, 40–41, 45–46, 47–86, 87, 89–97, 100, 102, 104–105, 110–111, 115, 127–130, 133–134, 143, 144, 145, 159–162, 165, 170, 172, 173–179, 183, 184, 190–199, 201–202
Thompson, Ella (character on *The Corner*) 18, 27–28, 94
Thompson, E.P. 73
Thorup, Mikkel 25
Times Square 144, 147, 166–168
To Kill a Mockingbird (novel) 137
Tony (character on *The Corner*) 161
Toyama, Koichi (character on *Treme*) 109
Treme (TV series) 1, 6–8, 11–12, 22–23, 51, 53, 56, 86, 87–114, 115, 146, 172, 176, 190, 192–193, 195, 199, 202

Trombley, Harold James (character on *Generation Kill*) 182–183, 185
True Detective (TV series) 23
Trump, Donald 169, 185–186
Tuck, Stephen 119
Tull, Jethro 122
Turner, Frederick Jackson 112–113

unions 52, 69–71, 74–76, 78–80, 115
United States Department of Housing and Urban Development 121
United States v. Yonkers Board of Education 125–126
University of Maryland 9, 196
urban crisis 2, 143, 145–146, 162–164, 166, 168, 202, 203
U.S. Court of Appeals 126

Valchek, Stan (character on *The Wire*) 74, 104
Vermont 165
Vest, Jason P. 44–45
Vietnam War 179–180, 184
Vint, Sherryl 63
Voting Rights Act of 1965 119–120

Wacquant, Loïc 144
Wagstaff, Melvin "Cheese" (character on *The Wire*) 77
Wagstaff, Randy (character on *The Wire*) 194
war on drugs 1, 3, 17, 45, 52, 57, 62, 76, 81–83, 85–86, 89, 94, 128, 134, 159, 177, 193, 200, 202
Ward, Brian 22
Washington, Sandra (character on *The Deuce*) 2, 160
Wasicsko, Nay (character on *Show Me a Hero*) 131–132

Wasicsko, Nick (character on *Show Me a Hero*) 3, 115–117, 122, 124–125, 130–133, 135, 137–139, 140, 145, 146, 193
Wasserman, Harvey (character on *The Deuce*) 151–154
Watkins, D. 9
Watts riots 163
Walon (character on *The Wire*) 83, 94
We Own This City (TV series) 8, 16, 23
Weeks, Johnny (character on *The Wire*) 74
Weems, Dukie (character on *The Wire*) 80
Westerns 63–69, 86
Williams, Linda 30–31, 47, 59, 102
Williams, Raymond 200
Williams, Robin 9
Wilson, William Julius 12–13, 24, 39–40, 43, 61, 75, 83, 173
Wise, Dennis "Cutty" (character on *The Wire*) 53
W.M. (character on *The Corner*) 24–25
Wolf, Bernie (character on *The Deuce*) 147–148
World War II 13, 163, 179–180
Wright, Evan 8, 179–181, 184
writers' room 7, 155, 179, 196–198
Wyatt, Harley (character on *Treme*) 111

Yonkers 115–127, 130–131, 133–134, 138–140

Zevin, Robert 162–163
Zorzi, William F. 115, 122, 129, 138, 139, 146, 193

EU authorised representative for GPSR:
Easy Access System Europe, Mustamäe tee 50,
10621 Tallinn, Estonia
gpsr.requests@easproject.com

www.ingramcontent.com/pod-product-compliance
Lightning Source LLC
Chambersburg PA
CBHW051611230426
43668CB00013B/2068